The history, traditions and rich cultural heritage of Arunachal Pradesh 'the land of rising sun' and its people have left an indelible imprint on my mind during my tenure as the Governor. Sonam Chombay's outstanding work *"In between the Blurry Lines"* offers profound insights into the historical background, culture and development of this geo-strategically important State. This book is a tribute to the remarkable journey - its challenges, achievements and the way forward of one of India's youngest States. A product of deep research, the book brings out the essence of Arunachal Pradesh and makes a compelling read.

Gen JJ Singh, Former COAS and former Governor of Arunachal Pradesh and bestselling author of 'A Soldiers's General' and 'The McMahon Line'

In Between The BLURRY Lines

14 Defining Moments That Shaped Arunachal Pradesh

Sonam Chombay

notionpress.com

INDIA · SINGAPORE · MALAYSIA

In memory of my

Ama la, Kesang Tsomu

Preface

If you've picked up this book, there's a good chance you're curious about the fascinating history of Arunachal Pradesh-a place as rich in stories as it is in scenic beauty. My inspiration to write this book arose from a noticeable gap in literature about this beautiful state, especially from the perspective of its own people. Despite the significance of many events that have shaped Arunachal Pradesh and in turn impacted our nation, there wasn't a single go-to book that captured these moments together.

This book isn't a typical history text but rather a collection of stories, woven with anecdotes and personal reflections, to present an engaging narrative. My aim was to create something informative and inviting, sharing real stories of trials, triumphs, and humbling moments that have contributed to Arunachal Pradesh's unique character.

Arunachal Pradesh, once known as NEFA (North East Frontier Agency), stands out not only for its breath-taking natural beauty but also for its strategic location and rich biodiversity. Bordering Bhutan, Tibet-China, and Myanmar, it holds immense significance for geo-strategists and scientists alike. Despite being India's most sparsely populated state, it attracts global interest-both for its natural allure and for its complex geo-political dynamics, including territorial claims and counterclaims.

This book is a humble attempt to be the go-to resource for anyone eager to understand the *Idea of Arunachal Pradesh*-whether you're a student exploring Arunachal's heritage, a scholar researching the region, a journalist writing about it, or simply a history enthusiast. Being a native who has spent considerable time outside the state and returned with a curiosity to explore my roots, I've infused these stories with a personal touch, making the journey feel like you're hearing them from a friend or neighbour.

Acknowledgments

They say it takes a village to educate a child. Little did I know it takes a community-of family, friends, mentors, and supporters-to write a book.

First and foremost, my gratitude goes to the people of Arunachal Pradesh, whose resilience across generations has made our state both beautiful and inspiring. You are the singular motivation behind this book. I owe a special thanks to my time at Donyi Polo Vidya Bhawan. Beyond earning a High School Certificate, this experience first introduced me to the "*Idea of Arunachal Pradesh*", helping me see that our state was so much more than I had understood. Even today, I am an unprepared student trying to decipher the riddle that is Arunachal Pradesh.

This book owes its depth to the works of many authoritative scholars and inspiring authors. I am eternally grateful to FM Bailey, Frank Kingdon Ward, Mani Lal Bose, PN Luthra, Brenece Rechard Guyot, Nari Rustomji, Verrier Elwin, Claude Arpi, and so many more. Their invaluable contributions have helped bring this narrative to life. Additionally, the Arunachal Pradesh State Archives provided a wealth of information and valuable maps. I owe a special thanks to KK Pandey, the Custodian, whose assistance was indispensable.

The British Officers' and Political Officers' tour diaries were also an integral source of information. My admiration goes to these individuals who meticulously recorded every detail of their journeys across the frontier. I salute their dedication and attention to detail.

A heartfelt thank you to Sadhana Deori, Anupam Tangu, Abu Tayeng, and Oken Tayeng for their encouragement. Sadhana and Oken generously shared rare books from their personal libraries, which feature prominently in my research. Many evenings with Anupam Tangu brought fascinating anecdotes from the 60s, 70s, and 80s to life, adding vibrant details to the book. My appreciation extends to Nob Tsering, Anupam Yadav, and Gumjum Haidar for sharing rare resources that find a place in this work.

Thanks to my brother Aaditya Tiwari for editing the third draft and my childhood friend Col Karma Wangchuk for meticulously scanning each page. Their "generous use of the red pen" helped trim the book into a leaner, more engaging read.

My dear colleague Ramesh was a pillar of support, sharing fascinating anecdotes from the 1980s when Itanagar was still largely wilderness. I also thank Sriram at Notion Press for his diligent editing and Saumya Chakravorty for combing through the ninth draft, helping refine the reading experience.

I am particularly grateful to Claude Arpi and Kai Friese for their careful review of the manuscript and insightful suggestions.

My deepest gratitude goes to PK Thungon La, Arunachal Pradesh's first Chief Minister, for graciously granting an interview. His reflections provide invaluable insights into the state's formative years, and my thanks to Sange for facilitating this meeting.

I am profoundly grateful to Pema Khandu La, Chief Minister of Arunachal Pradesh, for his support and for his rare candid interview, which offers a glimpse into his passion for our state.

On the family front, my father's scholarly support on Tawang and encouragement were invaluable. To my wife, Ten, my unwavering partner, and my children, Kunsang and Loden, who have patiently endured my endless discussions about the book-thank you. Special mention to my daughter Kunsang, who introduced me to the writer's tool, Hook, which I hope has served its purpose well.

Although the idea for this book had been brewing for a long time, real progress was slow. The extended break between recent elections and the announcement of results became a godsend, gifting me precious time to put in shape all my research and resources. I thank India's Elections-'Festival of Democracy' for this unintended benefit.

I am indebted to my alma mater, Hindu College. It was here, three decades ago, that a student of science dared to dive into the realm of Greek tragedies and English classics, an experience that unexpectedly equipped me for this journey. My two years at Jawahar Lal Nehru University further enriched my perspective and approach to research.

I thank Karan Singh for the cover design and Tasha Mimi for the author's photo.

A word of thanks to Puja and Joshua at Notion Press, whose patience and skill brought this book to life.

Finally, I extend my gratitude to the many well-wishers, both named and unnamed, who contributed to this book. This work is a product of a community, and I share its ownership with each of you.

Thank you, one and all.

Contents

Preface 7

Acknowledgments 9

Introduction 17

PART ONE

CAUGHT IN THE SHADOW OF THE ANGLO-CHINESE RACE FOR EXPANSION

1   **Inner line & Outer line: Towards Isolation and Exclusion** 25
     The Regulation 1 of 1873-What is it? 29
     Why the Inner Line?: A Dual Purpose Tool 30
     Impact on Arunachal Pradesh 35
     Looking Back and Looking Forward 36
     Citizenship Amendment Act and the Inner Line 37
     Political Dynamics and Amendments 37

2   **The Anglo-Abor War: A Confluence of Conflict and Colonial Ambition** . 43
     The Spark of Conflict 44
     British Military Response 46
     Indigenous Resistance and Adaptation 47
     Aftermath and Reflections 48
     The North-East Frontier Tracts is born: 48
     British Forward Policy takes shape 48
     Origins of Administrative Reforms 50
     Challenges and Implementation 50

3   **The Red (McMahon) Line: A Product of Bailey's Trail** 53
     Shadow Boxing becomes reality 53
     A Weak China and its fallout 54
     Bailey-Morshead Expedition 55
     Mapping the Frontier 56
     Drawing of the Frontier 59
     Northeastern Frontiers after the Simla Agreement 61
     Legality of the McMahon Line 64

PART TWO
THE FRONTIER IN THE FIFTIES AND BEYOND

4   Earthquake and the Benevolent State 81

5   Bob's Valour-Metoh Sahab and unfurling of the Tricolour at Tawang 93
Mystery, thy name is Tawang 93
Expansion begins, sans Tawang 98
Bob Khathing and the Unfinished Agenda of Tawang 100
Who exactly was Bob? 101
'Metoh Sahab' plants the Tricolour 102

6   Elwin's 'Philosophy for NEFA'-Securing Roots for a Stable Future 109
British Policy of Isolation of the Frontier 109
Post Independence Policy for NEFA 110
Post 1962 War: End of a Philosophy? 116

7   The Holy Exile – Ancient Indian Wisdom Returns 123
Two Asian Giants-Freedom & Liberation 123
Roof of the World-No longer Forbidden 125
Hindi-Chini Bhai Bhai-Five Principles of Deceit 126
Dalai Lama enters Tawang and brings along 128
Ancient Indian Wisdom 128

8   An Unprovoked War-The Wound that Won't Heal 133
Unexpected Conflict: A War Without Strategy 136
Psychology of the War 141
Tribal Loyalties Unmoved-Chinese Miscalculation 142
Post war Frontier Administration 146

PART THREE
LOST DECADES & MAKING OF A STATE

9   From NEFA to Arunachal Pradesh; Acronym adopts an Indic Identity . . 185
Growth of Bureaucracy in NEFA 187
From Shillong to Itanagar 190
The Political Transition 192
A Youthful State is Born, Albeit Prematurely? 195

10   Tongues of Harmony: The Quest for a Common Voice 223
NEFAMESE: A Pidgin Language 224
Linguistic transition in Arunachal Pradesh 225
Fusion and some Confusion 227

11 Development is the Best Defence; Ushering a New Dawn 231
The Sumdorong Chu Standoff 232
Prime Minister's Visit to China 234
Special Package Announcements of 2008: The Turning Point 236
The Push for Development: The PM's Special Package 236
The Strategic Shift and Confident Leadership 237
The Implementation Challenge: Turning Vision into Reality 238

PART FOUR
THE GOLDEN DECADE

12 From Trees to Treasure: The Green Boost 247
14th Finance Commission-The Game Changer? 250
Presenting a Convincing Case 250
Argument for a New Formula 251
Final Recommendations and Arunachal Pradesh 252
15th FC: Consolidating the formula of 14th FC 254

13 Touchdown in the Frontier: Giving Wings to Tribal Aspirations 257
Policy of Regular Ministerial Visits 259
Digital Governance: Connecting the Unconnected 261
Political Participation at the National Level 261
Frontier Villages as first Villages of the Country 263
Viksit Arunachal key to Viksit Bharat 264

14 Championing Change: Political Will for Transforming Lives 269

Epilogue

15 Towards the Future 283
Current Challenges and Opportunities in Arunachal Pradesh 284
In the National and Global Context 296
Some crystal gazing 297
Final Thoughts 298

Additional Readings 321

Select Bibliography 347

Endnotes 355

Introduction

Writing this book was anything but easy. I had to sift through more than a century and a half of written history-151 years, to be precise-and oral histories that stretch even further back, and select 14 events that I felt truly shaped Arunachal Pradesh. These events were chosen not only for their historical importance but also for their lasting influence on the state's development, culture, and modernisation. This isn't a history book in the strictest sense, but rather an exploration of pivotal events that highlight the state's journey through significant challenges and achievements.

To compile this narrative, I used a mix of primary and secondary sources. For events before 2010, I referred to academic books, British explorers' diaries, interviews with locals, and archival records from the Government of Arunachal Pradesh. For recent events, I drew from personal experiences and contemporary literature. My goal was to create an analytical yet accessible narrative, connecting historical events with their ongoing impact today.

During my research, I was fortunate to speak with people like PK Thungon La and Claude Arpi, having in-depth knowledge of these events, who offered insights into the multi-layered nature of Arunachal Pradesh's history. In some cases, the lack of credible records or the "noise" created by urban legends made it difficult to verify details. However, I hope this book will inspire researchers to delve deeper into these stories and unearth even more insights.

The involvement of local people in these historic events were of particular interest to me. Although I could access some resources about their contributions, I am certain that many of their stories remain untold. This aspect is one that future works should aim to highlight. In a way, this book, therefore, is a work in progress.

The book is organized around these 14 key events, each chosen to show a different dimension of Arunachal Pradesh's growth and resilience. Alongside the factual accounts, I have included some *"what if"* scenarios, imagining how things might have been different if events had unfolded in other ways. These reflections aim to help readers understand the implications of each episode, not only on history but on present-day life in the state.

So, as you turn the pages, I hope you find the journey through the defining moments of Arunachal Pradesh's history as intriguing and enlightening as I found while writing this book. Let's dive into the stories that have defined this enchanting place.

अरुण किरण शीश भूषण

कंठ हिम की धारा

प्रभात सूरज चुम्बित देश

अरुणाचल हमारा, अरुणाचल हमारा !

भारत मां का राजदुलारा अरुणाचल हमारा !

प्यार से दुलरायी तोहे तोड़ेंगे विपद सारा !

मन हमारा चंचल धारा होए ना कोई किनारा

प्रभात सूरज चुम्बित देश

अरुणाचल हमारा, अरुणाचल हमारा

- Bharat Ratna Dr Bhupen Hazarika

PART ONE

CAUGHT IN THE SHADOW OF THE ANGLO-CHINESE RACE FOR EXPANSION

This part of the book is set against the backdrop of a massive churning in Asia, where the 19th century witnessed perpetual shifts of power and territorial boundaries. As empires expanded and contracted, the geopolitical map of Asia was being redrawn. This era of flux had profound implications for the region that would become Arunachal Pradesh. The re-drawing of boundaries was part of this broader context, where colonial powers sought to secure their interests amidst the shifting sands of influence and control.

In China, the Qing Dynasty was making its last push for expansion further South. During the last decade of Qing rule, in 1910, the dynasty launched a military expedition to Tibet in an effort to reassert control over Lhasa and other Tibetan regions, including Dzayul and Pome, which were strategically important due to their geographical position along the Himalayan frontier. However, within a year, in 1911, 4,000 years of Chinese Monarchy and almost 300 years of Qing Dynasty were staring at an apparent decline, paving the way for declaration of the Republic of China in 1912; steered by Dr. Sun Yat Sen. Consequently, the *Ambans* installed by the Qing Dynasty *were* slowly losing their grip on Tibet. The expulsion of these Chinese officials from Tibet was complete by the end of 1912. For now, Tibet was to enjoy her *de facto* Independence. The rollercoaster ride of freedom and suzerainty, the waxing and waning of Chinese influence over Tibet, as we will see, reflected how strong or weak China was.

South of the Himalayas, the British East India Company would spread their influence and reach the Eastern Frontier, including the Assam Plains, to pursue their commercial interests. Tea, Oil and Coal of Assam would be strong enough attractions that the Battle of Yandaboo of 1826 and the consequent Treaty would determine British entrenchment in the region. With the Crown taking over the Company in 1858, the Eastern Himalayas became the hotbed for interplay and interaction between the two Powers. British India found Qing China's presence near the Eastern Himalayas was too close for comfort and something had to be done; Was the *British Forward Policy* the answer to this white man's predicament? We will see.

An expansionist China looked beyond the Himalayas. With the British already in the foothills, an intense dance of competition for expanding their respective spheres of influence was triggered. The Northeastern Frontier would be the playground for this protracted contest. This Part delves into this intricate dance of almost 100 years from 1826 to 1914 (between British India, China and initially with Burma) and how it impacted and influenced the Northeastern Frontier, resulting in three boundaries - *inner, outer and McMahon lines*, being drawn. The drawing of these lines would easily become the most defining moment for present day Arunachal Pradesh. In fact, present day Arunachal cannot be studied without knowing about these three administrative measures adopted by the British government[1]. Let us see how these lines came about and shaped the Frontier.

"Good fences make good neighbours."
– Robert Frost

1

Inner line & Outer line: Towards Isolation and Exclusion

'*Will give blood, but not our land*'. New writings on the wall begun to emerge…the protests started from Northeast India when the government announced its intent to move the bill to Parliament in early part of December 2019[2].

The protests were against the Citizenship Amendment Act (CAA). The Act, which granted fast-track citizenship to persecuted minorities from neighbouring countries of Afghanistan, Bangladesh and Pakistan, living in India prior to 2014. This sparked debates on identity, inclusion, and exclusion which are deep-rooted issues in Northeast India. But the roots of such exclusionary policies in India's Northeast run deep, tracing back to a lesser-known yet pivotal moment in 1873 when the British colonial government drew the "*Inner Line*." On the face of the debate, it felt like the two were at cross purposes. We will see how the Act and the Regulation reconciled, rather, how the latter shielded the former's implications in the region.

The Eastern Himalayas had for long remained the largest '*terra incognita*' in South Asia[3]. Prior to the beginning of the 20th Century, this region had limited contact with the '*outside*' world, only with the people of Assam Plains. The frontier tribes would often raid the plains for their needs. As a policy of reconciliation, it was the Ahom King Pratap Singha, who granted the right of *Posa* to many of these tribes.[4] The term Posa means allowances (sic) paid to certain hill tribes (Present tribes of Arunachal

Pradesh) to check their habit of raids and outrages against plains people for commodities. It was a kind of deals (deal) or settlement between the tribal chiefs and Ahom kings and later (the) British Government.[5]

In the aftermath of the Anglo-Burmese war between 1824 and 1826 and the *Treaty of Yandabo*, the East India Company gained access and control over Assam[6], enriching their commercial dominion over the region's vast resources. Coal and petroleum (1825) were discovered in Upper Assam and tea bushes were found in the jungles nearby (1823). Tea was an important item of import for Great Britain from China and a large amount of gold and silver bullion had to be exported from Great Britain to pay for Chinese tea. The successful cultivation of tea in Assam in the later half of the century had a decisive effect on the Company's policies in the North-East Frontier region. Moreover, the prospects of coal, mined since 1828, and petroleum, drilled from 1866, enhanced the value of Assam to the Company.[7] Assam quickly rose in prominence and economic significance for the British East India Company.

The British, succeeding the Ahoms, had no idea of the extent of their territory, which was not initially of much consequence. But now, with such huge economic interests, it was necessary that peace be maintained; this in turn required establishment of strict administrative control over the province as well as on the borders '….much of the troubles….was caused due to the unrestricted and undefined intercourse between the tribesmen and people of the plains'.[8]

Amidst these commercial pursuits, the British also had to contend with the strategic considerations posed in the Northern neighbourhood. The geopolitical dynamics of the region necessitated a careful balancing act, as the British sought to extend their influence without provoking outright confrontation. This delicate situation culminated in the drawing of *lines*, a process fraught with tension and negotiation. These boundaries not only delineated British control but also had profound implications for the indigenous communities, often disrupting established ways of life. This part of the book looks at how the British, local communities, and nearby powers interacted, covering their trade interests, strategic actions, start of early administration, and the often tense process of setting boundaries that changed the Frontier during this important time.

The numerous tribes living in these highlands were oblivious of the statecraft of the colonial powers and decisions driven by colonial interests, affecting the tribes and their unintended consequences even 150 years later. *The Regulation 1 of 1873* or *Bengal Eastern Frontier Regulation of 1873* was one such decision, ramifications of which would resonate for many years to come. The Regulation was the beginning of a series of events that would unfold in the Frontiers, primarily prompted by the competitive struggle for enhancing the sphere of influence between two imperial powers, British India and China. All activities around the Eastern Frontiers would be prompted to browbeat each other.

Thus comes the story of how a line drawn on a map more than a century and half ago, 151 years to be precise, shaped the destiny of what we know today as Arunachal Pradesh. This isn't just any line; it's a line that tells a tale of commerce, conflict, and colonial interests. Let's dive into the origins and implications of the *Bengal Eastern Frontier Regulations* (BEFR) of 1873, popularly known as Regulation 1 of 1873, which gave life to this ingenious concept of the '*Inner Line*'.

Following the revolt of 1857, power transitioned from the East India Company to the British Crown. This monumental change was solidified by the Government of India Act of 1858, ushering in a new epoch of British Raj over India. Its implications were bound to touch the Eastern Himalayas. Within fifteen years of Crown rule, came the most important legislation, the '*Regulation for the peace and Good Government of certain districts of the Eastern Frontier of Bengal, 1873*'. This legislation was not merely a rule; it aimed to regulate and restrict movement. It forbade individuals who were not native to specific regions from entering the designated districts without an authorised pass, issued under authority of the district's Chief Executive. This was aimed at regulating and limiting interactions between the plains and the hill regions. The Rule, which continues to this day, has profound impact on the social and economic dynamics of the Eastern Himalayan Frontiers.

The genesis of this Regulation was rooted in the economic realities of the time, particularly the unhindered extraction of rubber by European traders and settlers which became the immediate trigger. The extensive rubber extraction, which began without much regulation, prompted the British to establish more structured controls to manage both the economic benefits and the ensuing conflicts. In 1872, a resolution was passed by the Government of British India[9], that set off a year of intensive correspondences and deliberations between the Bengal Government and the Government of British India[10]. During this period, numerous drafts of the *Regulation* were debated and amended, with each amendment tailored to address evolving challenges and needs identified during these discussions.

Amongst the many amendments in the draft, one that stands out particularly was the insertion of the words '*or other person*' and the expansion of the scope of 'section 7 of the Regulation'[11]. This was primarily to include the Europeans-may be Italian, German or French within so that along with British subjects, they too could not acquire interests beyond the line. This emendation would also take care of Marwari or Bengali traders attempting to enter into agreements with tribals beyond the line to engage in speculations in forest produce like timber and rubber; thereby segregating classes within what would have been considered as natives of Assam.

This meticulous crafting of the *Regulation* was pivotal in creating a regulation that not only sought to secure the Crown's commercial interests by minimising disruptions but also aimed to define the cultural and geographic boundaries that continue to influence the region even today.

While seemingly administrative, these regulations were a direct response to the complexities of managing frontier regions-interwoven with strategic interests of the British Empire in maintaining control and maximising economic exploitation. The line drawn by the *Regulation* not only marked geographical boundaries but also set the stage for future interactions between the diverse communities of what would eventually be recognized as Arunachal Pradesh.

The Regulation 1 of 1873-What is it?

On August 27, 1873, under the crown's rule, the *Bengal Eastern Frontier Regulation, 1873* was introduced. This regulation, which came into effect on November 1 of the same year, was specifically designed for the frontier hill districts, the present day Northeast region of India. Its key features were straightforward but impactful:

- **Restriction of Entry:** No one could enter the defined area beyond the "*Inner Line*" without a special pass issued by the administration.
- **Land Ownership Restrictions:** Only natives of the district could acquire interests in land.

The East India Company arrived at the Eastern Frontiers looking for newer pastures for economic exploitation, tea and oil of the region being their favourites. Indigenous tribes, frustrated and threatened by loss of their lands, frequently raided the burgeoning settlements around the tea gardens and oil fields. These raids, which the British termed as '*savage disruptions*'[12] were desperate attempts by the tribes to reclaim their rights and protect their lands from foreign exploitation.

In retaliation, the British conducted several punitive missions to subdue the tribes. These military expeditions often involved harsh measures, including burning of villages and crops, which led to further alienation resulting in resistance and retaliation from the indigenous tribes. The British were looking for a solution to this 'menace', an unwanted interruption to their commercial expansion.[13]

A straightforward response to this was a simple one for the British authorities legislate a legal framework, creating a regulated line, restricting movement of indigenous people into key economic zones and limiting their interaction with the British and migrant workers. This segregation fulfilled their intention to protect British commercial interests from the incidence of tribal raids. In return, the British decided to continue the payment of *Posa*. The payment of compensation in the form of *posa* or assignment of a part of revenue was a pre-British system. The Ahoms had introduced the system to reconcile the hill tribes living on the frontiers of their kingdom.[14]

Why the Inner Line?: A Dual Purpose Tool

The concept of the *Inner Line*, as defined by the Bengal Eastern Frontier Regulation (BEFR) of 1873, was an ingenious colonial manoeuvre often referred to as '*British cartographic wizardry.*'[15] Ostensibly, this regulation was instituted to protect the indigenous tribes of Northeast Frontier from exploitation and cultural erosion by external forces. On paper, it promised to preserve their traditional ways of life, which were deeply connected to the forests, hills, and rivers of the region. However, beneath this veneer of protection lay a more strategic, economically-driven agenda aimed at bolstering the Crown's interests in the area.

The late 19th century was a period of aggressive expansion for British enterprises in the Eastern Frontier, particularly in Assam's tea, oil, and coal industries. The *Inner Line* was drawn to create a buffer zone that would prevent the indigenous tribes from accessing these burgeoning economic centres, thus reducing the frequency of tribal raids that had previously disrupted production and threatened investments. By restricting the movement of indigenous populations, the British effectively isolated their commercial ventures from the social and political complexities of tribal dynamics. The British administrators were conscious of the fact that the wall they had created by promulgating the Inner Line between the hills and the plains would suffocate the tribes unless some breathing spaces were provided for inhabitants of the hills. Therefore, the Government took initiative to bring the tribes to the annual fairs which were regularly held along the foothills.[16]

However, the drawing of the Inner Line had its share of critics. Col. Hopkinson was the first British officer who had the foresight to see that by the annexation of Assam, the British had accepted the obligation to undertake the administration of the tribes of the frontier and he criticised the Government for creating a wall of separation between the hills and plains of the province.[17] However, Delhi had other views and the Under Secretary to the Government of India wrote back "*I have seen the necessity of patience and forebearance, which I have studiously exercised towards them (hill tribes); these savages are utterly incapable of reasoning, and I fear they attribute our bearing towards them to timidity and either cannot, or will not understand our real motive.*" He went on to advise that "*what is of utmost importance in dealing with the uncivilised tribes is patience*".[18]

The *Regulation* is good only when the *Line* is in place on the ground. The Frontier Officials were to start the task of delineating the line on the ground. It was decided that the plan followed recently in demarcating the British India-Bhutan border[19] would be broadly adopted here. The difference, however, was that while the former was for laying borders with a foreign territory; the line drawn here was within British territory. Survey teams were constituted equipped with resources such as elephants and guards. Lieutenant Holcombe and Major Lance would play crucial roles in this exercise. Though it was decided that natural features would be the guiding principle for such a line, instances of tea gardens well beyond the line and land interests of tribes within the line in the plains would potentially pose a challenge to the survey team.

While the *Inner Line* was initially a tool for colonial economic preservation, its long-term effects on the social and political landscape were profound and multifaceted. By physically and legally separating tribal communities from colonially dominated urban centres, the British inadvertently solidified ethnic and cultural divides. This separation fostered a sense of isolation among the tribes, limiting their interaction with not only the British and other non-indigenous populations but also with neighbouring tribes that fell outside the Inner Line.

Over time, these enforced boundaries began to shape the identities of the people within them. For example, in what is now Arunachal Pradesh, the Inner Line still influences contemporary administrative and political boundaries. This has implications for local governance, resource allocation, and even electoral politics.

The *Inner Line* more than just restricted physical movement; it also played an unintended crucial role in the cultural preservation and identity formation of the tribes. By limiting external influences, the regulation allowed tribal communities to maintain their cultural practices, languages, and social norms without the direct imposition of British cultural assimilation policies. This led to a rich preservation of cultural heritage that might otherwise have been eroded or altered by more extensive and overwhelming contact with outsiders.

However, this isolation also meant that the tribal communities were left out of the broader economic and educational advancements occurring in other parts of India, contributing to disparities in development and access to resources that are still evident today.

Today, the concept of the Inner Line has evolved but is still in effect in various forms, such as the Inner Line Permit (ILP) system, which regulates the entry of non local Indian citizens into areas beyond the Line. For foreigners, the Protected Area Permit is in vogue. This continues to generate debate about the balance between protecting indigenous cultures and promoting economic development.

The *Inner Line*, therefore, serves as a stark reminder of the dual-edged nature of colonial policies: while they can offer protection and preservation, they can also impose segregation and economic disparity. As such, understanding the origins and implications of the Inner Line is crucial for policymakers and scholars who aim to address the complex interplay of development, cultural preservation, and regional security in Northeast India today. This rich historical tapestry provides valuable lessons in the challenges of managing economic interests while respecting indigenous rights and cultural diversity. The enactment of the *Regulation* has had lingering effects on the region's demographic and political landscape, influencing ethnic sparks and migration patterns even today.

The story of the *Regulation* is a testament to the complex interplay between colonial interests and indigenous rights. It highlights the enduring impact of colonial policies on indigenous communities in the region. Understanding these historical contexts is crucial for addressing contemporary issues of ethnic conflicts, environmental conservation, and social preservation.

The British also conjured up something called the *Outer Line*. It became evident to the colonial rulers that the administration of the large tracts of the Frontier was not possible, mostly because of the economic cost it entailed and also the difficult terrain. However, they also did not desire to completely close their eyes because there were bright economic prospects of forests in the hills, and therefore, they wanted to exercise indirect control over the areas and their natural resources. Hence, the originally undefined and ambiguous territory was to be kept with them through an imaginary line, the *Outer line*.[20] This imaginary line would be fungible and could wax or wane as per the convenience of British rulers.

"We only now claim suzerainty upto the foot of the hills. We have an Inner Line and an Outer Line. Upto the Inner Line we administer in the ordinary way. Between the Inner Line and Outer Line we only administer politically. That is, our political officers exercise very loose jurisdiction, and to prevent troubles with the frontier tribes, passes are required for our subjects who want to cross the Inner Line. The country between the two lines is very sparsely inhabited and is mostly dense jungle."[21] This was how in 1910, Lord Hardinge summarised the intent behind the two lines.

Lord Minto's view was to push northward the Outer Line to secure *"a good strategical (sic) boundary agreements being taken..... from the tribes within and beyond the line binding them to have no relation with foreign power, other than the British".*[22] This was a concern directed towards possible intermingling with the Chinese from the North. Through this outer line, British maintained 'loose' political jurisdiction over the tribal hills, till demarcation of the McMahon Line of 1914.

As if the purported isolation through the *Regulation* was not enough, the colonial powers introduced the concept of "*excluded*" and "*partially excluded*" areas. The Government of India Act of 1935 stands out as a significant chapter in the colonial history of India, particularly for its designation of "*excluded*" and "*partially excluded*" areas, which reinforced the seclusion fostered by the *Inner Line* of *Regulation 1 of 1873*. Essentially, under this Act, any law made for the British Indian Territory would not be applicable in these areas, unless stated otherwise. This piece of legislation not only sculpted the administrative landscape but also left a lasting imprint on the socio-political fabric of various regions, especially in the Northeastern part of India.

The decision to classify certain regions as excluded or partially excluded was ostensibly taken to protect the indigenous populations from external influences and to prevent their exploitation. The British authorities argued that these tribal communities were not yet ready to be integrated into mainstream legislative and administrative processes due to their distinct social and cultural practices. As a result, these areas were placed directly under the Governor's rule, who governed with the aid of advisors, often bypassing local inputs in administrative decisions.

Moreover, the distinctions created by the Act laid the groundwork for the ongoing complexities in the governance and integration of these regions into the Indian Union after independence. The legacy of the Government of India Act of 1935 is still evident in the administrative and political challenges faced by these regions, highlighting the enduring impact of colonial legislative frameworks on the modern Indian state. This formula continued post India's independence and found its way in the Constitution, in the form of scheduled areas and exceptions such as Article 371.

In 1935, during a debate in Britain's House of Commons, Winston Churchill expressed deep concerns about giving Indian leaders control over areas populated by tribal communities. He worried that the tribal areas might suffer under Indian rule, much like he worried about the safety of Europeans living in India. His words reflected a strong doubt among British officials about the ability of Indian leaders to manage regions with distinct ethnic and cultural identities. This doubt, sincerity notwithstanding, played a big role in how the British decided to govern these areas.[23]

Impact on Arunachal Pradesh

Arunachal Pradesh, known back then as part of the North East Frontier Tracts (NEFT), is a clear example of how these British decisions impacted certain regions. Unlike other parts of the Himalayas, where outside influences changed the local ways of life and economy, Arunachal Pradesh kept much of its tribal land and traditions. This was because of strict laws defining who could enter the area and who could own land there. These laws helped the innocent tribes keep control over their land and protect their way of life from being overwhelmed by outsiders.

Various communities residing in different regions of Arunachal Pradesh have preserved their unique cultural practices and governance structures, largely due to exclusion policies that limited external influences and land ownership. Apatanis, for example, are noted for their efficient land-use system involving paddy-cum-fish cultivation, which has thrived due to this isolation. Most tribes, known for their rich oral literature and religious practices centred around a naturalistic belief system, benefited from these restrictions that protected the cultural landscape vital for their traditions.

Similarly, all communities with a democratic governance system through village councils have successfully maintained their traditional social structures and cultural practices without outside interference.

Meanwhile, communities living in the higher reaches, renowned for their vibrant festivals and monastic traditions, saw their Buddhist cultural practices safeguarded by policies that curbed disruptive external influences. These examples highlight the significant role of protective policies in preserving the cultural identity and heritage of diverse groups within this region.

Reports and historical records show that while these rules protected Arunachal Pradesh's cultural identity, they also isolated it from the rest of India. This isolation had two sides to it: it preserved the region's unique cultural and social character, but it also prevented Arunachal Pradesh from developing economically and integrating with other parts of the country. For many years, this meant fewer roads, schools, and less business with other regions.

Looking Back and Looking Forward

January 20th of 2022 was a moment of reflection on how the British laws of 1873 and 1935 had profoundly shaped the State. The day was when Arunachal Pradesh celebrated her Golden Jubilee on attaining Union Territory Status and naming of Arunachal Pradesh. Interestingly, the year also marked 150 years since the *Inner Line* was introduced. These reflections showed that while the laws helped maintain cultural and social stability, they also slowed modernization. Today, as some urban areas in Arunachal Pradesh start to modernise, most of the region still holds on tightly to its traditional values and lifestyle.

In short, the *Inner Line* of Regulation 1 of 1873 and the "*excluded*" and "*partially excluded*" areas of Government of India Act of 1935 did more than just control how these regions were governed. It significantly shaped the lives and futures of places like Arunachal Pradesh. The law protected these regions from outside influences at the cost of keeping them isolated, a decision that still affects their development and how they interact with the rest of India today.

Citizenship Amendment Act and the Inner Line

The Citizenship Amendment Bill represents a significant chapter in India's ongoing narrative of addressing historical and social challenges. Introduced by the Government in 2019, the Bill aimed to provide a faster pathway to citizenship for persecuted religious minorities from Pakistan, Afghanistan, and Bangladesh[24]. This initiative, rooted in the idea of correcting perceived injustices arising from the Partition of India, stirred a complex mix of responses, especially in the Northeastern states.

The influx of refugees and immigrants has been a contentious issue for decades in the region and more so in Arunachal Pradesh, intertwining with concerns about cultural preservation, employment, and social harmony. The initial proposal of the Bill ignited widespread protests across these regions, reflecting deep-seated fears about the potential alteration of demographic balances and erosion of indigenous cultures.

Political Dynamics and Amendments

The Bill's journey through the legislative process was anything but smooth. It faced significant opposition initially and lapsed in the Rajya Sabha (Upper House of the Parliament of India). Influential political figures from the Northeast, including the Chief Ministers of few Northeastern States, were pivotal in articulating the concerns of their constituents. Their advocacy brought national attention to the unique challenges faced by the region, eventually contributing to the re-evaluation of the Bill.

Recognizing the sensitivities involved, the Government reintroduced the Bill with crucial amendments which read as 6B (4) *"Nothing in this section shall apply to tribal area of Assam, Meghalaya, Mizoram or Tripura as included in the Sixth Schedule to the Constitution and the area covered under "The Inner Line" notified under the Bengal Eastern Frontier Regulation, 1873".*[25] These modifications specifically excluded areas under the Sixth

Schedule and those protected by the Bengal Eastern Frontier Regulations (BEFR) of 1873. Arunachal Pradesh figured in the exclusion, where the BEFR has historically regulated the movement and settlement of outsiders, thereby preserving the demographic and cultural fabric of the state.

The revised CAA, with its exclusions, was eventually passed in 2019, marking a significant moment in India's legislative history. This outcome not only reflected the compassion displayed by the central leadership towards the sensitivity of the fragile demographic fabric of the region but also underscored the continuing relevance of colonial-era laws like the BEFR in contemporary governance. These laws, once designed to manage the frontiers of the British Empire in India, are now pivotal in balancing modern India's national priorities with regional sensitivities.

As Arunachal Pradesh and other Northeastern states navigate the complexities of modern governance, the legacy of the BEFR and its implications on the CAA represent layers of historical and legislative evolution. These regulations not only shape the legal landscape but also influence how communities perceive their place within the broader national context. Imagine the political landscape and evolution of Arunachal Pradesh without the BEFR and the exclusion accorded under the GOI Act, 1935. Episodes like the CAA helps us appreciate the present day unintended positive consequences that unfold in favour of Arunachal Pradesh.

One need not look far, but in our near neighbourhood, to see how native tribes have become minorities in their own land. Perhaps, in the absence of a regime like the *Inner Line*, Arunachal Pradesh would have gone a similar way and the various tribes would have been reduced to minorities in their own land. Whatever the intent, the Regulation has been singularly responsible for the preservation of the sanctity of the Tribes, secure with their lands, waters, forests and rich composite culture.

Looking ahead, the challenges for policymakers will be to continue adapting these historical frameworks to meet contemporary needs while ensuring that the rights and identities of indigenous populations are respected and preserved. This delicate balancing act will likely continue to shape the political and social dynamics of the region in the years to come.

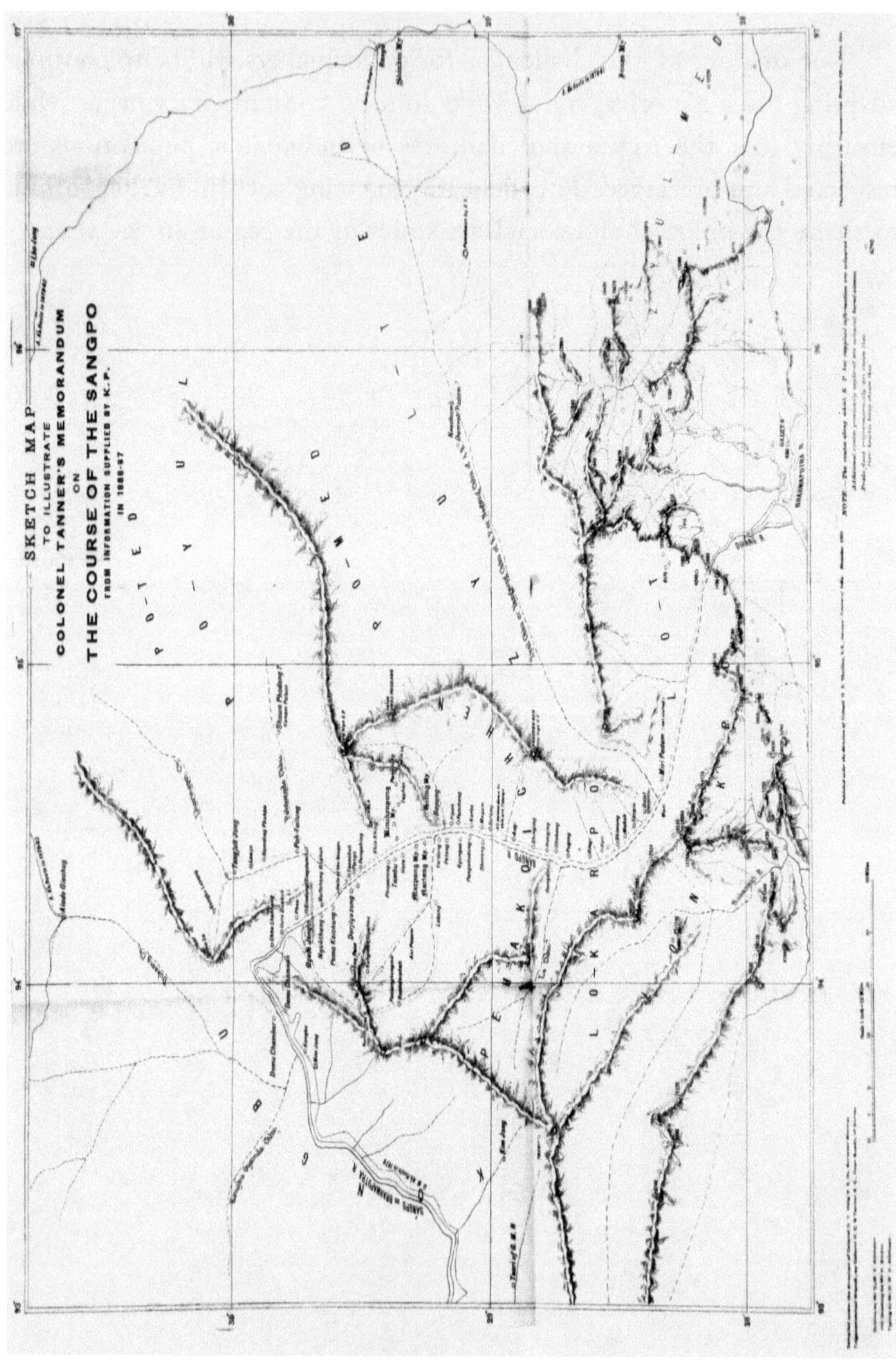

▲ **Map 1:** The Course of Tsangpo (1886-87) to illustrate Colonel Tanner's Memorandum (Source: Directorate of Research, Government of Arunachal Pradesh)

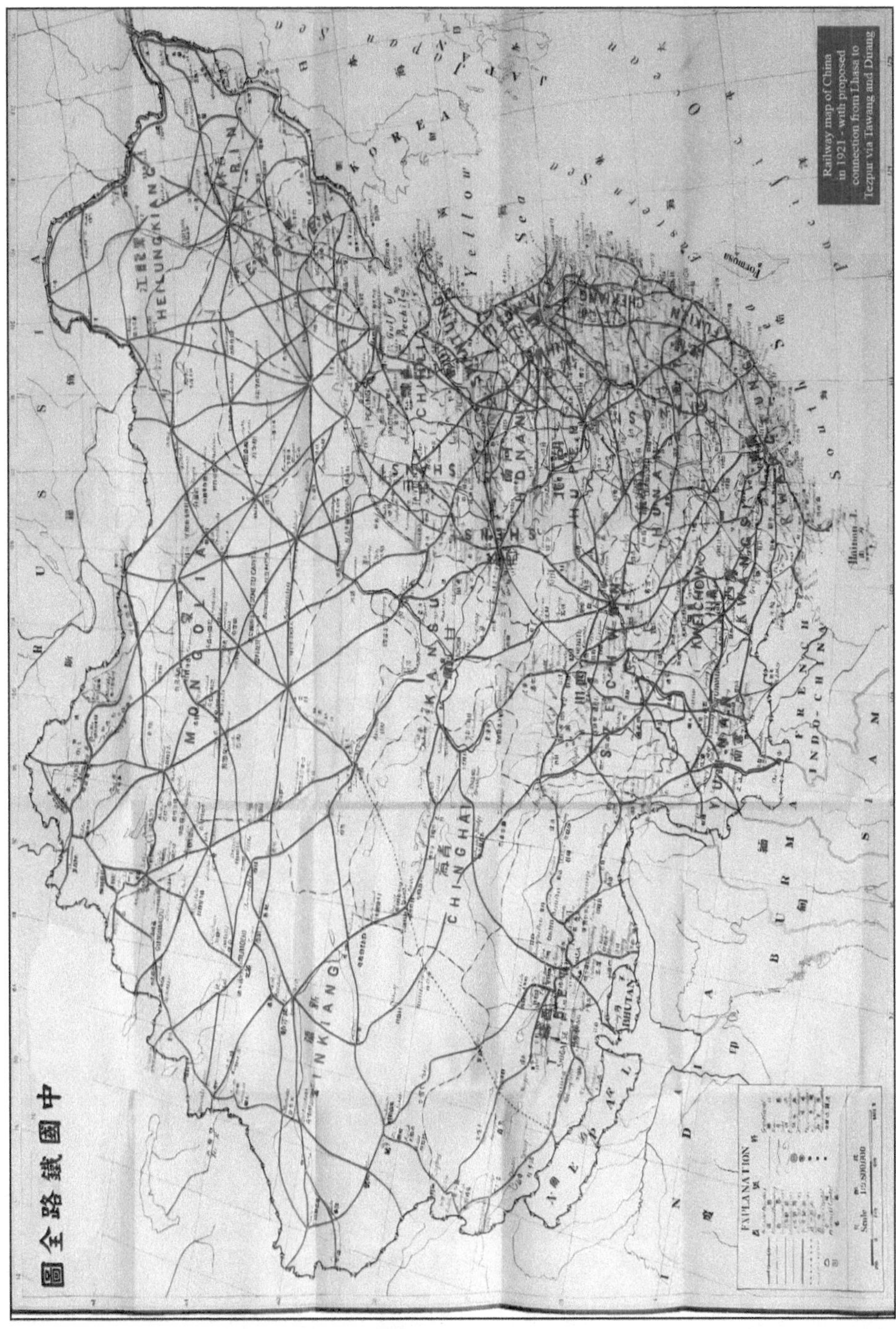

▲ **Map 2:** Railway Map of China showing proposed Line from Lhasa to Tezpur via Tawang and Dirang, 1921 (Source: Claude Arpi)

"Empire expansion is not about the settlement of moral scores, but about the material settlement of foreign lands and peoples."
– Richard Drayton

2

The Anglo-Abor War: A Confluence of Conflict and Colonial Ambition

The British may have viewed their mission to the Abor Hills as a routine expedition, but beneath the surface, a far more dangerous game was at play. Unbeknownst to Noel Williamson and Dr. Gregorson, their deaths would ignite a fuse not only for the Anglo-Abor War of 1911 but for a larger clash of imperial ambitions and tribal resistance. As the British grappled with growing Qing Dynasty influence and the Adis hardened their stance against foreign encroachment, this small corner of India became the battlefield for forces far greater than themselves. Hidden in the shadows of this remote frontier, an ancient people would stand defiantly against one of the most powerful empires in history. The question was: who would break first?

The Anglo-Abor War of 1911, a notable yet often overlooked conflict in the annals of British colonial history, provides a vivid tableau of the tensions that characterised the British expansionist policies in Northeastern Frontier of India. It all began when Noel Williamson and Dr. Gregorson were on a tour to the Abor Hills which went horribly wrong leading to the murder of both the Englishmen. Their excursion was rather an exploratory mission authorised to study the extent of Tibetan influences in the region. But beneath this, it is said that he also wanted to be the first to solve the biggest mystery of the time, to establish the Tsangpo-Brahmaputra linkage. Initially, the British Government of India had prohibited expeditions beyond the *Inner Line*. However, the growing influence of Zhao Erfeng, Military Commander of the Qing Dynasty, in the Dzayul area led Delhi (British India) to grant limited permission to venture beyond the *Inner line* strictly for information gathering, provided it did not lead to complications[26]. This nuanced approach was aimed at better understanding the dynamics at play without escalating tensions.

The earliest documented interactions between the British and the Adis, dating back to 1830, began with Captain Neufville commissioning David Scott to build guard houses to manage disputes over land between the Adis and the Mishing areas[27]. By 1840, David Scott acknowledged the Adis as one of the relatively cooperative tribes of the region, signalling a period of initial congenial relations. However, tensions escalated in 1847 after a night attack on Captain Vetch's camp in the Adi land, marking the start of a deteriorating relationship. Subsequent conflicts, including the Kebang Clan's attack on the Beehas in 1858, prompted British expeditions and intensified efforts to establish control. By 1878, a guard post at Nizamghat underscored ongoing British efforts to assert authority, while Chief Commissioner Sir Charles Elliot sought official engagement with the Adis and other frontier tribes, reflecting a shift towards formal political management and governance strategies in the region. That was not to be, yet.

In 1882, Jack Francis Needham arrived in Sadiya, a British Base, as the Political Officer, and by 1884, he ventured into the Abor Hills to initiate political engagements. However, towards the end of the 19th century, the Adis grew increasingly unsettled, persistently raiding the plains. The 1894 expedition led by Captain Maxwell and Needham further strained relations. These strained interactions between the British and the Adis would significantly influence events in the following years.

The Spark of Conflict

Noel Williamson, serving as the British Political Officer in Sadiya since 1904, navigated the intricate balance of diplomacy and authority essential for maintaining relations with the tribal communities of Northeast Frontier. Renowned for his diplomatic finesse and the ability to foster alliances among tribal leaders, Williamson's expeditions into the Abor hills, first in 1905 (where he went without escort) somewhat thawed the acrimonious relation. In 1908 he marched from Pasighat through Ledum and further westward[28], tours which were critical to the British strategy for mapping these regions. These efforts were aimed at bolstering the northeastern frontiers against the backdrop of the Qing Empire's weakening control over China and the encroaching Russian influence on China, as seen in the developments following the successful British expedition to Tibet in 1904 led by Francis Younghusband[29].

By 1906, with the signing of the Anglo-Chinese Treaty which recognized Chinese suzerainty over Lhasa[30], and the subsequent Qing expansion under Zhao Erfeng reaching Kongbo by 1910, British unease over China's advances grew. The situation was further aggravated by their active presence in Dzayul, prompting British India to reconsider its stance against northward exploration. Initially reluctant, the British eventually allowed limited and low-risk reconnaissance missions to monitor Chinese activities.

In March 1911, amidst these geopolitical tensions, the murder of Williamson and his party at Komsing, including Dr. Gregorson at the Pangi camp[31], dramatically shifted the scenario. This event, far from being an isolated act of violence, was a stark manifestation of the larger regional dynamics and British anxieties about Qing encroachments. The massacre not only challenged British authority but also demanded a recalibrated response, pushing Delhi and the London Office to sanction further actions to assert control of the Frontier and prevent any future escalations.

Looking back, this was not the first faceoff between the Adis and the British Raj. *Bitbor Mimak of 1858, Bongal Mimak of 1859, Nijom Mimak of 1894*[32], all local names for the Anglo-Abor conflicts, were all precursors to the 1911 Anglo-Abor War which played out at Kekar Monying (present day Siang District of Arunachal Pradesh). The deep distrust towards the outsiders by the people of the Adi Hills culminated in this incident, which sparked a major retribution. This would sow the seed for major changes in the political landscape of the region, accelerating the entrenchment of the British into the Frontier.

The immediate trigger was when Williamson asked the villagers to present before him the persons guilty of stealing provisions and some liquor from the camp. The Adi version is that Manmur Jamoh had conceived the murder in 1908, when during his earlier visit, Williamson had insulted Manmur Jamoh in his own village.[33]

British Military Response

After extensive deliberations, heightened by the Qing Empire's ambitious advances close to the Eastern frontiers, the British Government recognized the urgent need for a decisive response. On July 24, 1911, the London Office authorised a shift from its previous policy of non-interference to active engagement, motivated by competitive concerns over regional control[34]-a strategic decision reflecting the stark reality that dominance in the area would rest either with the Qing or with the British. The choice was clear for the British Crown. This strategic decision was hastened by the murder of the two Englishmen representing the Crown in the Eastern Frontier.

Under the command of Major-General Bowers[35], the British military launched a robust expedition. This force, consisting of several battalions and equipped with modern artillery, was not only tasked with punitive actions against the Adis but also aimed to solidify the British presence through the establishment of stockades and thorough mapping and exploration of the territory. The mission faced significant logistical challenges due to the rugged terrain and the onset of the rainy season, which complicated and delayed their operations. This military initiative marked a critical moment in asserting British influence in the face of growing geopolitical competition. The '*Terra Incognita*' was now to be exposed to the British colonial power.

"*It is of prime importance that we should take advantage of the opportunity afforded by the expedition to carry out surveys and explorations as may be possible, in order to obtain knowledge requisite for the determination of a suitable boundary between India and China in this locality.*"[36] This was the direction from the Viceroy to the Secretary of State for India Henry McMahon stating the real objective of the punitive expedition.

In response to the Qing forces' plans to invade Pemako and Pome, areas bordering Tibet in the Siang Basin by the spring of 1911[37], the British military adopted a strategic two-pronged approach to counter the advancing threat and assert their regional dominance. The main column of the British force advanced through the Dibang valley, penetrating deep into the heart of the Abor Country. Simultaneously, a smaller column was tasked with securing the flanks, a crucial move to encircle and diminish the capacity of the Abors to resist[38].

This strategic deployment aimed not only at subduing the Adis but also at achieving critical geographical and strategic objectives. These included surveying the region comprehensively and establishing a more defined and enforceable boundary with Tibet. This military manoeuvre was a direct counter to the Qing's aggressive expansion, representing a calculated effort by the British to maintain control over the soon to be contested border regions.

Indigenous Resistance and Adaptation

The Adis employed guerrilla tactics, leveraging their deep knowledge of the terrain to launch ambushes and raids against the advancing troops. For the Adis, the conflict came to be known as *'Poju Mimak'*, or the Anglo-Abor War of 1911[39]. Despite their initial resistance, owing to less fighting power, inferior weaponry, the overwhelming military might and strategic operations of the British gradually could garner a truce of sorts. Nonetheless, it must be acknowledged that the fight lasted for three long months. The war, which erupted in October 1911, concluded by New Year's Eve of the same year[40]. This marked an important turning point, ushering in a new era of British presence and influence over the previously indomitable frontiers and its people. This period not only represented a shift in control but also signalled the start of a new chapter in the history of the region under British Administration. The conflict was marked by numerous skirmishes and the establishment of British outposts deep inside the previously autonomous tribal areas. The murder was a culmination of the widespread discontentment of the Adis against the British. Therefore, the entire movement can be compared to any other nationalistic movement that was directed against British imperialism in different parts of the country.[41]

Aftermath and Reflections

By early 1912, the immediate objectives of the expedition were largely achieved. The Adi villages were subdued, significant territories were mapped, and a semblance of peace was restored, albeit tentatively. The British also conducted trials and meted out punishments to those involved in the massacre, further cementing their judicial and administrative reach into the region.

The war, though ultimately deemed a truce between the Adis and the British Army, was indeed a pyrrhic one. It starkly exposed the vulnerabilities inherent in British colonial strategies, specifically highlighting the formidable challenges associated with governing distant territories characterised by deeply entrenched tribal identities. Moreover, the conflict underscored the substantial costs-both in terms of human lives and resources that were required to maintain control over such remote regions. This revelation not only questioned the sustainability of such colonial endeavours but also spotlighted the intricate dynamics and resilience of the local tribal communities in the face of external pressures.

The North-East Frontier Tracts is born: British Forward Policy takes shape

This event was an important milestone in the opening of the *'Terra Incognita'* or the unknown land to the lights of the modern world. The policy of non-intervention now gave way to the policy of active intervention[42]. Following the tragic events of the Anglo-Abor War, there was a significant shift in British policy towards the frontier areas, the *British Forward Policy* was operationalised. One of the immediate outcomes was a notable change in the administrative hierarchy of the Frontier Administration. Previously, Political Officers (POs), tasked with overseeing frontier areas, reported to the nearest Deputy Commissioner. However, in the aftermath of the conflict, on their request, the approval of reporting directly to the Provincial Governor was received[43]. This streamlined administrative processes and facilitated a quicker, more direct line of communication and decision-making.

Additionally, this shift heralded the introduction of some semblance of administrative machinery in the frontier areas, which later evolved into an official entity known as the North East Frontier Tracts (NEFT). This development represented a critical step in formalising British administration in these remote areas, significantly altering the governance landscape of the Eastern Frontiers; meanwhile the tribal communities had their own introduction to life under British Authority.

The Anglo-Abor War, apart from others, sowed the seed and laid the foundations of administrative machinery in the Eastern Frontiers. The first half of the 20th century was thus a period of substantial administrative reforms and territorial demarcation within British India in the frontier territories. The establishment of the North-East Frontier Tracts (NEFT) in 1914 marked a crucial evolution in British strategies in the Frontier. This significant shift from the Policy of Non-Interference was specifically designed to strengthen the British hold over an area renowned for its complex mosaic of tribal cultures, rugged terrain, and significant geopolitical importance. The NEFT was organised into three divisions: the Central & Eastern Frontier Tract, the Lakhimpur Frontier Tract, and the Western Frontier Tract[44] to address the unique challenges and dynamics of its respective area, further solidifying British control over these strategically vital frontiers.

The Northeast Frontier, with its diverse array of ethnic groups and challenging geographies, presented a unique administrative challenge to the British Raj. Prior to the formation of NEFT, the region was a loosely defined frontier, managed under various political offices with overlapping and sometimes conflicting jurisdictions. The area was fraught with resistance to external control, evidenced by frequent tribal uprisings and the difficulties faced in penetrating the region.

The decision to create the **North-East Frontier Tracts** was driven by several factors. Professedly, the foremost among these was the need for a more efficient administrative system that could integrate the region more effectively into the British Indian framework. On the contrary, it was primarily because of growing concerns over the influence of neighbouring countries like China and Tibet, making the stabilisation of this frontier a priority for strategic and security reasons.

Origins of Administrative Reforms

In 1912, in response to these challenges, the British government formalised the boundaries of what would be known as the North-East Frontier Tracts, two years later. This new administrative entity amalgamated several areas, including the erstwhile Abor Hills, Mishmi Hills, and unadministered areas along the Assam-Tibet border. The primary aim was to create a manageable and cohesive administrative unit that could oversee and coordinate the British policies effectively across the Northeastern Frontier.

The governance structure was designed to be flexible yet authoritative, allowing for a degree of autonomy within local tribal contexts while establishing firmer British oversight. This dual approach was intended to mitigate resistance by respecting traditional tribal hierarchies and customs, thereby facilitating smoother governance and lessening occurrences of conflicts.

Challenges and Implementation

The implementation of this new administrative tract was not without challenges. The diversity of the tribes, each with their distinct dialects, cultures, and social structures, posed significant difficulties in establishing a one-size-fits-all administrative protocol. Moreover, the remoteness and inaccessibility of the region made it hard to enforce policies effectively or to respond swiftly to local issues.

British officials appointed to manage the NEFT had to navigate a complex landscape of tribal politics, cultural sensitivities, and logistical hurdles. These administrators, carefully appointed and preferred with experience in frontier management, were tasked with the dual role of governance and diplomatic engagement with tribal leaders. Their responsibilities included everything from handling local disputes and overseeing development projects to ensuring the security of borders.

Over time, the NEFT helped in bringing a semblance of order to a region previously marked by volatility. With more engagements and British presence, it laid the groundwork for future administrative delineation and opened up avenues for more systematic exploration and mapping of these frontier areas. The NEFT also played a crucial role during the later stages of the British Raj and the early years of independent India in defining the contours of the Northeast Frontier's political and administrative identity. It was the beginning of more frequent and to some extent, more intimate interactions between the Raj and the Frontier population and would sow the seeds for the commencement of a deep-rooted governance structure in days to come.

In retrospect, the formation of the North-East Frontier Tracts, triggered by the *Poju Mimak*, is a testament to the challenges of colonial administration over diverse and isolated regions. It shows how tricky it can be to govern frontier areas. They are not just far-off places on the map; but an area with rich cultural mixes that need thoughtful and delicate ways of being governed and included.

Consider this. Had Zhao Erfeng not advanced southwards, and the Williamson murder not occurred, the British might have hesitated to adopt the Forward Policy with the urgency they did. In this alternate scenario, the frontier might have remained more isolated, with delayed British administrative inroads. This could have led to a significantly different historical trajectory, where the integration of the frontier areas into the Indian administrative framework occurred at a much slower pace. The absence of a strong British presence might have allowed local powers and allegiances to evolve, potentially leading to a more autonomous or distinct regional identity. The geopolitical dynamics of the region, without the immediate influence of British policies, could have charted a vastly different course, altering the region's place in the broader narrative of Indian history.

———— ◆ ————

"The drawing of borders is not merely an act of delineation but a declaration of destiny."
— **Cecil Rhodes**

3

The Red (McMahon) Line: A Product of Bailey's Trail

Shadow Boxing becomes reality

We have seen that the beginning of the 20th Century was marked by a complex geopolitical dance. The weakening of Chinese control over Tibet and fears of Russian influence growing in the region spurred the *British Forward Policy*[45], to increase British presence northwards, including Lhasa. The British administration was particularly alarmed by the Russian encroachment, fearing Tibet might fall into what they termed a "Russian Orbit."[46] This concern led to the Younghusband expedition in 1904, which, while temporarily asserting British dominance, irritated the Qing Chinese and provoked them to secure the Kham region under Zhao Erfeng, General of the Qing Dynasty, known as "The Butcher."[47] The quick Chinese advance southwards was not to the comfort of the Frontier Officials and certainly not Assam and Delhi.

By December 1911, in the rugged terrain of the Eastern Frontier Himalayas, British counter colonial ambitions were intensifying. WCM Dundas, newly appointed Political Officer at Sadiya, embarked on a significant reconnaissance mission up the Lohit Valley. Guided by intelligence from Tungno, the village head of Pangum, and Mezanon, the Digaru Mishmi headman, Dundas was investigating reports of Chinese activities in the valley. Seizing this opportunity, Dundas fostered and reinforced peaceful relations with the local Mishmi tribes. The tour reports of Francis Needham submitted earlier had already raised alarm bells in Delhi and London. Later reports of O'Callaghan substantiated this. In fact, he removed the markers, repositioned them upstream, near Kahao, just south of the McMahon Line.[48]

Upon reaching Menilkrai, Dundas encountered unmistakable signs of Chinese encroachment: flags adorned with four-clawed dragons and a wooden board declaring "*The Southern frontier of Dzayul on the borders of the Szechuan Province of the Chinese Empire.*" Additionally, he discovered fifteen 'Warrant of Protection' documents issued by Zhao Erfeng, found with the headman of Delei Valley. These documents were meant for presentation to Chinese officials during trade trips to Tibet or when dealing with British authorities[49].

In response, Dundas established a cairn and placed a bilingual notification asserting British territorial claims, in response to which Chinese officials from Dzayul installed a Qing pillar next to Dundas's cairn, immediately on Dundas' return. Backed by reports of these encounters and the strategic significance of the area, the Delhi Office, with little resistance from London, agreed to strengthen the administrative base at Sadiya. Plans were set in motion for expanding British presence, including establishing posts at Menilkrai, constructing a bridle road up to Walong, another trek to the Dibang Valley, and a telegraph link to connect Sadiya with these new outposts, thus solidifying British influence and responding to the geopolitical shifts in the region[50]. How quickly was this plan achieved? We will see later in the Book.

A Weak China and its fallout

This era of exploration and expansion coincided with significant political shifts in the region, particularly following the fall of the Qing Dynasty in 1911. The establishment of the Republic of China on January 1, 1912, led to widespread revolts against the Qing Army, creating a Chinese vacuum in Tibet and its bordering areas. Tibet, under the 13th Dalai Lama, rejected all overtures from the new Republic and declared its independence[51].

Conscious of the need for a clearly defined boundary to prevent future complications and ensure stability, Tibet was open to negotiating a Sino-Tibetan border, aligning with the British desire to clearly delineate the frontier with Tibet. The British, recognizing the strategic importance of stabilising the volatile Kham boundary, protecting the Assam hinterlands, and establishing a buffer zone, were prepared to provide the necessary external support for these negotiations. This backdrop of mutual interests eventually compelled Beijing to the negotiating table in October 1913, under the veiled British threat to cut financial support and deny diplomatic recognition to the new Chinese Republic[52]. Further, the ongoing war at Kham and the Tibetan advances in the area forced the Chinese to take a seat in the negotiations. While the round table was set, the first imperative to decide borders was a map-not table-drawn cartography by armchair cartographers but one which had its heels dug on the high ranges of the Himalayas.

Bailey-Morshead Expedition

From the Sadiya base, in the late 19th century, British India officers often made bold, albeit mostly unauthorised, attempts to penetrate the '*Inner Line*'-the northern frontier shrouded in mystery and home to the Adi and Mishmi tribes. The dense jungles and fierce resistance from these tribes made any significant progress difficult.

Among these various attempts, the expedition led by Frederick Marshman Bailey and Captain Henry Morshead in 1913 stands out. Frederick Bailey, born in Lahore in 1882 and a veteran of the British Indian Army, had an extensive background in political and intelligence operations. After participating in the 1904 Tibet invasion, he served as the British Trade Agent in Sikkim. His interest in the region deepened after a failed 1911 attempt to trace the reported 150-foot waterfall on the Yarlung Tsangpo, first brought to light by Kinthup[53], a Sikkimese explorer. Kinthup, originally working as a servant for a British expedition in the 1880s, became a key figure when his daring solo journey through the Tsangpo

Gorge revealed significant geographical details. Despite enduring extreme hardship, his findings intrigued the British and led Bailey to continue his search for the elusive waterfall.

Henry Morshead, his contemporary, also born in 1882, joined the Indian Army and later served with the Survey of India. His expertise in cartography was pivotal during their joint expedition, which focused on mapping the Frontier and the elusive Tsangpo Gorges[54].

Frederick Bailey and Henry Morshead embarked on a monumental journey that would span 1,680 miles over the course of six gruelling months, from May to November of 1913. This expedition was not just a journey through the unknown but a groundbreaking effort to chart the mysterious connections between major rivers and to map the contours of a frontier that had baffled explorers for decades.

Mapping the Frontier

Their route took them from Mipi in the Dibang Valley, in the East, cutting across the rugged terrain of Tibet, and finally emerging in Tawang, at the western end. Throughout their trek, they encountered not only the physical challenges of the landscape but also made significant contributions to the understanding of natural history and the geographic mysteries of the Tsangpo Gorge-famously linking it to the Brahmaputra River.

This arduous journey laid the groundwork for what would become one of the most significant geopolitical decisions of the era-the delineation of the *McMahon Line*, which today marks the boundary between India in Arunachal Pradesh and Tibet-China. The efforts of Bailey and Morshead during this expedition became crucial in shaping the face of Eastern Asia.

Bailey, in his later years, chronicled this adventure in his 1957 memoir, *"No Passport to Tibet."* Reflecting on the expedition, he acknowledged the indispensable role of his partner, Morshead, whose enthusiasm and expertise were vital to the success of their mission[55]. It was an endeavour that, in today's context, might seem risky-yet in 1913, it was a bold and a necessary undertaking.

Before this landmark expedition, Bailey had already been part of a lesser-known solo expedition in 1912, which caught the attention of Sir Henry McMahon, the then Foreign Secretary. McMahon was contemplating an international treaty to settle the boundary issue between Tibet, China, and British India-a task that necessitated a detailed map of the region. In Bailey, McMahon saw the man cut out for the mission.

Bailey's previous experiences and his deep understanding of the Tibetan landscape and its people were instrumental as he prepared for the 1913 mission. He knew that a solo journey would be impractical for the ambitious goals he had in mind. Fortuitously, he found in Morshead not only a colleague but a kindred spirit, equally driven to push the limits of known geography.

Together, they planned to navigate from Showa village, traverse westward along the Tsangpo Valley, and meticulously map the Himalayan watershed up to the junction with Bhutan. From there, they would head south back to Assam, carrying with them the critical data that would eventually help Sir Henry McMahon propose the historical boundary.

This expedition was not merely about mapping an unknown land; it was about securing a future, about understanding a mysterious territory that had long stood as a buffer between empires. Bailey and Morshead, through their dedication and daring, turned what could have been mere footnotes in colonial archives into pivotal moments that shaped the future of a region. Their journey was a testament to the power of exploration and the enduring quest for knowledge.

On 14th November 1913, the duo reached Rangiya and Morshead records, 'At Tamulpur we got 3 buffalo carts, on which we travelled at night, reaching the railway station at 2:30 AM, after a journey of 1683 miles from Mipi in Dibang Valley'[56]. After completing their ground-breaking expedition, Frederick Bailey received a telegram from the Foreign Secretary while recuperating in Calcutta, urging him to travel to Simla as quickly as possible. This message marked the beginning of a crucial chapter in the geopolitical history of the region, India and the World.

The Simla Conference had already commenced in October 1913, but it faced delays as the Tibetan and Chinese representatives hesitated, each waiting for the other to make the first move. The situation prompted the British Indian Government to notify China that they would proceed with negotiations with Tibet alone, if necessary. This led to the rapid arrival of Ivan Chen from China. Between 13th October 1913, when it formally convened, and 3 July 1914, when it dispersed, the Simla Conference held eight formal sessions. The first two took place at Simla on 13 October and 18 November respectively; the next three at Delhi, on 12 January, 17 February and 11 March (1914); and the last three again at Simla, on 7 and 22 April (re-convened on 27 April) and 3 July.[57]

The negotiations progressed slowly, hindered by the need for the Chinese and Tibetans to consult their respective governments at every turn. For the Tibetans, this was particularly challenging due to the lack of telegraphic communication with Lhasa. This delay, however, afforded Morshead the necessary time to complete the detailed map[58] that would become crucial for the negotiations.

After six months of tripartite discussions, the 1st Simla Convention was held and was signed on April 27, 1914, by representatives from Tibet, China, and India[59]. The key points were:

- **Division of Tibet:** Tibet was divided into "Inner" and "Outer" regions. Outer Tibet, roughly corresponding to the present-day Tibet Autonomous Region, was recognized as autonomous under Tibetan rule, free from interference from China or India. However, the British retained the right to station trade agents and a few troops.
- **Chinese Suzerainty:** The agreement acknowledged Chinese suzerainty over the entirety of Tibet but included an undertaking from China that Tibet would not be converted into a Chinese province.
- **Rights in Inner Tibet:** The Government in Lhasa retained its rights over Inner Tibet, which would roughly include Amdo and eastern Kham, but China could send troops, officials, and establish colonies.

However, by June end, the territorial dispute between the Outer and Inner Tibet cropped up. Eventually in the 2nd Simla Convention on 3rd July 1914[60], the Indo-Tibet Border agreement was signed between McMahon and Lonchen Paljor Dorje Shatra.

A critical aspect of the Simla Conference was the negotiation of the frontier between Tibet and present day Arunachal Pradesh. This frontier stretched from the East of Bhutan along the Eastern Himalayan crest to the point where China, Tibet, and the Burmese hinterland meet-a frontier that had never been clearly defined before now had a clear map agreed to by all stakeholders.

Thanks to the efforts at Simla, it became possible to establish a boundary along the Eastern Frontier spanning over eight hundred and fifty miles through challenging and perilous terrain. This newly defined boundary set the frontier about a hundred miles from the plains of India, incorporating difficult hills and valleys that would serve as a formidable barrier.

Drawing of the Frontier

Drawing the frontier was a complex process. As negotiations proceeded, the Tibetans made certain concessions to the Government of India, which in turn guaranteed the Simla Convention. Notably, following the watershed and the highest ridge principle, regions such as Tawang and Dirang Dzong were to be within the Indian Territory[61]. This demarcation later came to be known as the McMahon Line, named after Sir Henry McMahon, who played a pivotal role in steering the agreement. Claude Arpi in our conversation, however, strongly advocates that the line should ideally be called the *McMahon-Shatra Line,* as both were signatory of the agreement. It actually makes a lot of sense.

However, the process was not without its share of challenges. Ivan Chen, representing China, did not initial the 'final agreement'. Apparently, disagreements between Tibet and China over the Sino-Tibetan border further complicated matters. Disagreement stemmed on the boundary of

Inner Tibet (China insisted on the boundary set by Zhao Erfeng at the height of his Campaign-which includes the whole of Kham, Dzayul and Pome; Tibet and Delhi both insisted on recognizing the general watershed as it stood between Tibet and Qing China at the beginning of the 20th century).

The boundary encompassed several key regions, including the strategic areas of Arunachal Pradesh (then part of the North-East Frontier), the high-altitude passes of Nathu La and Jelep La, and the contested territories along the McMahon Line. Both parties viewed this natural division as crucial for defining the frontier, particularly in regions such as Tawang, which held religious and cultural significance, and the Tibetan plateau, which served as a buffer between British India and Qing China[62]. With no zone of potential agreement in sight, the trilateral turned to bilateral negotiations.

Despite these obstacles, on July 3, 1914, Lonchen Shatra and the British representatives signed the agreement. This version included conditions that the agreement would not grant any privileges to China until they agreed to sign it. Simultaneously, a new trade agreement, which superseded the 1908 agreement, was also signed between Tibet and British India[63].

The boundary outline of the Agreement was about 1400 KM (850 Miles) extending from the Northern edge of Bhutan in the West to Upper Myanmar. Accordingly, Walong was positioned below the line in Lohit. Most of Mónyul (Tawang) in the West now fell clearly under the British Indian Territory providing *'a good clean line on the map'*[64]. This was a significant achievement of the agreement, as this *'Wedge'*, as seen by the Political Officer at Sikkim, had clear signs of Chinese covet. The advantages British India gained in this 'Wedge' included, the shortest route to Lhasa from Assam, an area with less inclement monsoon, and good agriculture potential. The compromise was accepted by the Tibetans after the British Plenipotentiary promised to pressure the Chinese Government to approve the demarcation of the border between Tibet and China'.[65]

The purported 'compromise' was not true after all. It is interesting to note here that the location of the customs house just north of the range suggests that the Tibetans did not consider Tawang as part of Tibet proper. This idea is rather confirmed by the discrimination made between the merchandise going to the south and that coming from the south of the range. Had it been just an internal toll house, no such discrimination would have occurred. Thus, though the Tawang tract north of the Se La seems to have been under a greater degree of Tibetan control than the country south of the Se La, the Tibetans themselves do not seem to have considered this northern part as within Tibet proper.[66]

Bailey's biographer recalls *"Morshead continued working on his maps, calling in Bailey for consultation whenever necessary. It was very gratifying to feel the glow of official approval, and a fortunate chance that the information acquired on the expedition should have proved so vital to the political negotiations. Without it, the Indian Government would have been negotiating a treaty regarding territory both unexplored and unmapped"*[67]. Indeed, the duo's efforts were central to the entire negotiations.

Northeastern Frontiers after the Simla Agreement

On ground, the problems of the *Line* continued to irritate the Frontier Administrators. The long tour of the duo was not sufficient to fully understand the geography of the Eastern Himalayas-physical and human. The watershed or the highest ridge principle was easier drawn on map than delineated on ground. The absence of clear guidelines and cartographic inaccuracies made it challenging to establish the McMahon Line on the ground. With the precise location of the line undefined, the full extent of the issue went unnoticed by the authorities at the time.

McMahon had recommended immediate takeover and control of Tawang. Assam Officials concurred[68]. However, there was in fact no clear intention both at London and Delhi to administratively strengthen presence in the Eastern Frontier. The period of 1914-1935 were decades of a lull in the colonial presence in the region, evidently due to little or no threat of Chinese expansionism. And there was the World War I for 4 years, which took full attention of Britain.

Along the Sino-Tibet border, China's refusal to recognise the 1914 Simla Convention, led to resumption of conflict in 1917 in Chamdo. Facing military defeat, British diplomat Eric Teichman was requested by China to mediate a ceasefire agreement with Tibet, which culminated in the tripartite Rongbatsa Agreement of 1918. This agreement defined the border between Tibet and China.[69] It is another story that China later refuted the Agreement.

During this period, more so during the 1920-1930s - a stronger Tibet began to assert control in the outlying areas, especially Tawang, the Nah area of Subansiri and as deep towards the Ramos, Pailibos and the Adi Country[70].

While the Eastern Frontier was now sandwiched between two lines- the Inner and McMahon, in 1919, pursuant to the Chelmsford Reforms, lines of administrative territories of the Frontier were also redrawn, to make critical amendments in administering these areas-the Sadiya Frontier Tract (Central and Eastern Sections), the Lakhimpur Frontier Tract and the Balipara Frontier Tract (Western Sections)[71] were to be the new Administrative Entities.

The much-touted Buffer Logic of the British Indian Government for the Eastern Himalayas, restrained their aim only to achieving '*External Sovereignty*'[72]. To that end, roads, outposts and other infrastructure were restricted to the bare minimum, only to fulfil the buffer requirements. When the Chinese Checker moves recessed, London and Delhi turned to 'more pressing' needs elsewhere.

The handful of British outposts decaying and eventually disappearing, were some of the immediate consequences. Many territories gained out of the Agreement did not see any presence of the State till the 1940s. The majority of the Monpas, lived in blissful ignorance of their masters till 1951-another landmark event, which will unfold later in the book.

Frederick Bailey reflected in his memoir on the broader context of these events. He speculated that if not for the outbreak of the First World War, the Simla Convention might have stabilised the region and provided

Tibet with the peace it needed. However, he noted that China continued its aggressive policies, just as he had feared during his discussions in Tsetang.[73]

Interestingly, the Simla Agreement remained relatively obscure for years. It was not included in the authoritative *"A Collection of Treaties"* by C.U. Aitchison in its 1929 edition. Why? Was it deliberate or an oversight? There is no straight answer to this. The First World War had begun and the British were not in favour of antagonising the Russians. Naive as it may seem, the British held a view that the unnecessary publicity[74] of the agreement could also renew Chinese interest in Tibet and raise questions about British Imperialism.

On the ground, Frontier Officers noticed no significant changes in the situation, and the McMahon Line remained largely overlooked until a pivotal incident in 1935 rekindled interest in the Agreement. This resurgence of attention can be credited to Olaf Caroe, who was serving as the Deputy Foreign Secretary at the time. The trigger for this renewed focus was an episode involving Frank Kingdon Ward, a renowned plant hunter and explorer who, in late 1935, ventured into Tawang and crossed into Tibet without the necessary permissions[75]. This unauthorised expedition irked Tibetan officials in Lhasa, prompting them to send a stern letter to Delhi. This incident drew the attention of the British to the ongoing control and presence of Dzongpons in Tawang, starkly contradicting the terms of the Simla Agreement. After a lapse of two decades, the McMahon Line was not yet stabilised on ground. With a stronger China in sight, Caroe had to fix this and do so quickly.

In 1938, during the Viceroyalty of Lord Linglithgow, upon receiving affirmation from the Government of India, Caroe had the Agreement published in a revised volume of Aitchison's Treaties. The previous year, the Survey of India had published a map that showed the McMahon Line demarcating the border from East of Bhutan along the Himalayan crest up to the trijunction of Tibet-British India-Burma, North of what is now Arunachal Pradesh. Caroe's contributions were so significant that some scholars have suggested the boundary be referred to as the '*McMahon-Caroe Line*'.

Even after publication of the map, limited printing and circulation proved problematic as many American and few British maps did not adhere to the McMahon Line; 'Apparent Forgetfulness'[76] or deliberate apathy-this attitude left behind a difficult legacy. British *'Sovereignty Goals'* in the Eastern Himalayas, to say the least, were at best half-hearted and reactionary to Chinese Moves.

The implications of the Simla Agreement continued to unfold over decades. In 1938, Captain G.S. Lightfoot[77] travelled to Tawang and informed the local monastery that Monyul was an Indian territory, which caused some unease amongst the Tibetan Dzongpons from Tsona. Lightfoot submitted a detailed report along with a host of recommendations for bringing effective administration in the area. According to him, the tract had about 80 villages with about 2,140 houses. Despite this declaration and recommendations, Civil Administration reached Tawang only in 1951. We will see later, how.

The endeavour of Bailey and Morshead, which began as a daring exploration, laid the groundwork for these significant diplomatic achievements. Their six-month-long ordeal provided essential data that underpinned the Simla Agreement, even though China which agreed and signed the initial Agreement ultimately did not sign it.

Legality of the McMahon Line

There was no doubt that the McMahon Line (so called after McMahon, the British representative at the conference) merely confirmed the natural, traditional, ethnic and administrative boundary in the area. No boundary in the world have (sic) been as free from dispute, so well established by tradition, so free from dispute and administration, as the India-China (*Tibet*) boundary.[78]

The legality of the McMahon Line came under question for the first time on 23rd January, 1959, when Chou Enlai wrote to Nehru: *"Firstly, that the Sino-Indian boundary had never been formally delimited and that no treaty or agreement had been concluded between the Chinese Central Government and the Government of India. Secondly, that the McMahon Line was a product of the British policy of aggression against the Tibetan Region of China. Thirdly, Zhou admitted that the Tibetan Local authorities had signed the Convention but were dis-satisfied with the 'unilaterally drawn' line. Nevertheless, Zhou asserted that 'the Chinese Government finds it necessary to take a realistic attitude towards the McMahon Line".*[79]

This was amplified in his second letter dated 8th September 1959, '*the so-called McMahon Line was never discussed at the Simla Conference, but was determined by the British representative and the representative of the Tibet local authorities behind the back of the representative of the Chinese Central Government through an exchange of secret notes at Delhi on March 24, 1914, that is, prior to the signing of the Simla treaty.*'[80]

The Indian Prime Minister Nehru, in one of his letters to the Chinese Premier, dated March 22, 1959, pointed out that this line was drawn after full discussion and confirmed subsequently by a formal exchange of letters. There was nothing to indicate the dissatisfaction of the Tibetan authorities with the agreed boundary. The Chinese representative signed the document without any reservation.[81]

The Chinese representative, Ivan Chen, not only fully participated as a delegate, but on an equal footing with the Tibetan representative. All arrangements at Simla were made with the knowledge and consent of the Chinese and the Chinese Foreign Minister wrote to the British government on 7 August 1913 that the Chinese plenipotentiary would proceed to India to '*open negotiations for a treaty jointly with the Tibetan and British plenipotentiaries*'.[82]

The two maps of 27 April 1914 and 3 July 1914 showing the India-Tibet boundary bear the full signatures of the Tibetan Plenipotentiary. The map of 27 April 1914 bears the full signature of the Chinese Plenipotentiary, Ivan Chen. The British Plenipotentiary, McMahon initialled the map of 27 April 1914 and the Convention of 3 July 1914, but signed in full the map attached to the 3 July 1914 Convention as also the Trade Regulations of 3 July 1914.[83]

Later, on 13 June 1914, the Chinese made fresh proposals to the British government on the Inner-Outer Tibet boundary. There was no mention of the India-Tibet boundary. Similarly, five years later, on 30 May 1919 the Chinese again made fresh proposals suggesting modifications of the Simla Convention. These again related to Inner Tibet and Outer Tibet and Inner Tibet and China. Significantly, there was no reference to India-Tibet boundary [McMahon Line]![84]

The Atchison Treaties Series, XIV, 1929, published this convention and the McMahon Line was shown in the official maps published from 1937 onwards. Since China did not raise objections to it, it was inferred that China had accepted it.[85] Even the official Chinese maps of 1893, 1917 and 1919 showed the boundary in this area as depicted in official Indian maps today.[86] The dispute, therefore, was more to do with the Sino-Tibet border and not the settled Indo-Tibet Borders.

The objection to the McMahon Line came *only* after forty-five years of signing the agreement. The International Laws are clear (by limitation of time) that China had renounced the right to dispute the Line. And that is why Zhou rejected Nehru's offer outright to take the dispute to the International Court of Justice (ICJ), as conveyed in his letter of 1 January 1963.[87]

Today, Arunachal Pradesh stands as a testament to the journey of Bailey and Morshead, defined through the Simla Agreement and marked by the McMahon Line. This historical border not only authenticated the map with on ground realities but also substantiated Arunachal Pradesh as a crucial part of the Indian Union, sealing it as an indelible part of the country's fabric.

Consider this counterfactual. What were the odds China and Tibet would come to the negotiating table if the Qing Empire had not collapsed and therefore not been replaced by the Republic of China? What if Tibet had not sent their strongly-worded letter to the British protesting Frank Kingdon Ward's illegal entry into Tibet? Would the British Indian Government ever have known that the territory south of the McMahon

Line was illegally under Tibetan control, in contravention of the Simla Agreement? Without these events, would Caroe been motivated to include the Simla Agreement in the 1929 Atchinson Report? How might these factors have reshaped history of the Eastern Frontier?

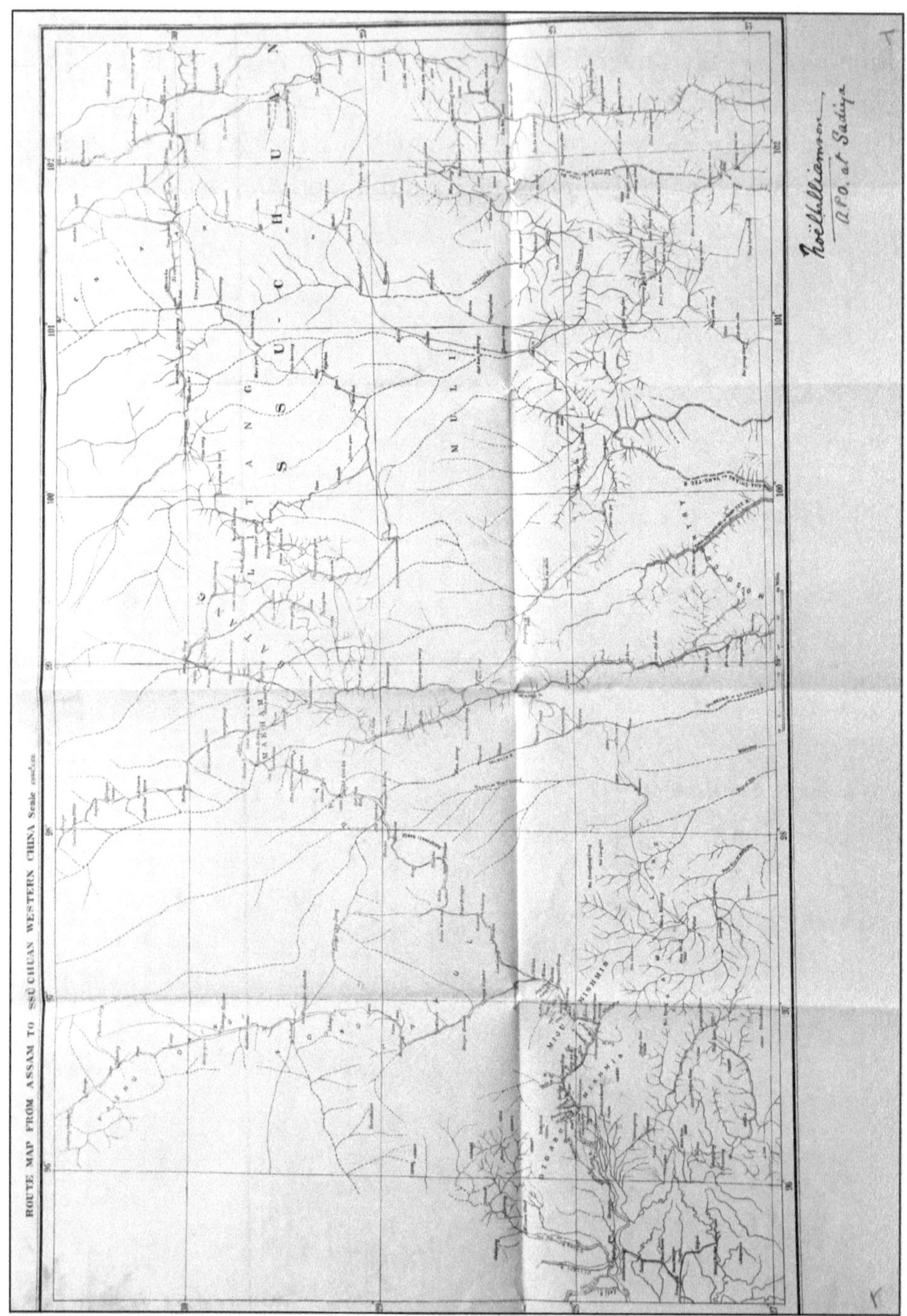

▲ **Map 3:** Route Map from Assam to Sichuan Province, China prepared by Noel Williamson

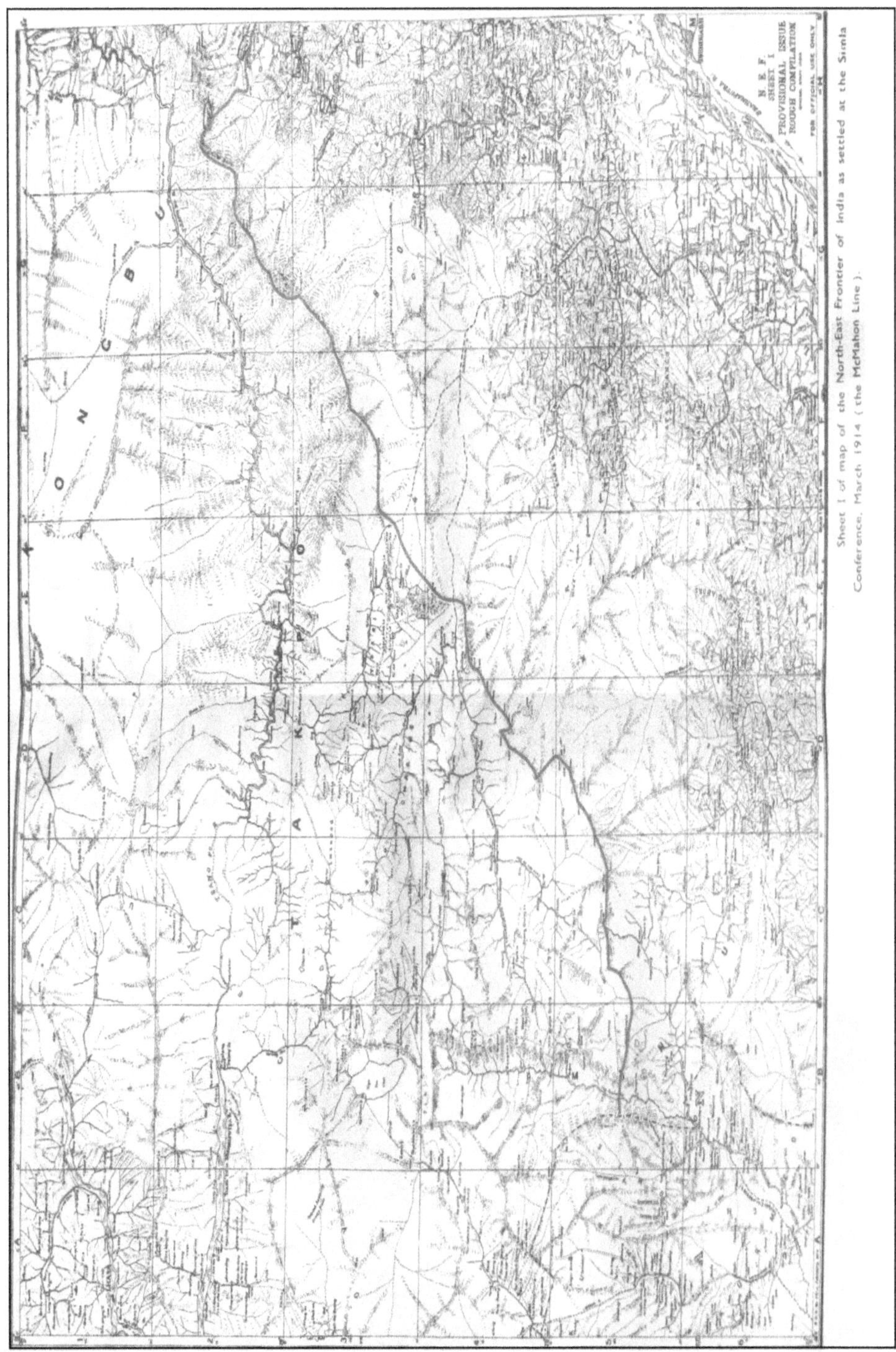

▲ **Map 4:** Sheet I of Map of the Northern Frontier of India as settled at the Simla Conference, March 1914 (the McMahon Line) (Source: 1960 Atlas of the Northern Frontier of India, Ministry of External Affairs, GoI)

In Between The Blurry Lines

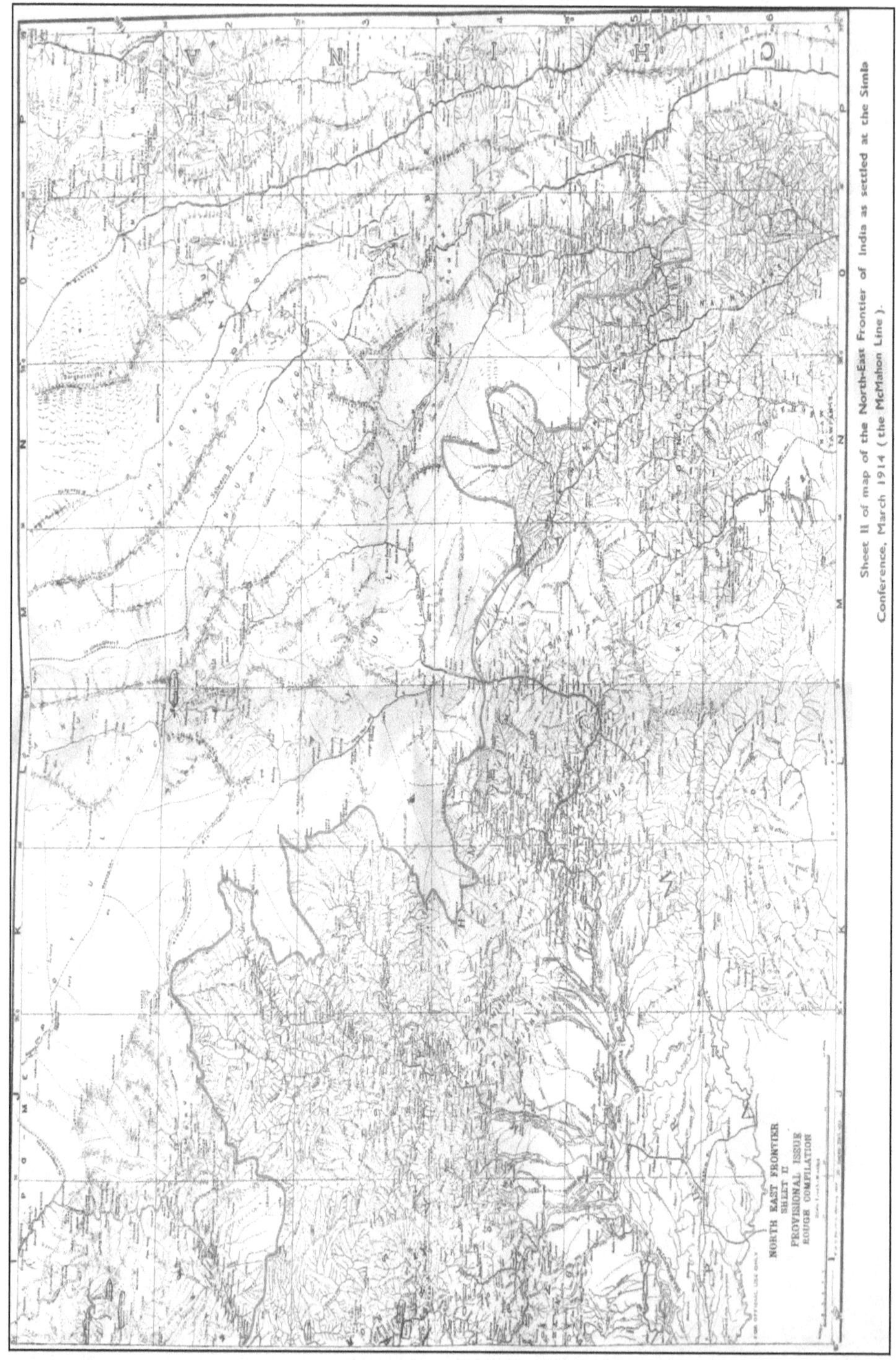

▲ **Map 5:** Sheet II of Map of the Northern Frontier of India as settled at the Simla Conference, March 1914 (the McMahon Line) (Source: 1960 Atlas of the Northern Frontier of India, Ministry of External Affairs, GoI)

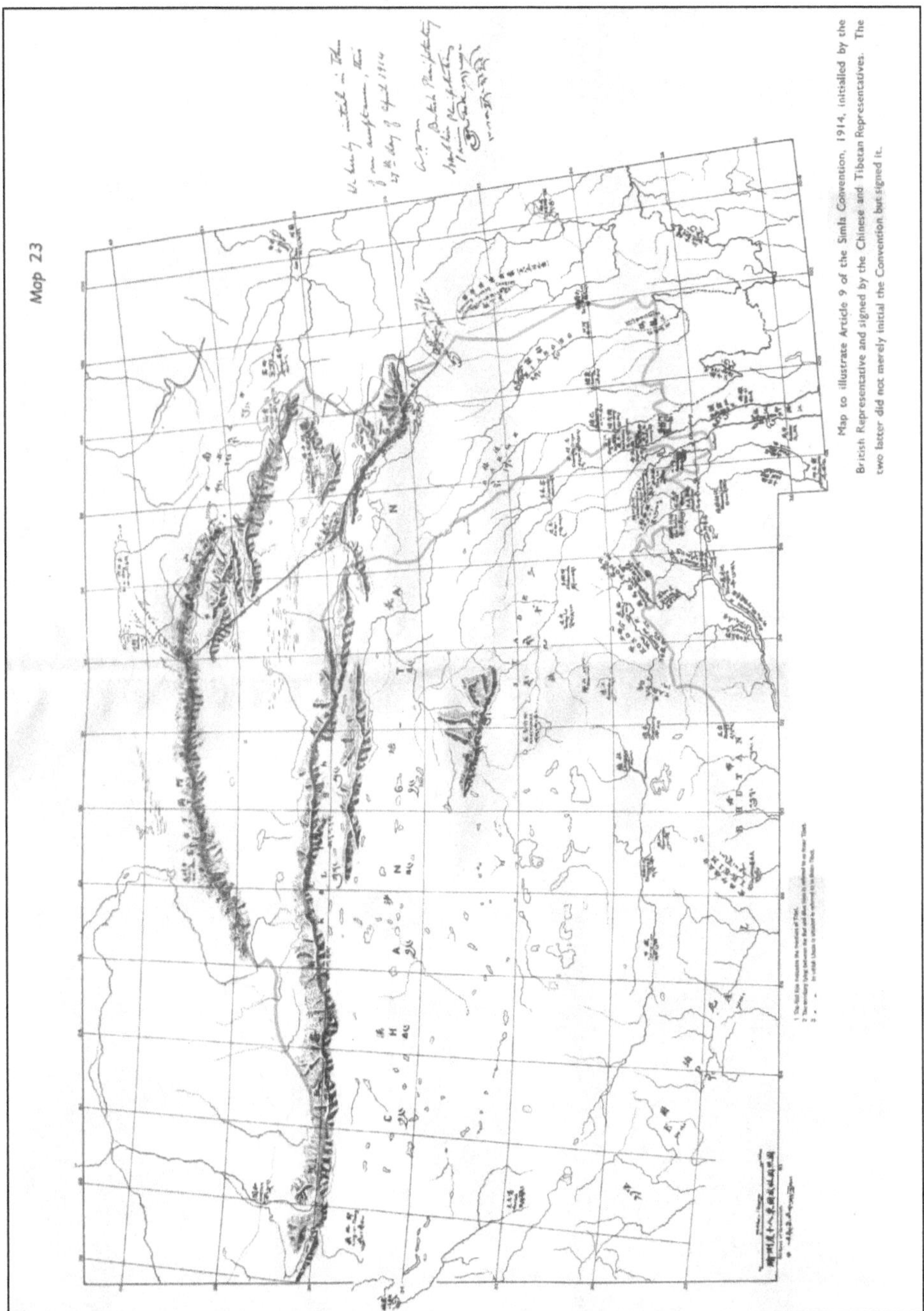

▲ **Map 6:** Map to illustrate Article 9 of the Simla Convention, 1914, initialled by the British Representative and signed by the Chinese and Tibetan Representatives. The two latter did not merely initial the Convention but also signed (Source: 1960 Atlas of the Northern Frontier of India, published by the Ministry of External Affairs, GoI)

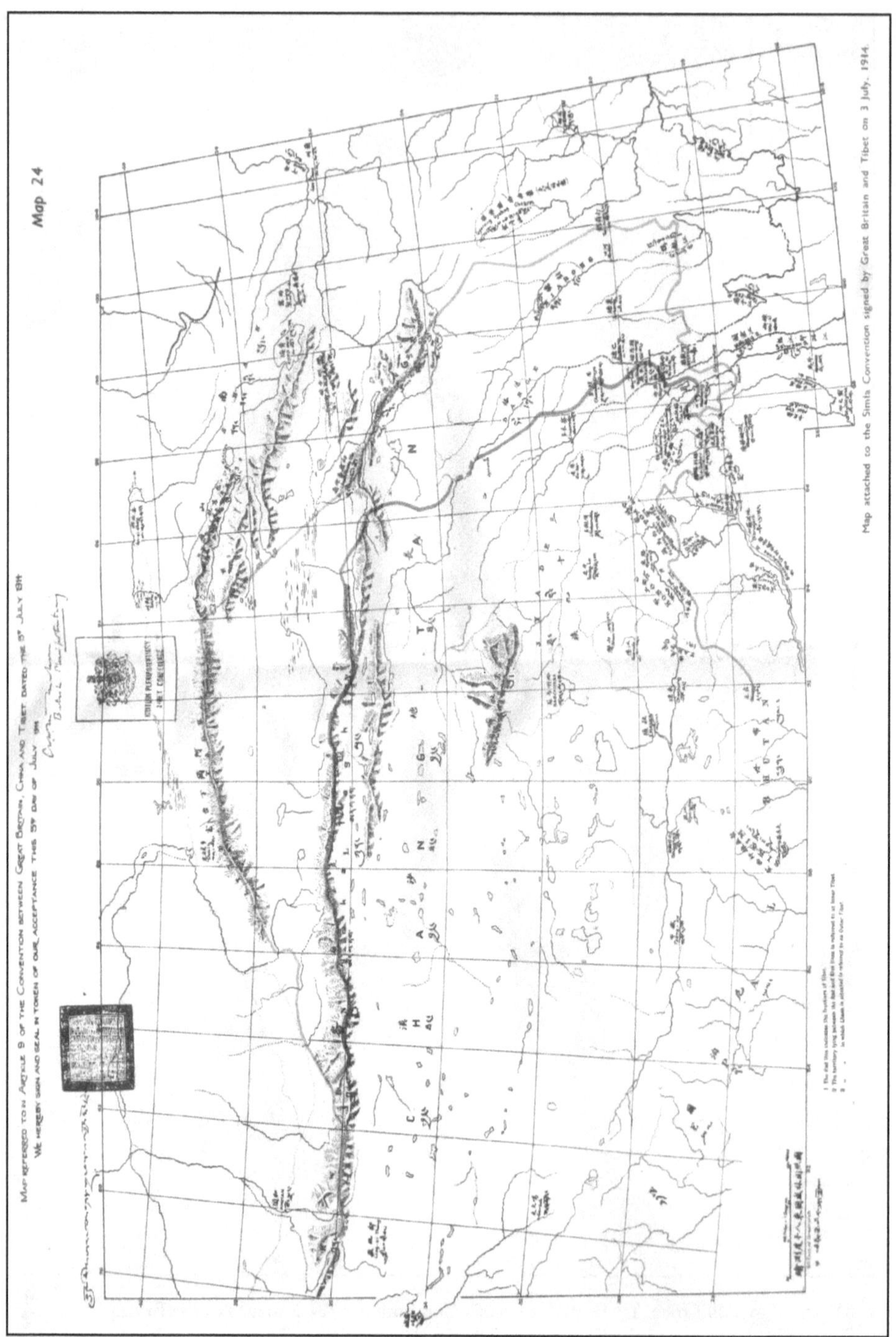

▲ **Map 7:** Map I attached to Simla Convention signed by Representatives of Great Britain and Tibet, 1914 (Source: 1960 Atlas of the Northern Frontier of India, Ministry of External Affairs, GoI)

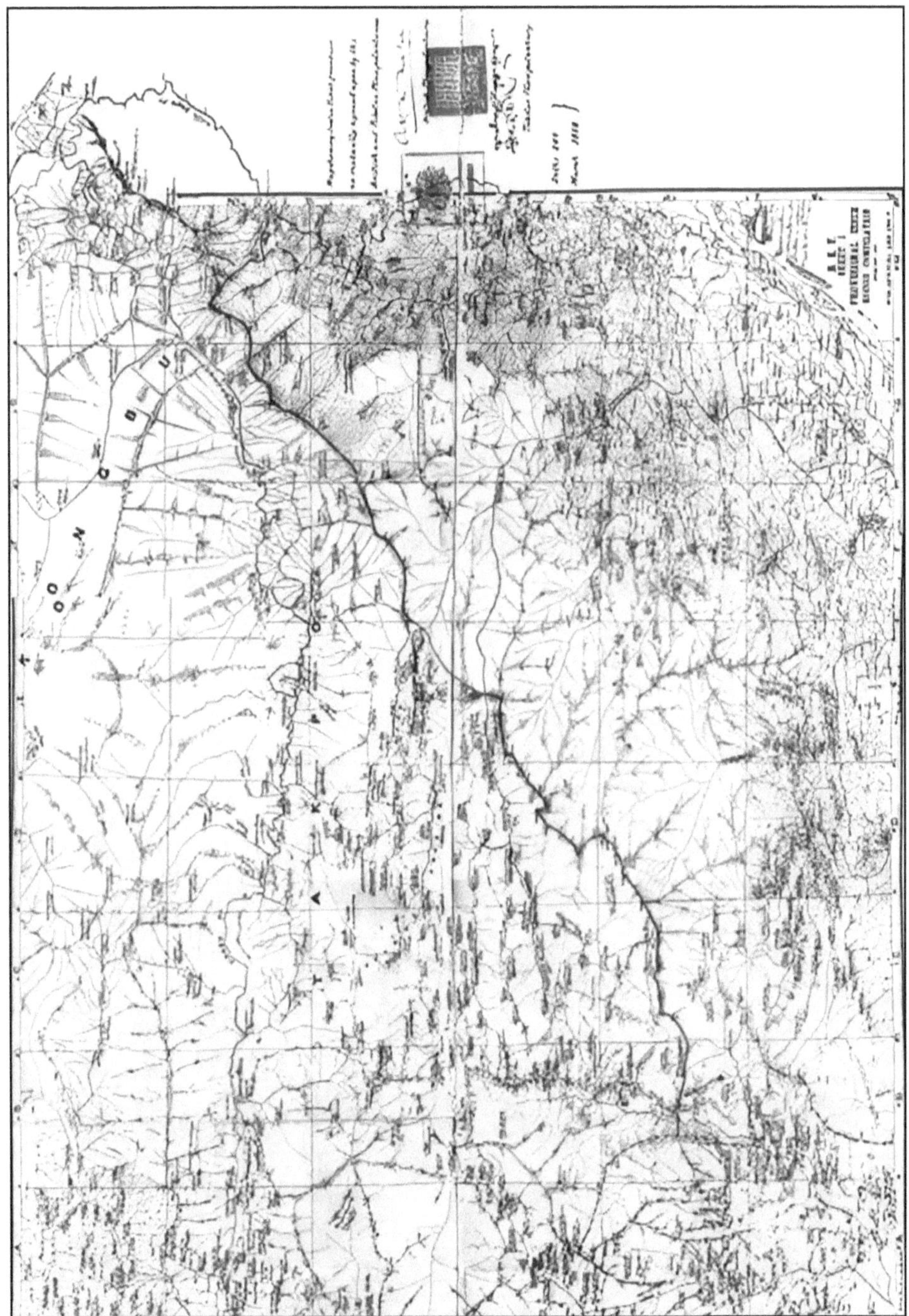

▲ **Map 8:** Map II attached to Simla Convention signed by Representatives of Great Britain and Tibet, 1914 (Source: 1960 Atlas of the Northern Frontier of India, Ministry of External Affairs, GoI)

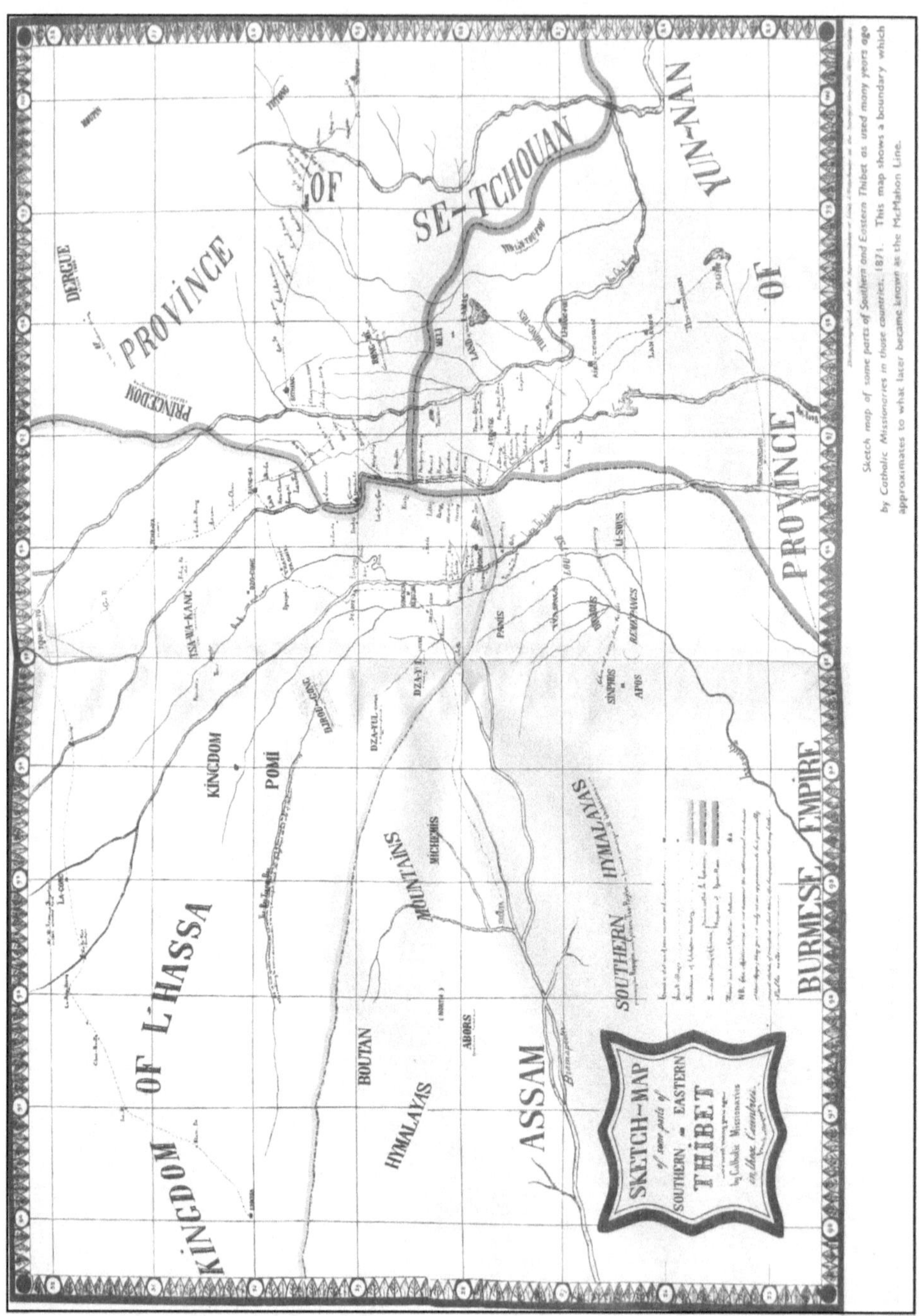

▲ **Map 9:** Sketch Map of some parts of Southern and Eastern Tibet as prepared by Christian Missionaries in 1871. The boundary shown in the map approximates to what later became known as the McMohan Line (Source: 1960 Atlas of the Northern Frontier of India, Ministry of External Affairs, GoI)

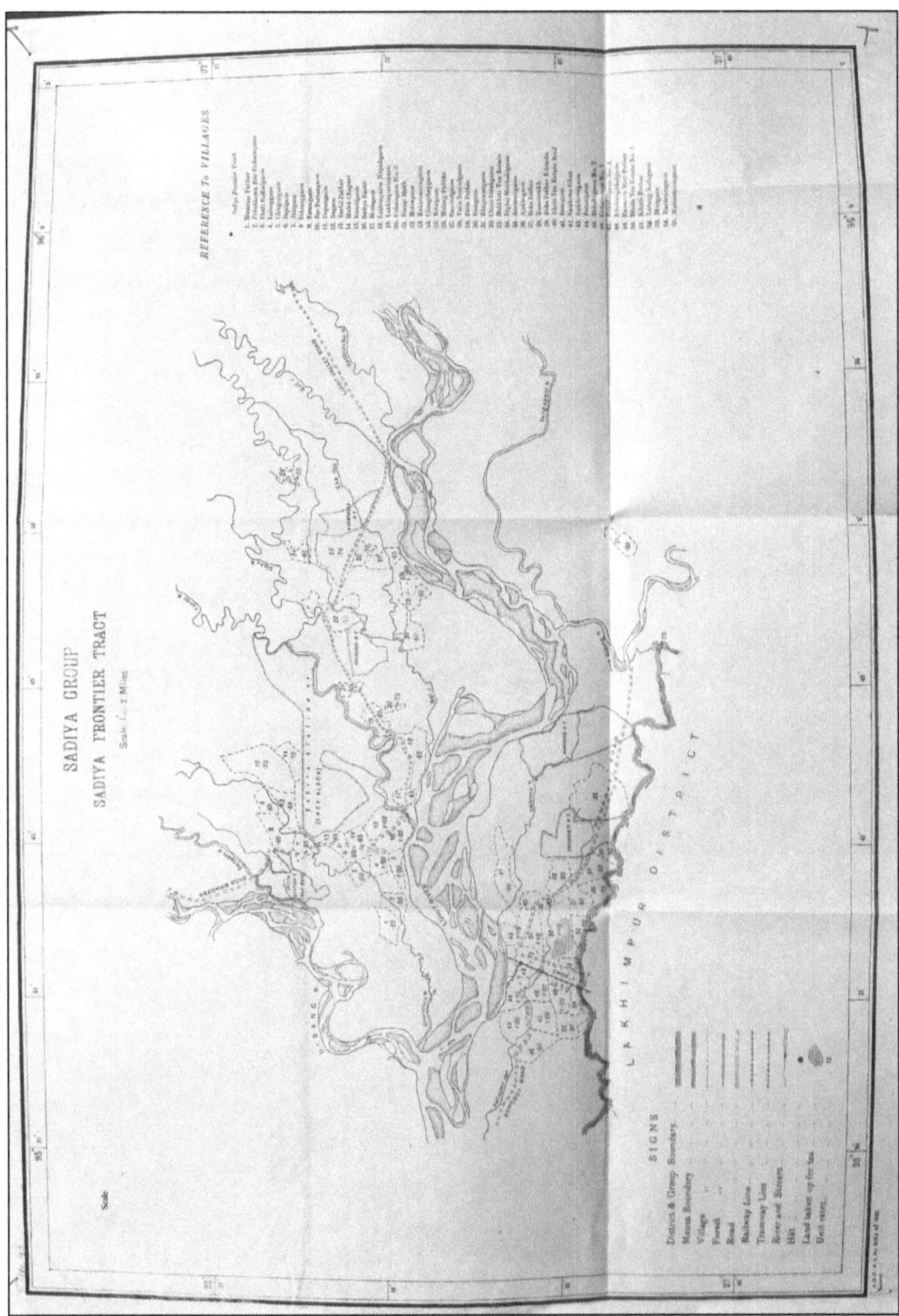

▲ **Map 10:** Map of Sadiya Frontier Tract– 1933
(Source: Directorate of Research, Government of Arunachal Pradesh)

PART TWO

THE FRONTIER IN THE FIFTIES AND BEYOND

With the emplacement of the three lines-*Inner, Outer & McMahon*, the Frontier became a complex tapestry, sandwiched between these lines. The lines were blurry on ground and the *outer line* was at best imaginary. These delicate demarcations set the stage for a rich and often contentious interplay of peoples, landscapes, and ecosystems.

For the Northeastern Frontier, the second half of the 20th Century could easily be termed as the most eventful and yet the most stressful time for the innocent local population. This decade has been a canvas of tragedy, jubilation, and spiritual upheaval, all while laying the groundwork for an impending and dreadful war.

Around this time, Asia was undergoing a momentous power and ideological shift. The 13th Dalai Lama had passed away in 1933; a vacuum of sorts was felt in Tibet. By 1942, the Japanese Army overran Burma and headed westwards to the Eastern Himalayas, while from the North, Lhasa was asserting herself in the Monyul region, forcing British India to undertake '*effective control*' of the Eastern Himalayas.

Republican China under Chaing Kai Shek was facing a revolution, thrusting a civil war between the Goumindang Party and the Chinese Communist Party (CCP) in 1946, paving the way for Communism in China. The CCP, winning the Civil War in 1949 with Mao Zedong at the helm, proclaimed the People's Republic of China. This was the end of 37 years of Republican China. The young 14th Dalai Lama was in Lhasa, keenly watching this development. Maoist China's imminent threat of occupation of the Tibetan Plateau was looming, an event which was only a matter of time.

At the same time, South of the Himalayas, the British Colonies were gaining independence, of which the Indian story of 1947 stands out, with Nehru becoming her first Prime Minister. In the midst of this colossal transformation, in the North East Frontier, the Indian Administration was trying to make sense of what they inherited from the British-administratively and politically. What would be the best course for integrating the Frontier region into India? This was a dilemma weighing heavily on the minds of Independent India's administration.

With this geo-political background, the following chapters delve into a decade marked by profound adversity and resilience, a period etched into the collective memory inhabitants of the eastern Himalayas. This tumultuous era began with the shattering force of a devastating earthquake of 1950 that razed villages and left countless families grappling with loss and despair. The aftermath of the quake tested the region's capacity to rebuild, both physically and emotionally, as communities rallied together amidst the rubble, seeking solace and strength in unity. The seismic scars of this natural disaster were soon followed by the political and social upheaval of consolidating a small yet significant territory, a process fraught with tension and confrontation. The Eastern Himalayas were formally christened NEFA or North East Frontier Agency in 1954.

Amidst these tangible transformations, this period was also marked by a profound philosophical debate regarding the integration of the indigenous people into the broader fabric. The Achingmori Massacre, a year prior, in 1953, triggered an intense debate. The appointment of Verrier Erwin as Advisor for Tribal Affairs to the NEFA Administration would take this debate to a direction which would decide the fate of the frontier population for years to come.

This discourse centred on finding a balance between preserving the rich cultural heritage and traditions of the indigenous communities and fostering a unified national identity. Some advocated for policies that promoted cultural preservation and autonomy, while others pushed for a more assimilationist approach. We will explore how this debate unfolded.

As if these trials were not enough, the frontier found itself thrust into an unprovoked war, a brutal confrontation that brought further sorrow and hardship. The unrelenting conflict strained resources, tested loyalties, and plunged the region into a state of uncertainty and fear.

This Part recounts these key events of the ten arduous years and beyond, highlighting the trials faced by the people and the remarkable resilience they demonstrated in the face of relentless challenges. Through tales of pain and sorrow, we uncover the indomitable spirit that emerged from these dark times, setting the stage for the NEFA's eventual recovery and people's unwavering determination to forge a better future.

"We learn geology the morning after the earthquake."
– Ralph Waldo Emerson

"Out of chaos, find simplicity. From discord, find harmony. In the middle of difficulty lies opportunity."
– Albert Einstein

4

Earthquake and the Benevolent State

In the quiet of an ordinary evening, as families gathered around their hearth and the sun dipped below the horizon, the earth decided to tell its own story. August 15, 1950, was not just another Independence Day in the Eastern Frontier; it was the day the ground beneath trembled with a force so deep that it altered the course of many lives and landscapes. At 7:39 PM, the Assam-Tibet earthquake erupted, ranking as one of the most formidable seismic events of the 20th century. With a magnitude of 8.7 on the Richter scale, this earthquake not only shook the physical world but also the psyche of a region.

Oshong and his 28 classmates[88] had just returned to their school hostel near Pasighat after celebrating Independence Day under the heavy August rains. Exhausted from the day's festivities, they settled in for what they thought would be a quiet night. But just as the rain eased, the earth rebelled. A violent rumble shattered the stillness, and the ground beneath them seemed to twist and heave. It was an earthquake!

In the chaos, they scrambled out of the hostel, their hearts pounding, unsure if they'd make it out. And then, moments after they reached safety, the hostel collapsed into a pile of rubble. They stood there in the pouring rain, soaked and terrified, staring at the ruins that had been their home. The tremors didn't stop. All night, the ground kept shaking beneath their feet. It was like the earth had come alive, cracking open, spitting out mud and water, a haunting reminder of its power. It was a night that seemed to stretch on forever.

By dawn, the tremors had subsided, but the damage was done. After scavenging whatever food they could from the wreckage-a meagre breakfast of salvaged rations-the group set off toward Pasighat, hoping to find some semblance of safety. But what they found was devastation. The once-standing British-built structures were reduced to rubble, entire sections of the town washed away, and the receding waters of the Siang River spoke of a greater disaster yet to come.

Upstream, a landslide had blocked the river, and the water, now held back by debris, was ready to break free. And when it did, it unleashed a torrent that swept through Pasighat, taking with it homes, buildings, and the hopes of the townspeople. The destruction was total. What followed was almost as deadly-a near-epidemic of diarrhoea spread through the region as people consumed fish that had been stranded on the riverbanks, poisoned by the sudden change in their environment. Food became scarce, and desperation grew until government airdrops finally brought relief to the suffering region. For Oshong and his friends, the memory of that night would never fade-the night the earth tore itself apart and their lives changed forever.

The bloody partition of 1947 and the birth of East Pakistan made Assam and the Eastern Frontier a victim of the 'geo-political accident' and suddenly the Region was landlocked. It was only recently connected with the mainland through the narrow Siliguri Corridor, the only land link to the mainland, often referred to as *the Chicken's Neck.'* Assam was also slowly limping back to normalcy from the partition induced riots. Furthermore, Assam had on 5th August lost its popular leader and Chief Minister Gopinath Bordoloi. In the Frontiers, a crucial road project conceptualised by the British during the early years of the 20th Century-Lohit Valley was connected up to Walong-the first major project of the Frontiers to see completion. The Nation had given to herself earlier that year a *'Freshly Minted Constitution'*, *'emphasising a new development and a modernising paradigm*[89]. The earth shattered, when the region was trying to come to terms with so many events unfolding.

The earthquake was a dramatic demonstration of the ongoing clash between the Indian plate and the Eurasian plate. The High Himalayas, young fold mountains towering in the backdrop, are a direct result of this monumental tectonic activity. Below the surface, the immense stress accumulated from the pushing plates periodically releases, leading to seismic events. The tectonic dynamics in the Himalayas are unique. The collision of the Indian plate with the Eurasian plate doesn't simply push one plate beneath the other as seen in typical subduction zones. Instead, it's a chaotic dance where sections of both plates jostle and thrust against each other, creating a complex web beneath some of the world's most rugged terrains. Interestingly, the epicentre of this quake was near Rima, a location in Tibet, *making it not strictly an Indian earthquake.* The only on-the-spot observations we have were from F. Kingdon-Ward, who was in Rima at the time with his wife. His account, while limited, highlighted the violent shaking, extensive landslides, and the dramatic rise of streams. The immediate challenges he faced were more about survival and escape rather than detailed scientific observations.

It was the fifth biggest tremor ever recorded. The last big quake in Assam was in 1897, while a tremor was also witnessed in 1949, the previous year. With a seven minute long quake and forty one tremors, it must have felt like eternity for the people. Aftershocks continued to rattle the region for months, till November, many strong enough to be of note. Dr. Tandon[90] used these aftershocks to delineate the seismic activity's broad geographical spread and the epicentre of the main quake near the eastern margin. As Dr. Tandon and his team worked to map the aftershocks, tracing the quake's reach across longitudes, the earthquake continued to unsettle the region. This relentless seismic activity not only highlighted the broad geographic impacts but also exacerbated the already precarious situation. The fragile terrain, weakened by the main quake and numerous aftershocks, became prone to landslides, setting the stage for further tragedy. This cascading series of events was about to take a dire turn, directly affecting communities along the Siang, Dibang and the precarious Subansiri Rivers.

Landslides, triggered by the quake, were primarily responsible for significant loss of lives and damage to property. One particularly severe landslide blocked the Subansiri river, creating a temporary dam. For a week, this natural dam held, a silent threat looming over lives downstream. The communities living along the riverbanks, already dealing with the aftermath of the quake, suddenly found themselves in a race against time, unaware of the danger that was coming their way. Then, the dam burst. It released a torrential wave, seven metres high, a furious, unstoppable force that swept through villages in its path. The deluge was ruthless, claiming over 500 lives in its wake, washing away homes, and leaving a scar on the landscape that would be remembered for generations.

After the terrifying rupture of the natural dam along the Subansiri River, which sent a massive wave crashing through the surrounding villages, the focus quickly shifted to the urgent need for relief and reconstruction. As the communities dealt with the aftermath of this huge event, different groups jumped into action to lessen the impacts of the disaster. The response was coordinated on many fronts, with local and national efforts to give quick aid and start the long journey of rebuilding the lives and homes lost in the disaster.

The Assam Rifles were quick to act, setting up shelters for those who had lost their homes and working tirelessly to repair buildings and tracks. This was crucial for re-establishing connections between Battalion Headquarters and their outposts. Local volunteers, alongside staff and students from the Medical College at Dibrugarh, were instrumental in the relief and reconstruction efforts. Frontier Administration deployed their men who were familiar with the terrain and would therefore expedite the rescue and rehabilitation of the affected persons.

Prime Minister Jawaharlal Nehru addressed the nation, detailing the ongoing relief operations. Indian Air Force Dakota planes braved adverse weather to airdrop rice and other essentials to the affected areas, while smaller aircraft conducted reconnaissance missions and delivered officers to remote locations.

The Rashtriya Swayamsevak Sangh (RSS) and related organisations stepped up as well. The Marwari Relief Society of Calcutta (a close associate of the RSS) sent some workers for relief and the Assam branch of the RSS organised the Assam Bhukamp Pidit Sahayta Samiti (The Assam Earthquake Sufferers Relief Society) that distributed food, clothes and provided shelter to several victims of the earthquake.[91]

This disaster provided a significant opportunity for the Indian state to reinforce its presence in the region. It was a chance not just for nation-building but also for redefining Assam and the Eastern Frontier's role within India's political geography. The involvement of state agencies like the Indian Air Force helped enhance the visibility of the Indian state in these remote and sensitive areas, reinforcing state authority. The Frontier tribals witnessed first hand the benevolent side of State and its machinery, their first encounter with '*the sircar*'[92] (the government). This was to have a lasting impact.

Chow Khamoon Gohain (Namshum) was appointed the head of the government relief committee for Lohit Frontier Division to provide immediate relief and help to the affected people... He worked day and night to provide succour to the needy[93].

Moreover, the engagement of organisations like the RSS in relief efforts did more than just provide immediate aid; it also familiarised people with the organisation and set the stage for new social associations, aligning social welfare goals with broader national objectives and furthering national unity and integrity.

The earthquake undoubtedly reshaped the region's physical and economic landscape, shifting the Brahmaputra riverbed and destroying valuable infrastructure. The state's proactive role in the rebuilding and rehabilitation efforts was critical in mitigating these impacts and helping restore normalcy to this shaken region.

As the initial shock of the disaster settled and local efforts to provide immediate relief were underway, the scale of devastation caused by the 1950 Assam earthquake captured global attention. The plight of the affected communities resonated worldwide, catalysing a surge of international support. Countries near and far rallied to aid the stricken region, offering a testament to the universal spirit of humanitarianism. This outpouring of international aid not only supplemented national and local efforts but also brought new resources and attention to a region that was always consigned to the footnotes of Indian political imagination.

The 1950 earthquake resonated across the globe, sparking a wave of compassion and action from the international community. Countries as varied as Ethiopia and Lebanon sent messages of sympathy, and offers of aid poured in. The Indian Association of Djibouti was quick to contribute, sending 5,000 rupees through the Indian Consulate. Even the United Nations stepped up, with the Secretary-General inquiring about the specific needs that could be addressed by the UN and its agencies[94].

From the United States, there was a promise of six tons of emergency relief supplies along with over 427,000 tons of food grains. Contributions also flowed in from the Indian community in Addis Ababa, and Burma reached out with offers of help. The Watnumull Foundation in San Francisco extended its support to the quake-hit region[95]. Internationally, the response was generous, with offers of help coming from various countries and organisations.

Volunteer groups, both people from NEFA and from beyond Assam, were pivotal in the relief and reconstruction efforts. Their work was widely lauded, showcasing a spirit of cooperation and solidarity that stood tall in the disaster's aftermath. NEFA administration compiled a list through the Political Officers, of all people contributing to and rising to the occasion during and after the disaster. They were duly recognised and given certificates and cash rewards[96].

The Frontier administration and people came together to overcome this catastrophe. Few acts of bravery by tribals of NEFA, like the valour of Taravlum Yun, who went to a Tibetan village near Rima, on the day after the quake, risking his life to procure rations for those marooned on the McMahon line, were recognised along with several local porters of the Mishmi Hills who carried rations for the stranded. Thamaloka, Empi and Palum assisted by Sangazup Zakring, Dapti and many others rescued Mrs. and Mr. Kingdon Ward[97], who was on a *Botanising Spree* in the area.

In the Siang Hills, the story of courage displayed by Interpreter Obat Tayeng in venturing North up to Siyom to collect news of the extent of damages despite ill health and immediately later leading an Assam Rifles team to successfully rescue a stranded team near Daring Village are inspiring. He also visited a few remote villages to assess the damage and provide relief. He was aptly recognised by the Administration. Tati Lego had successfully led a stranded platoon from Riga to Pasighat under extreme conditions post the calamity when all the bridges were washed away. River Siyom was brimming with floodwaters, and the route was blocked by landslides, forcing the creation of temporary bridges and paths. Guidam Yomsa, a Political Jamadar who the first to come down to Along to give news of the damage in Yomcha also volunteered to go to the Subansiri valley and Bori areas to ascertain damage when the earth was still shaking. The bravery of Tomi Riba, Tage Gamboo, Tage Mira, Bollung Mengu, Mannya Kaye, Ram Gobin Lohar and Baburam Saikia of the Laimakuri Area[98] were exemplary for braving the post-quake floods and providing essentials to the affected.

Osang (Oshong) Ering, the school boy displayed extreme courage by consoling and encouraging his terrified schoolmates after their school was totally damaged. At Nizamghat, the bravery of Ita Pulu, Lango Menda, Tako Mena, Eangi Lingi, Ekola Mitayun[99] were recognised.

This catastrophe also fast-tracked the integration of Assam, especially its Himalayan borderlands, into India's national framework. It led to an unprecedented expansion of state presence in the region's Frontier Tracts, which had previously been on the margins. The concerted relief and rehabilitation efforts not only reordered Assam's place within India's political geography but also underscored the region's strategic significance and highlighted the urgent need for improved infrastructure and disaster preparedness.

As the international community rallied to provide aid in response to the catastrophic events of the 1950 earthquake, the focus shifted to the specific impacts on regions like Arunachal Pradesh. This transition from broader international relief efforts to localised recovery highlighted the unique challenges faced by this Frontier State. Tawang Monastery, a revered spiritual and historical site, along with many stone houses, suffered damage. The 1950 earthquake left a significant impact on the region, particularly in Arunachal Pradesh, especially its eastern parts, which bore the brunt of the devastation.

Official records[100] reveal the severe aftermath in the Sadiya Frontier Tract, covering 17,000 square miles, where the earthquake affected over 2,25,000 people. Pasighat, a crucial town in the region, saw parts of itself submerged, with its main access route partially washed away. While Pasighat eventually recovered, Sadiya wasn't as fortunate. The earthquake caused the Dibang River to change its course dramatically, leading to the slow submersion and decline of this old administrative town, the most important British Base for NEFA and the last few remnants of British presence, later shifted to Tezu in Arunachal Pradesh.

This natural disaster initially appeared to undo the Government's efforts in developing the state machinery in these frontier areas, posing a significant setback. However, the reality was slightly different. While the physical signs of the state's expansion in the eastern Himalayas were lost, the earthquake inadvertently provided momentum for further state-building[101]. This disaster necessitated a focus on recovery and reconstruction, particularly targeting infrastructure such as roads, bridges, and railway lines in areas like Dibrugarh, and North Lakhimpur, which had suffered extensive damage.

The quake also caused a significant loss of life, with official reports recording 1,526 deaths in Assam alone. Including those in Arunachal Pradesh, the total death toll was estimated to be around 4,800. The region's economy, especially the vital tea industry, faced near ruin, with losses estimated at Rs. 20,000,000 for Assam's industries[102].

One of the more significant outcomes of the earthquake was the accelerated integration of NEFA into India's broader national framework. In response to the disaster, the Indian Government expanded its presence in what were considered the marginal Frontier Tracts. This not only aided the immediate recovery efforts but also tied NEFA more closely to central mechanisms of governance and development.

Assam and its Frontier was seen and even treated as *'the administrative and cultural appendix to Bengal'*[103], but the quake forced the region to be redrawn in the mental map of Indians; Nehru in his air broadcast was pointing the area on map, educating the people, showing where exactly the disaster happened in India. PM Assam Relief Fund and Governor's Earthquake Relief Fund were in place and relief, rehabilitation and state expansion worked hand in hand, accelerating State making and Nation building. The calamity brought the Indian state and frontier populations into unprecedented interactions. For the first time the State was seen as *'potential provider of tangible goods and benefits; contrast colonial coercive military promenades and punitive expeditions'*.[104]

Within a year, nine outposts were made operational from a mere two posts in the Eastern Frontier. Assam Rifles took possession of Tawang in 1951 and a Monpa Cleric was installed in Tawang Gompa (Monastery). Expeditions to Ramo and Pailibo country in Abor and Gusar in Subansiri were undertaken and Assam Rifles and Administrative centres flourished in Pangin, Mebo, Damro, Mariyang and Mechukha. State making was in a hurry, as if Frontier officials wanted to eagerly make up for the lost time. A model village was established in Pasighat to settle the Pasi, Minyong & Pangi population of the interior and Wet Rice Cultivation was introduced.[105]

Though the region transitioned from margins and came to prominence, Assam was stereotyped as a region of uncertainty; at the mercy of nature, with quakes and annual floods or at best romanticised as a hunting ground of Rhinoceros; this despite her tea, oil and coal. Frontiers were labelled as a jungli place; savage, separate and inferior. These stereotypes of the region would accentuate over time and would even impair Centre-State relations, much to the detriment of the population of the region, resulting in stunted development, ethnic strife and insurgency in many parts of the Region[106].

Though the Frontier Administration looked towards Assam during relief operations, the relationship ebbed by end of 1951 with even the Governor and the Advisor's Office not forthcoming in sharing updates about the Frontier and their unwillingness to merge with Assam became apparent. The Inner Line regime was strictly enforced, restricting unwanted movement and the 'British Raj's *old imperial frontiers*' became naturalised within the Indian national space'[107]. This sowed the seeds for shaping a distinct entity for the Frontier people.

In her thought-provoking paper, Rechard concludes that *'rather than the product of top-down, well planned strategies, state-making and nation building are often reactions to extraneous events and crises.*'[108] The earthquake of 1950 was indeed one such event for the Eastern Frontier.

In the aftermath of the earthquake, Arunachal Pradesh emerged not only as a region that had endured great trials but as one that found a renewed path toward development and integration. The tragedy brought an increased governmental focus to the area, catalysing efforts that would, in time, strengthen the resilience and infrastructure of this frontier state. Thus, the 1950 earthquake marked a pivotal moment in the history of Arunachal Pradesh, signifying a period of significant transformation and renewal. As we turn our attention from the broader impacts of this natural disaster, we next explore the specific case of Tawang-a region that embodies the challenges and triumphs of Arunachal Pradesh in the face of both natural calamities and political changes

◆

"Geography has made us neighbours. History has made us friends. Economics has made us partners, and necessity has made us allies. Those whom God has so joined together, let no man put asunder."
– John F. Kennedy

"One man's courage can make a difference when the odds are stacked against him."
– Anonymous

5

Bob's Valour-*Metoh Sahab* and unfurling of the Tricolour at Tawang

Mystery, thy name is Tawang

As the first light of dawn shines through the towering Himalayan peaks, casting long shadows and lighting up the ancient paths of Tawang, it uncovers a land rich in history and complexity. Here, among these massive sentinels, unfolds the tale of a small yet crucial region—a story influenced by diplomacy, spirituality, and the changing landscape of geopolitics.

Exploring Monyul's rich history takes us on a journey back to the mid-7th century AD, tracing a tapestry woven from waves of migration, cultural exchange, and the spread of Buddhism. Starting with seven distinct waves of migration from Tibet, the story of Monyul, including Tawang, began to unfold, reaching a defining moment with the banishment of Prince Tsangma in 830 AD[109]. Since then, Monyul has been a crossroads where Tibetan, Monyul, and Drukyul traditions intertwined. Buddhism began to take root, thanks to figures like Khandro Dowa Sangmo, the Queen of Monyul in the 6th century AD.

The Nyingma guru, Padmasambhawa, is also said to have imparted Buddhist teachings in Monyul, while Bon and Kagyu traditions also spread. The Gelukpa tradition, however, arrived later between 1391 and 1474, when Tsangton Rolpai Dorjee, a disciple of the First Dalai Lama, was sent to establish monasteries in the region. Among these, Aryak Dung

Gompa, the first Geluk monastery, stands as a landmark. The Gompas of Monyul, Merak, and Sakteng came under the Ganden Phodrang-the Office of HH Dalai Lama, causing unease to the Karmapa sect of Bhutan, triggering a sectarian war for religious dominance in the Valley[110]. Today, these Monasteries remain testament to the enduring spiritual and cultural legacy that flourished here over the centuries.

In 1644, the 6th Dalai Lama proposed to the Merak Lama and an officer of the Tsona District that certain rights and privileges would be provided to them if they brought all land and Gompas of Monyul under Tibet by peaceful means. They accepted the offer. However, a turf war broke out between Monyul and Bhutan that same year. In 1680, under the guidance of the 5th Dalai Lama, the foundation of the Tawang Gompa was laid. To facilitate the construction of the Gompa, the 5th Dalai Lama directed the abolition of all taxes on laymen in Monyul. Over the years, Tawang Gompa became the de facto seat of Tibet's spiritual and temporal Government in Monyul, although administrative oversight remained with the Dzongpons from Tsona Dzong. This established Tawang as a significant spiritual centre, deeply influencing the region's religious and administrative landscape[111].

Tawang has another distinct historical feather in her hat. The 6th Dalai Lama, Tsangyang Gyatso was born here, one of the only two reincarnations to manifest outside of Tibet, (the other was in Mongolia). Tsangyang Gyatso, also remembered as 'the Great Sixth', was born in 1682, around the same time when the Tawang Monastery was built.

With this background, and as we fast forward three centuries, we pick up Tawang's story which begins again with the Simla Agreement of 1914, where boundaries between India and Tibet were defined based on the watershed principle along the Himalayas. Signed by the Plenipotentiaries of British India and Tibet, this agreement seemed straightforward on paper but was quite complex in practice, especially for Tawang.

Tawang is not just any town; it's a monastic town inhabited by the Monpas who practise Himalayan Buddhism strongly influenced by Vajrayana traditions. It is home to India's largest monastery and the second largest in Asia, after the Potala in Lhasa. Historically, the area was 'under seasonal' Tibetan administration and subjected to monastic tributes.

In the Simla Agreement, the line was drawn north of Tawang, clearly making it an Indian territory. The circumstances under which the McMahon line came into existence have already been covered in the previous section. However, despite these agreements, the reality on the ground remained different for Tawang and the Tibetan monastic influence of its gompa could extend as far south as the edge of Assam Plains.[112]

The boundary issue remained dormant for about two decades until it caught attention again in 1935 when British botanist Frank Kingdon-Ward made an unauthorised entry[113] into Tawang via the Se La Pass on June 3, and later entered Tibet through the Tulung La Pass. This journey not only sparked a diplomatic standoff but also highlighted that far from respecting the McMahon Line, Tibet still held a sort of *Seigniory* over Tawang and its influence even reached South of the Se La Pass.

Kingdon-Ward's travels, driven by his botanical interests, unveiled a troubling scenario in Assam's Frontier Tracts, where the agreed boundaries were not being honoured. His journeys revealed that Tawang was still very much under Tibetan influence, a revelation that caused considerable unease within British administrative circles.

Prompted by the confusion and the realisation that the McMahon Line was being disregarded, the Foreign Office and the India Office began to dig through archives for records and maps that could clarify the situation. This led to more frequent visits by British officers to Tawang, signalling a renewed interest in asserting control and understanding the dynamics of this strategically important region.

This period is described as *"The Return of the Fair-Weather State,"*[114] capturing the essence of the British response which fluctuated with the politico-geographical climate of the time. This incident not only brought the complexities of Tawang's political status to the forefront but also underscored the challenges of managing frontier territories in the shadow of great powers. It is relevant to mention that Captain GA Neville, the Political Officer of Western Section accompanied by Captain RS Kennedy, had toured Tawang during 1st- 9th April, 1914. The tour was short and without any follow up.

As the complexities of Tawang's political landscape continued to unfold, the British intensified their efforts to assert control and clarify boundaries. In April 1936, Captain G Lightfoot, the Political Officer from Balipara, visited Tawang to assess the situation firsthand. His journey took him to the Lumla (Lungla) area, where he played a crucial role in settling the Indo-Bhutan border. This negotiation with the Bhutanese led to the successful conclusion of the Central Monyul Boundary. During his visit, local representatives of the Tsona Dzongpons were informed that the area was under British Indian jurisdiction. Lightfoot's tour not only provided valuable insights but also resulted in detailed correspondence from the Assam Administration to the British Indian Government, particularly focusing on the taxation patterns in Tawang and the adjoining Monpa areas.

Encouraged by the findings from his initial visit and with approval from London, Captain Lightfoot embarked on a second expedition to Tawang, arriving on April 30, 1938[115]. This time, his stay extended to nine weeks, allowing him and his team to tour most of the major villages in the region. The conditions they observed were eye-opening. The Monpas, described by the British officers as peaceful and friendly, were noted to have "no warlike instincts" and were seemingly oppressed under Tibetan Feudal domination, which they both hated and feared.

During this extended visit, Lightfoot engaged in further discussions about the border alignment with his Bhutanese counterparts. Adjustments were made that slightly favoured Bhutan, but these were agreed upon and have remained the agreed border to this day. Concurrently, the renowned botanist Frank Kingdon-Ward also made his second journey to the region around this time, adding to the growing British presence and interest in Tawang.

Captain Lightfoot's thorough exploration led to a comprehensive report accompanied by several recommendations aimed at bringing more effective administration to the area. His findings indicated that in the Tawang area there were about 80 villages, each with an average of 15 houses while in the Dirang area there were about 15 larger villages of about 40 houses each. Around Kalaktang, some 15 Monba villages were surveyed with 12 houses each plus two Sherdukpen villages of 160 houses. Lightfoot's conclusion was that there were roughly 2,140 houses[116].

As the focus on the Tawang region intensified, the Assam Frontier Authorities were keen to conduct more comprehensive tours to solidify their presence and control. However, the impending global conflict shifted priorities dramatically. With war against Germany looming on the horizon, London and Delhi began to reconsider their expansionist strategies in the eastern Himalayas. The financial and political costs of an activist policy in such remote areas suddenly seemed less justifiable, and soon, the concerns about the McMahon Line began to fade into the background.

In the winter of 1942, four years after Captain Lightfoot's detailed expedition had seemingly cemented British interests in Tawang, a new development threatened to undo that progress. Two Tibetan Generals, or Depons[117], with troops, arrived in Tawang on a mission that underscored the ongoing complexities of regional politics. Their task was to arrest migration between Tawang, Tsona, and Bhutan, reflecting a direct exercise of authority over the area. They conducted a thorough inspection, listing all inhabitants and property, and even communicated their expectations of compliance to Bhutan, directly from Lhasa. The Military Commanders issued summons to the Chiefs of Dirang Dzong, Talung Dzong, Sher and Rupa Gaon (Monyul's Chieftains) to immediately present themselves before him. Rupa and Shergaon Chiefs did not comply, perhaps drawing strength from the Assam Rifles post at Rupa, and instead went South to their traditional winter camp.

This action by Tibet was alarming to British officials, particularly Olaf Caroe, who saw it as a clear breach of India's protectorate over Bhutan and a flagrant disregard for the McMahon Line. Tibet's actions highlighted a persistent challenge: despite previous agreements and the presence of British officials, Tibet still exercised considerable influence in Tawang and did not fully acknowledge the boundaries that had been negotiated decades earlier. This situation not only revived concerns about the McMahon Line but also raised questions about the effectiveness of British policy and the future stability of border arrangements in this strategically vital region.

This triggered a series of correspondences between and among the Political Officers of Sikkim and the Balipara Frontier Tract, the Governor of Assam, the diplomatic emissary at Lhasa, the Foreign Office in Delhi and finally the India Office in London.

The parleys were broadly on securing British territory of Tawang and other northern borders of the Eastern Frontiers from Tibetan encroachments. The ideas mulled ranged from the retrocession of Tawang to Tibet, taking a military expedition to Tawang through Trashigang in Bhutan, giving control of Tawang to the Political Officer of Sikkim, aerial reconnaissance, and sending troops up to Dirang Dzong. Terming Chinese plans to takeover Tibet as their '*Post-war Desiderata*'[118], British India was prompted to take urgent action on securing the boundaries in the Eastern Frontiers.

Expansion begins, sans Tawang

As tensions simmered and strategic necessities grew clearer, a significant shift in policy impacting the eastern Himalayas was brewing. On April 16, 1943, Secretary of State for India endorsed a forward policy for this region and agreed to shoulder its costs[119]. For the first time, there was unanimous agreement across all levels of the colonial hierarchy to assert 'effective control' over the Eastern Himalayas. This marked a watershed moment, heralding a new era of expansion.

However, this green light came with several important caveats. Frontier officials were instructed to ensure that their advances in the Eastern Himalayas would not impede the ongoing war efforts, and that military clashes with Tibet were to be avoided at all costs. This delicate balance led to heated discussions about the fate of Tawang. Could it be relinquished to secure the broader strategic '*Red Line*'- the McMahon Line? The Political Officers of Sikkim and Assam strongly opposed the transfer of Tawang to Tibet, and it was ultimately decided that, [for now], the expansion would proceed without including Tawang[120].

To facilitate this expansion, a new position was created-Advisor to the Governor specifically for expansion in the Eastern Himalayas, with J P Mills appointed as the first incumbent. He swiftly reorganised the Frontier Tracts, creating two sub-agencies in Balipara-Subansiri, and another South of Se La. With a renewed sense of urgency, the consolidation process began, extending from the Se La Sub Agency to the Lohit area.

Meanwhile, as the case of Tawang was put on hold, representatives from the Tsona Dzongpon continued to collect monastic tributes from the Monpas.

As these administrative and strategic changes unfolded, a major historical shift was taking place: India gained her independence on the stroke of midnight, August 15, 1947. The British officially left, handing over the reins for India to decide her own destiny. In the tumultuous months and years that followed, the newly independent nation grappled with the vacuum created by the hurried departure of the colonial administration, consolidation of its territory, and the deep wounds of partition.

Amid these monumental changes, there was one small town, seemingly detached from the dramatic developments-a town under the *de facto* control of the Tibetan administration from Tsona Dzong. This town, Tawang, remained loosely tied to the broader narratives of the new nation, almost oblivious to the radical transformations shaping the rest of the country.

Bob Khathing and the Unfinished Agenda of Tawang

At the dawn of the 1950s, as the maps of many nations were redrawn in the wake of World War II, a less noticed but equally significant boundary discussion was shaping up in the remote Himalayas. This conversation would not only redefine the borders of India and Tibet but also influence the political fabric of Asia for decades to come. Here, in the shadow of the majestic Tawang Monastery, a story of courage and strategic foresight unfolds-highlighting a pivotal moment in India's history.

As the geopolitical landscape of the Himalayan sub-continent underwent a drastic transformation with the Chinese People's Liberation Army reaching Lhasa by the end of October 1950, India found itself preparing for direct borders with China. This shift brought the strategic importance of Tawang into sharp focus.

KM Panikkar, India's Ambassador to China, and GS Bajpai, Secretary General of the Ministry of External Affairs, were central figures in shaping India's China policy during this critical period. Their views diverged significantly: Panikkar advocated maintaining good relations with China, while Bajpai adopted a more pragmatic approach, focusing on the implications of China's takeover of Tibet for India's frontiers[121].

Amidst these discussions, Sardar Patel, recognizing the gravity of the situation, penned a prescient letter on November 3, 1950[122], only four days after Bajpai's note, warning of Chinese intentions in the Himalayan Frontier. It is said that the letter was drafted by GS Bajpai. Unfortunately, Patel passed away a few weeks later, and with his demise, the urgency of his concerns were somewhat overshadowed by the burgeoning Hindi-Chini Bhai Bhai sentiment.

In response to the evolving situation, the Himmatsinghji Committee was formed to study and recommend preventive actions on the ground. 'It was the Ministry of External Affairs that moved the recommendations of the Himmatsingji Committee that civilian administrative control to ensure the welfare and development of tribal population inhabiting its border regions should be expanded......sent out instructions to the government in Assam that administrative presence in Tawang should be established forthwith'[123].

It was against this backdrop that Major Bob Khathing was instructed by Governor Jairamdas Daulatram to move towards Tawang. On January 17, 1951, Major Bob, accompanied by 200 troops from the Assam Rifles and later joined by 600 porters, embarked on his crucial mission.

Who exactly was Bob?

Major Bob Relangnao Khathing, born on February 28, 1912, was a Tangkhul Naga from Ukhrul, Manipur. Initially, he was drafted into the 'V'(Victor) Force during the Second World War, a guerrilla type force to collect intelligence on the Japanese with orders to recruit volunteers. Acknowledging his daring feats he was honoured with the Order of *Member of the British Empire (MBE)* and awarded the *Military Cross (MC)*[124].

In May, 1950, on instructions from the Government of India, Daulatram, the Governor of Assam asked Bob to join the 2nd Battalion of Assam Rifles as Assistant Commandant at Sadiya.

While he was on a reconnaissance patrol accompanied by Maj DK Roy and Capt B Gupta of the Kumaon Regiment at Chingwinti area, the earthquake of 15th August, 1950 occurred. Bob was deeply engaged in restoration and relief efforts post the devastating 1950 earthquake and ensured that the road in the strategically critical Lohit was restored[125].

In October of 1950, when he had just been appointed as an Assistant Political Officer-I (APO) of NEFA, he was tasked with taking administration to Tawang. While being briefed by the Governor on the strategic importance of the Tawang Mission, *'to avoid a repeat of our folly in Kashmir'*, Bob had no clue whatsoever about Tawang-its people, terrain and climate[126].

Later, after a thorough brief from Major GT Allen, the Political Officer of Se La Sub Agency, at Charduar (Headquarter of Se La Sub Agency), Bob and a team consisting of Captain Hem Bahadur Limbu, Asstt Commandant 5 Assam Rifles and Doctor Captain Modiero set out for the Mission on 17th January 1951. After a week's halt at Dirang Dzong, getting reinforcements and ration stock, the Mission marched for Tawang on 1st February. The long caravan crossed Se La Pass at about 14,000 feet on the cold winter morning of 3rd February; with personnel suffering high altitude sickness[127].

'Metoh Sahab' plants the Tricolour

By February 6, Bob, fondly named as *Metoh Sahab* (Metoh meaning flower in Monpa dialect), reached Tawang and set up camp above the Gyangkar Dzong, the seat of the Tsona Dzongpon. The next couple of days were spent in scouting for a suitable site for a permanent Headquarters and also to gather intelligence. Anecdotes suggest that sensing the reluctance of the Tibetan officials to accept Indian Authority by the Tibetan Officials, Army Personnel in full battle uniform undertook flag marches and rounds of the town, as a show of strength.

A camp was set up later in *Cham leng*, the dance ground adjacent to the Tawang Monastery, which was traditionally used by monks for training in monastic dance, where the public meeting was to be held on 9th February. This strategic positioning near the monastery underscored the significance of Tawang not only geopolitically, but also culturally and spiritually.

The meeting with Tibetan Officials was also scheduled for 9 February. It was the time of the Tibetan New *Iron Rabbit* Year (Lo-Sar) and Tawang wore a tense festive mood. The flag march, ordered by Bob, apparently had a salutary effect and the Tibetan Officials with local elders came in the evening. Bob urged compliance, telling them categorically of the intent of his mission, and that henceforth, Tsona would have no role south of Bumla.

While the stage was being set, in the background hectic parleys were at play through diplomatic channels between Delhi, the Consul General at Lhasa through Gangtok and the Advisor for NEFA on how Bob ought to act, with concerns not hurt Tibetan susceptibilities and prevent internationalisation of to issues. After two rounds of futile musical chairs, Bob was getting impatient and sent a stern message for clear directions, else he would pack his bags. He however stayed and accomplished the Mission and the rest is history[128].

When the Tibetan Officials sought time for orders from Lhasa, Bob invoked the 1914 Simla Agreement and insisted that they leave soon from Indian Territory.[129] Hence, without firing a single bullet, with tact and authority, for the first time, the Tricolour was unfurled in Tawang. The Tibetan Officials were escorted respectfully out of the Indian Territory through Khin-Dza-Mane.

On the Centenary of the McMahon Line in 2014, Lobsang Tenpa wrote a paper, wherein the peaceful formal control over Tawang in 1951 has been dealt in detail. Few paragraphs of importance are reproduced here:

"Border Defence Committee" to recommend a "pushing forward the post to Tawang" (Chakravarty 1953: 35). Therefore, on 10th December 1950, Joint Secretary to the GOI informed the "Advisor" of the Government of Assam that "we should effectively occupy it." The matter was taken seriously under the Governor of Assam with the help of the "Adviser" N.K. Rustomji in 1951, which asked Major R. Khating to lead a column of Assam Rifles with eight "instructions" to implement the 1914 Simla Convention's spirit.

Although it took nearly four decades for the GOI to fully assert a direct administration in the region, the change of regime took place between the Assam Rifles Major R. Khating and the last Tibetan administrator - Bla gnyer Thubbstan chos 'phel (r. 1949-51) at Tawang monastery was successful. The latter was locally called gnyer tshang, to whom Khating states that "the Nyertsang or Accountant of the monastery, who is Deputy from Lhasa may become the only thorn in the administration of the monastery in future, [and notes that] he is cunning and well informed" (Chakravarty 1953: 36). Indeed, his return to Central Tibet in early 1951 marked the change of regime, while Major Khating had accompanied three Monpa representatives from Tawang "to express to His Excellency [Governor of Assam] their gratitude" at Shillong in 1951. Since then, Monyul's two districts were not left untouched by the GOI and they steadily developed over the last six decades.

At same time, Tsona rdzong dpon "entered our territory [Tawang] without previous permission", and on formality ground an objection was lodged in April and September 1951 to Khating (Chakravarty 1953: 38). Khating states that the Tsona rdzong dpon objected to Khating's "annexing" of Monyul in their formal meeting, and later upon requests by the Tsona rdzong dpon, he had given them the last and only "written reply" on 27th April. It was further rejected on 2nd September 1951, which was the last possible objection raised by the Tsona rdzong dpon to Khating (1951b). However, it is not known what is stated in that "written reply" given by Khating. It could be probable that the privileges were offered, if they–the Tsona rdzong dpon stayed back in Monyul. Since then, no further objection was raised by the GOT. Thus, the peaceful incorporation of Monyul into the union of Indian states was a gradual process. As briefly mentioned before, the last Tibetan official, Thub bstan chos 'phel (1988) accepted the change of situation in February 1951 and left to [for] Lhasa within some weeks after then. The remaining (Tibeto-) Mon officials of the "Council of Four/ Six/Seven" (bzhi/drug/bdun sbrel) filed ["acceptance cum] requisition" to the GOI, which was endorsed by the newly appointed "Assistant Political Officer" of the "Sela Sub Agency" in July 1952.

The new agreement reiterated the rights of the defunct Tawang officials, and where the "requisition" was partially based on the 1844 and 1853 treaties and the 1680 edict issued by the fifth Dalai Lama. Probably, it was the last time that they were exercising their autonomous status in their history. And the 1952 document records it being part of the Union of Indian states by the ["acceptance cum] requisition" to the Asst. Political Officer, who represents the GOI. Thus, the Water-Dragon year (chu'brug) document marks an important point in comparison to the "17th Point Agreement" document of 1951. The only difference between the two documents is that the latter was forced to be "signed and accepted," while the former was ["acceptance cum] requisition" to maintain the status quo of the social-political system of their respective regions. Therefore, the former is intact, but changed gradually in the last sixty years, while the latter was abolished completely by the People's Republic of China in 1959. However, it is to be noted that historically Monyul is known to British India since 1844 and 1853 at the imperial to chieftainship level, which proves crucial to Monyul being "legally" incorporated into Indian nation-states in 1914 at the international level and in 1952 at the national level.[130]

Whatever may be the sequence of events culminating in the formal possession of Monyul by India, to build confidence, immediately thereafter, Bob began construction of the Permanent Administrative Headquarters and Assam Rifles Post along with a small dispensary. While the process of consolidation was almost through, Bob provided galvanised sheets for roofing the Main Prayer building of the Tawang Monastery, which had been damaged by the recent earthquake. This act sent signals of the Indian State as a benevolent one, respectful of local religious and cultural ethos, further reinforcing the integrating elements towards India[131].

The air sorties that ensued brought in the essentials and rations. This had a soothing effect on the locals, boosting their confidence that this time the Indian Government was here to administer.

Bob did not rest on his recent successes, but went on a sixteen day tour to Bum La and Tulung La ranges to demarcate the McMahon Line of ground and set up check posts along trade routes of Bumla, Chuthangmu and Chuna near Mago. In 1952, he was promoted and succeeded Maj Allen as the Political Officer of Se La Sub Agency. It was then, the Headquarters of Se La Sub Agency was shifted from Charduar to a forested area, now Bomdila. Bob was later inducted into the prestigious Indian Frontier Administrative Service (IFAS).[132]

Ms. Neeru Nanda, an IAS officer, who served in Tawang in the 70s, in her reminiscence of the Bob expedition, writes how the village elders were perturbed that the Indian Government had imposed no tax, and hence, doubted the seriousness of Indian Govt's claim on Tawang.

This impression of *'what good is a Government, if it doesn't tax'* was an imbibed trait from the Tsona experience. Further, many earlier promenades of British Officers and claim over Tawang were not followed by any form of State presence, while the Tibetan Dzongpons continued their rule, much to the detriment of locals who sided with the British Indian Representatives. The scepticism stemmed from previous bitter experiences of the Lightfoot and other such *'Tip and Run Expeditions'* and the act of the *'Vanishing Govt'*.

The village elders, not convinced by Bob's explanation of benevolent welfare governance, urged him to impose a minimum tax to authenticate the Indian Government in Tawang. Accordingly, Bob reluctantly imposed Rs. 5 per household as annual tax[133].

While anecdotes are plenty, few questions will need more research. How did the mission seek prior intelligence on situation in Tawang? Who provided the inputs? Were they monpas? Did they facilitate Bob's entry into Tawang? Who were those brave monpas, if any, who risked the danger of being tortured by the Dzongpons and assisted the mission? Who were the monpas who accompanied Bob to meet the Governor in Shillong?

Nari Rustomji, the then Advisor to Governor, in his memoir, *'Enchanted Frontier'*, while describing the sequence of events that resulted in the decision on Tawang, reminisces, *'We selected Bob Khathing for the task–and could not have made a better choice'*, feeling vindicated on the decision. Nari Rustomji, further in adoration for and acknowledgement of Bob, writes. *'And we did not think twice before deciding that Bob was the man for the job. In Nagaland, Tawang, Bomdila, in the face of the Chinese aggression in 1962, wherever there was trouble afoot, the heavens might fall, but Bob, we knew, we could always depend on. If any officer deserved his Padma Shri, it was this tough, redoubtable Tangkhul Naga from Manipur'*[134]. This was indeed a fitting tribute to a great man that Bob was. His deft and diplomatic skills displayed in the smooth transition of formal control over Tawang into the Indian Union, among others, may have been a crucial basis, while he was being considered for the high office of Ambassador of India to Burma.

> *'There is no reason why I should not love*
> *My motherland in which I was Born!*
> *She has lovingly nurtured our forbearers,*
> *She has withstood heat as well cold,*
> *Even now, without forsaking us all*
> *Like the hen she still broods over us'*

> **– Bob's Lyrical anthem for his Tribe**[135]

If Jairamdas was, as I had once described him, the 'High Priest' of NEFA, Verrier Elwin was its administering herald angel'. The popular image of the tribal may have been of an uncouth savage. For Elwin, he was all magic, love and beauty. Verrier's first and most important offering to the cause of the frontier tribals was his 'Philosophy for NEFA', which was soon accepted as 'the frontier officer's bible'.

– Nari Rustomji,
Advisor to Governor of Assam in his book
'Imperilled Frontiers'

6

Elwin's *Philosophy for NEFA*-Securing Roots for a Stable Future

Building on Bob Khathing's story and the evolving agenda in Tawang, the tale of NEFA's transformation after 1947 is another fascinating piece of India's Northeastern frontier mosaic. As India emerged from the shadows of colonial rule, the democratic Government faced the formidable challenge of integrating the North East Frontier into the nation's broader framework.

British Policy of Isolation of the Frontier

Let's consider the British policy of isolation in the North-eastern frontier of India. This strategy is quite intriguing because of the way the British treated this region as a strategic buffer-a protective barrier between their empire and the neighbouring powers such as China or the regions bordering Myanmar. The field officers strongly advocated for a forward push and taking administration deep into the Frontier, not for love of the tribes but mostly, for strategic reasons. However, owing to a lack of funds, London and Delhi's lack of intent, the *lost opportunity* was indeed, a blessing in disguise.

Back in the day, the British rulers saw this lush, remote area as a sort of cushion-a buffer zone-between their empire and the neighbouring powers that might pose threats, like China or the regions adjunct to Myanmar. Their strategy? Keep it isolated. This meant not only limiting how much

109

outsiders could interact with the region, but also how much development they allowed there. The idea was simple: less development meant fewer external influences and, hopefully, fewer complications in managing these areas.

You might be curious, "Why maintain this seclusion?" Well, by keeping the Northeast disconnected from the hustle and bustle of the colonial economic centres and even from the advancements in infrastructure that other parts were seeing, the British were essentially trying to maintain a controlled environment. They believed this would prevent any political or social upheaval that could complicate their hold over India. Therefore, tribal isolation was also partly to insulate them from the freedom movement, with the motive that the frontier remain a *'British Preserve'* in perpetuity. No wonder, the idea of making the frontier a *'Crown Colony'*[136] was seriously considered by the British Government.

It's almost like they treated these regions as a drawer full of old, valuable maps that they didn't want anyone else to get their hands on. By doing so, they hoped these tribal areas would remain untouched and easy to govern, despite the rich cultures and diversity that thrived there, unseen and unappreciated by the wider world for a long time.

Thus, while this policy might have appeared strategically sensible, it also meant that the tribes and communities in these areas were segregated from the progress unfolding elsewhere-not only in technological terms but also in socio-economic and political spheres. It's a profound reflection on how historical policies have shaped the lives of many, secluded in their mountains and forests, hidden from the world's view.

Post Independence Policy for NEFA

As we move past the British era into the dawn of Indian independence in 1947, the approach to the Northeastern frontier underwent a significant transformation. With independence, the new Indian government faced the complex task of integrating these previously isolated regions into the broader fabric of the nation.

The untouched realm was rendered a place where only essentials were sufficient for the tribals. With no roads and limited tracks, tours to the frontier from plains would mean months of arduous treks; which would entail arranging rations all along, porters to carry it and additional ration for the porters. Locals kept themselves busy with their daily chores, unavailable for porterage. Hence it was a logistic nightmare even to plan a visit into these territories. These unique circumstances provided the *'Breathing Space'*[137] for both the tribals with their way of life and the Administration, as it looked for the best way to administer the North East Frontier Agency (NEFA), being mindful of the far-reaching implications of taking administration to these pristine societies.

This integration was about more than just establishing administrative control; it was fundamentally about weaving these diverse tribal cultures into the democratic and developmental agenda of free India. For decades, these areas were intentionally kept at a developmental standstill, marked by minimal external interference and engagement. Now, the focus shifted towards not only incorporating these regions into the Indian state but ensuring that their unique cultural identities were respected and preserved.

Verrier Elwin, an anthropologist whose journey from missionary work to advocating for tribal rights in India is as fascinating as it is impactful, brought a refreshing perspective to the treatment of tribal communities in the NEFA. His philosophy was ground-breaking for its time, proposing that tribes should have the space and freedom to evolve at their own pace, rather than being rushed into conformity with the broader society. If his Philosophy was to be described in a single phrase, it was *'Hastening Slowly.'*[138]

Harry Verrier Holman Elwin was born in Dover in 1902 to Henry Edmund Elwin, Bishop of Sierra Leone. A graduate from Oxford, with a first class degree in English, he took up Theology in accordance with his family traditions and was ordained a priest in the Church of England. His journey in India began in 1927 when he joined a small sect, the Christa Seva Sangh in Pune apparently tasked to 'indigenise' Christianity. Here, on frequent visits to Sabarmati Ashram, he was impressed by the Gandhian approach and eventually became an adopted son of sorts to Gandhi.

Contrary to his missionary calling, he entered Central India and worked for the tribals, with a focus on preserving their culture and preparing them to face the hailstorm of cultural change. He then, on the request of Nehru and Daulatram Jairamdas, reached Shillong on New Year's Eve of 1953 and worked as Advisor for Tribal Affairs to the NEFA Government. On the personal front, he gave up both his religion and citizenship, became an Indian Citizen in 1954. He married twice, both times to tribal ladies and lived till 1964. Three years before his demise, he was awarded with the third highest civilian award, the '*Padma Bhushan*'[139].

Elwin believed deeply in the inherent capacity of tribal societies for self-governance. He argued that these communities should be entrusted with the autonomy to shape their own future, an idea that contrasted sharply with the more overwhelmingly intrusive policies which many advocated. His approach was not merely theoretical but intensely practical, advocating for policies that respected the unique cultural identities and traditions of each tribe.

Elwin had his fair share of critics. Many accused him of being a British '*isolationist*', '*trying to divide mother India on communal lines*'.... Creating a '*Aboriginilistan*' to be ruled by ethnographers like himself, while others denounced him for contributing to '*Balkanisation of Bharat*'. The other line of thinking was around the insecurities surrounding '*the mongoloid stock*' of the frontier and their loyalties during crises. Hence settling more outsiders and ensuring quick assimilation to mainstream culture was their common refrain. It was a totally ill-conceived idea and rightly rejected, for it would have led to sure extinction of rich tribal culture and maybe even tribes because of the low population.

One author's claim "*that he [Elwin] was chiefly responsible for the turmoil in the Northeast*'. This was rightly rebutted that "*There are seven states in India's North-east. All with the exception of Arunachal (where Elwin's policy recommendation holds sway) are hotbeds of secession and insurgency*". In support of his argument, he further quotes from an author about Arunachal Pradesh, "*it is an island of peace,' with a 'degree of stability not witnessed elsewhere in the Northeast*'[140].

Building on the strong foundation of administration laid by Jairamdas Daulatram, Elwin became the guiding star of the policy for administration of NEFA. He started by setting up a Research Department and began publishing monographs on tribes and made it available to the administrators as easy reads. This made the officers aware of customs, beliefs, rituals, superstitions, art, culture and history allaying many avoidable troubles arising out of ignorance. These documents also educated the wider public, refuting misconceptions of frontier tribes being *'backward and primitive'*[141].

Elwin would often say, 'whilst not opposed to change in principle, we were opposed to change for the sake of change'. The Philosophy was *'near missionary in its intensity and sincerity'*[142].

The impact of Elwin's Philosophy on NEFA was profound and multifaceted. At a time when the region was transitioning from a history of isolation under British rule to integration within an independent India, Elwin's ideas influenced the newly formed Government's approach to tribal areas. The policies that emerged were infused with a respect for tribal customs and languages, recognizing them as vital elements of India's diverse cultural tapestry rather than relics to be modernised.

Education and healthcare programs were introduced under the influence of Elwin's philosophy, but with a twist-they were designed to be culturally appropriate and sensitive. Schools were encouraged to incorporate tribal elements such as folklore, local heroes in curriculum, and healthcare initiatives were adapted to align with local practices and beliefs. Elwin's Research Department laid the framework for these initiatives. This not only helped in preserving tribal cultures but also ensured that development was perceived positively by the tribal communities, fostering a sense of involvement and ownership.

These initiatives underpinned by Elwin's philosophy did not merely seek to bring change to NEFA but aimed to empower the tribal communities to lead that change themselves. This was a shift from viewing tribes as passive recipients of policy to active participants in their own development narrative. Small yet significant care was taken to bring about dignity. The insulting nomenclatures used by plainsmen such as *'uncouth Abor'* became a thing of the past and replaced by more respectful utterances such as *"Adis, Denizens of the Hills'*, as a token of fresh and more enlightened approach acknowledging the people of NEFA as equal and respected partners of the Nation[143]. Oken Tayeng, a legislator and founder of Abor Country Travels and Expeditions, passionately articulates that the term "Abor" is anything but derogatory. Instead, it embodies the indomitable spirit of the Adi people. He elaborates that "Abor" translates to "the indomitable," a tribute to their resilience and determination.

The legacy of Elwin's work is still evident today in how tribal policies are framed and implemented, even in other tribal areas in India. His advocacy for respect, autonomy, and cultural sensitivity laid the groundwork for a development approach that is more inclusive and affirming of India's rich tribal heritage. Within these broad narratives, the philosophy as advocated was losing its relevance with each passing day. Of course, for the first few years, immediately post-independence, the people of the frontier were not ready to intermingle 'freely', thanks to the isolation imposed by geography which was accentuated by the *Inner Line* and the policy of *'excluded and partially excluded areas'*. At that juncture, the *Elwinian Philosophy* for mainstreaming at the pace chosen by the tribes was a necessity of the times.

It is also a fact that, while the philosophy to govern came in writing in 1954, Nari Rustomji and many other frontier officials, since 1948, were already thinking of the problem of *'introducing change without being destructive of the best values of the old life'*[144] and his ideas were already put in practice on ground. Rustomji and Elwin, both accused of being romantics, given their similar thinking on the tribal question, would often condemn *'reckless'* talks of *'uplifting and civilising'* the tribes. Elwin in his autobiography quotes Rustomji's writing of 1953 for the frontier officials approvingly, *'Much of the beauty of living still survives in these remote and distant hills, where dance and song are a vital part of everyday living, where people speak and think freely, without fear or restraint. Our workers must ensure, therefore, that the good that is inherent in the institutions of the hill people is not tainted or substituted by practices that may be 'modern' and 'advanced', but are totally unsuited to their economy and way of thinking. The hillmen has, essentially, a clean, direct and healthy outlook; he is free, happily, from the morbid complexes induced by the unnatural life of a city folk.*

The greatest disservice will be done, therefore, if in an excess of missionary zeal, our workers destroy the fresh creative urge that lives, strong and vital, within the denizens of the hills. For, if we wish to serve, we must show that we have respect for the hillmen and their institutions, their language and their song: and, in showing such respect, we shall secure their confidence in the work that lies ahead. For this reason, everyone should make it his first task to familiarise himself with the local language, take interest and come to understand the customs and usages of the people and share fully in their life, not as a stranger from without, but as one of themselves. [145]

Even with the passage of seven decades, the words of Rustomji still stand relevant to this day and the essence of serving in Arunachal Pradesh still reverberates around these profound thoughts and continues to be the true guiding principle.

The bringing of the entire 84,000 square km of the frontier into administration in the shortest possible time, that too without any predicament, save for one incident was an achievement Rustomji considered a success, like none in history. A credit to the Frontier Officers and the guiding light of Elwin.

To summarise, the tenets of the Elwinian philosophy for the government administration in NEFA: if anything was to be done, it would be only in consultation with the tribes. There would be zero tolerance for the *'patronising attitude'*-assuming that officials know better than the tribals. Respect tribal culture and not impose alien culture to destroy it. Aim for positive and constructive ways to prepare the tribal communities to meet the inevitable future challenges, prepare them to be competent to assess and make choice balancing traditional values and the new values.

Post 1962 War: End of a Philosophy?

The philosophy of Verrier Elwin, which had guided the approach towards the North East Frontier Agency (NEFA) with a focus on cultural sensitivity and autonomy, faced a dramatic shift post-1962. The tranquillity and progressive ethos cultivated by Elwin's insights were sharply disrupted by the tremors caused by the Sino-Indian War. The policy of *'hastening slowly*[146]*'* was reviewed and overtaken by concerns of security.

This conflict, which underscored the strategic vulnerabilities of NEFA, prompted a radical re-evaluation of priorities. The Indian government, recognizing the critical need to fortify the region against potential threats, shifted its focus from cultural preservation to national security. The landscape of NEFA, once marked by educational initiatives and healthcare programs that respected tribal identities, began to change. Infrastructure developments surged, not for economic growth or social welfare, but for strategic and military purposes. The military presence in the region was significantly increased, marking a departure from the previously minimal interference.

This period marked the end of an era where Elwin's philosophies were a cornerstone of policy-making in NEFA. The ideals of autonomy and cultural respect gave way to a more assertive stance from the central Government, where geopolitical considerations took precedence. This transition reflected a broader shift in policy as the Government sought to secure its borders and maintain sovereignty at the cost of the unique cultural integration strategies that had been employed.

However, with time, the tribes, especially the youth, with access to education and healthcare, and enhanced levels of education and exposure began seeking mobility and were more than eager to venture outside NEFA. This was an indication, in a sense, of the need to accelerate the pace of mainstreaming, and also bridge the wide gap caused by isolation over the years. The events that unfolded in 1962 and the urgency to militarise the frontiers pushed the Philosophy for NEFA to the backdrop. Roads, bridges, airstrips and all ancillary infrastructure came to the fore with large military presence. This meant closer and frequent interaction with the '*Harings*', '*Ayings*' *and* '*Kyas*'-pejorative names for outsiders, each learning from each other, changing the social landscape. Thankfully, by then, across fifteen years, NEFA tribals had not only secured stable roots to face with confidence the overwhelming onslaught of '*civilising*' forces but were ready to rise to the higher echelons of success. With a strong and solid foundation laid and a set of tribal leaders already in place to face the situation by taking a balanced view, NEFA was ready to move forward. It is interesting, that owing largely to this Philosophy, tribals of NEFA saw mainland as a friend and a guide and not an aggressor, either territorial or cultural. This ensured easy integration and spared NEFA the bloodshed and distress that were the sad pages of history in the near neighbourhood.

Elwin was of the firm view that the '*real protector of the aboriginal is knowledge. … [which] can convince administrator and reformer alike that they are … human beings like themselves and escort them safely through the perilous passage of acculturation*'[147].

In that spirit, the NEFA administration continued to support the frontier population, particularly the first generation of college students. A NEFA hostel was established in Shillong to accommodate boys from NEFA pursuing higher education. These students received meticulous guidance from the frontier officials, including the Governor himself, ensuring they were well-supported during their academic journey. This initiative exemplified the administration's commitment to fostering education and development in the region.

Remember Oshong Ering, the boy whose heroic act during the 1950 earthquake was recognised by the Frontier Administration? He was one of the pioneers who reached Shillong seeking a degree from St. Edmunds College, and would later retire as an Indian Administrative Service officer. He recalls his conversation with Dr. Elwin in 1955 on why Elwin did not like the idea of converting the rhododendrons of high mountains to lilies of the plains and [why] at the same time converting of dwarf lilies to robust rhododendrons, was a mockery of natural beauty[148].

Other pioneers such as Daying Ering, a Cotton College educated gentleman, under the close guidance of NEFA administration, from Pasighat, rose to the heights as the Deputy Minister in the central government, while another young boy from Pasighat, Jamat Matin Tangu made it to St. Anthonys College and graduated from there, rising to helm of affairs and retiring as Commissioner. An orphan, Jomin Tayeng, from Dambuk, a small subdivision which had no road connectivity till as recently as 2016, ventured out and became the first IAS officer of NEFA in 1968, later retired as the Chief Secretary of Meghalaya State and a Legislator in the Arunachal Pradesh Legislative Assembly. Kuru Hassang from the Apatani Plateau became the first Indian Air Force fighter Pilot of Arunachal Pradesh. Col Rimmo Karbak from Kamba qualified for National Defence Academy through UPSC in 1967 to become the first Defence Officer from Arunachal Pradesh. There are many such Pioneers, who against all odds dared to move out and pave way for the future fellow tribal sisters and brothers.

The story goes that the Governor and Advisor would often send their ambassador cars to invite these first-generation scholars to their residences, at Shillong, where they would engage in long discussions about the future of NEFA. During these visits, the scholars were also taught small etiquettes, such as tying a tie knot and using spoon and fork.

On one such occasion, Jamat Matin Tangu, a boy from Pasighat pursuing higher education in Shillong, was driven in a black ambassador car to meet Rustomji. Upon arrival, Rustomji said, *"Let's go, young man, and visit the Shillong Jail."* Perplexed but curious, Jamat followed without questioning. To his utter surprise, Rustomji took him to meet one secessionist leader. The excited young man got talking and commented that NEFA might face similar issues, suggesting that NEFA-educated officers must be given opportunities in the administration, including the coveted IFAS, to avert such an eventuality.

Rustomji immediately picked up on the hint and assured Tangu that he would take up the matter, recognizing the importance of integrating local talent into the administrative framework to ensure the region's stability and development.[149]

In 1965, three gentlemen from NEFA got into the Indian Frontier Administrative Service. They were AJ Tayeng, Toi Dai and Takap Ringu, pioneers from the frontier to have been inducted into the elite Services. Two retired as Chief Secretaries, while one retired as Additional Chief Secretary. It is difficult, though, to ascertain how much the Tangu-Rustomji conversation contributed to this development. Tangu, himself, got into Government Service in 1963 as Assistant Political Officer-II[150].

It's clear that while Elwin's philosophies had a profound impact on the approach towards tribal regions during their time, the exigencies of national security and international politics eventually overshadowed these non-traditional policies. Could it do so? The legacy of Elwin's philosophy, a debate of cultural pluralism versus homogeneity, however, continues to inform debates and policies concerning tribal rights and integration in India, reflecting his enduring influence on how cultural sensitivity and autonomy can be balanced with national interests. Hence, though the 1962 aggression and the subsequent developments, wrote the epitaph for the Philosophy, it continued to silently influence the shape of things to come for Arunachal Pradesh; many tenets of the philosophy are still finding relevance in the State.

It is also intriguing why Elwin, a cleric with missionary intent, had a change of heart and worked contrary to what is expected of a missionary. The *'Savaging of the Civilised'* will always remain a mystery for us all. Nonetheless, the *Elwin Affair* with NEFA had a mentoring effect on the *gentle hand* administration over the NEFA people, a *sine qua non* then.

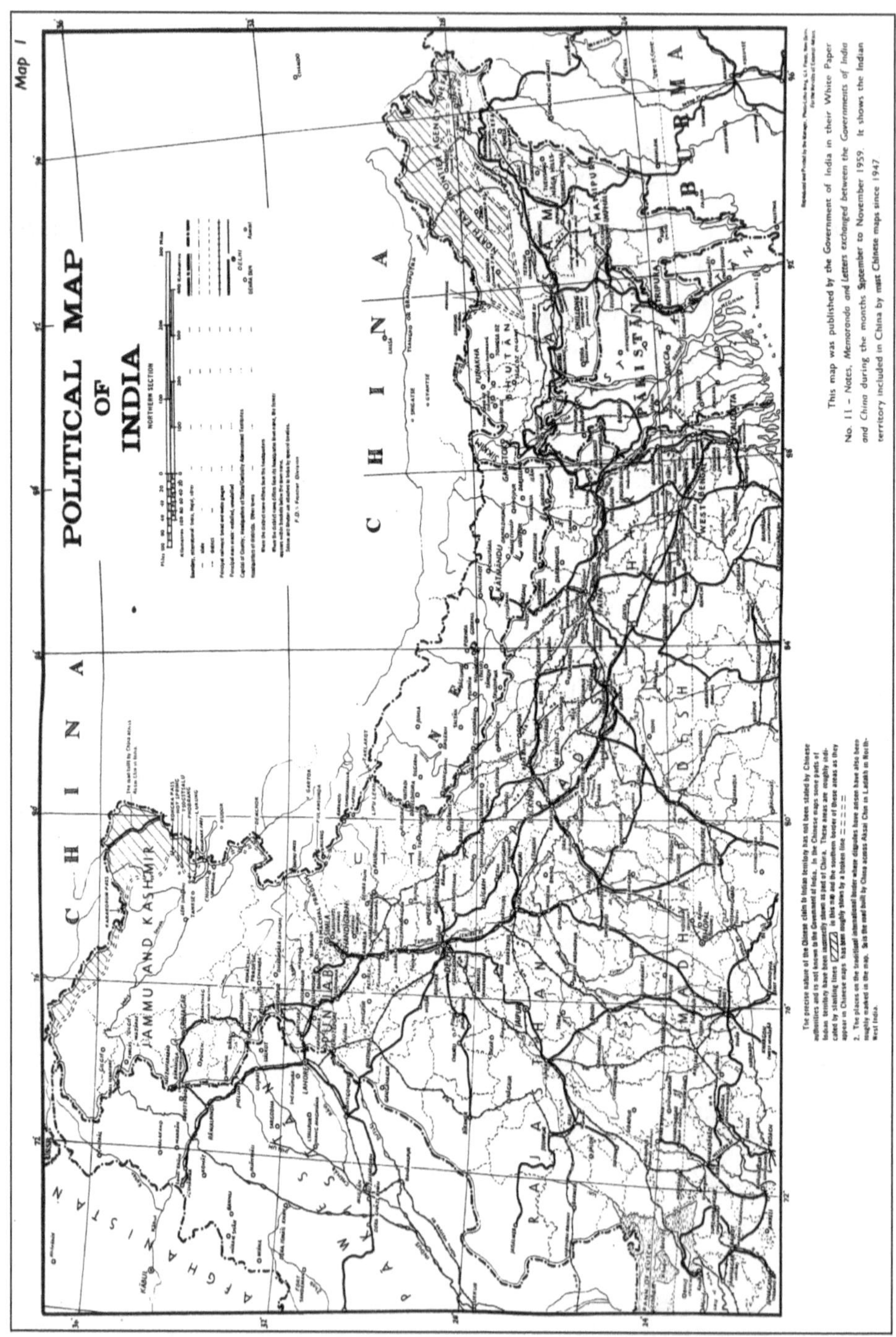

▲ **Map 11:** Political Map of India, 1959
(Source: 1960 Atlas of the Northern Frontier of India, Ministry of External Affairs, GoI)

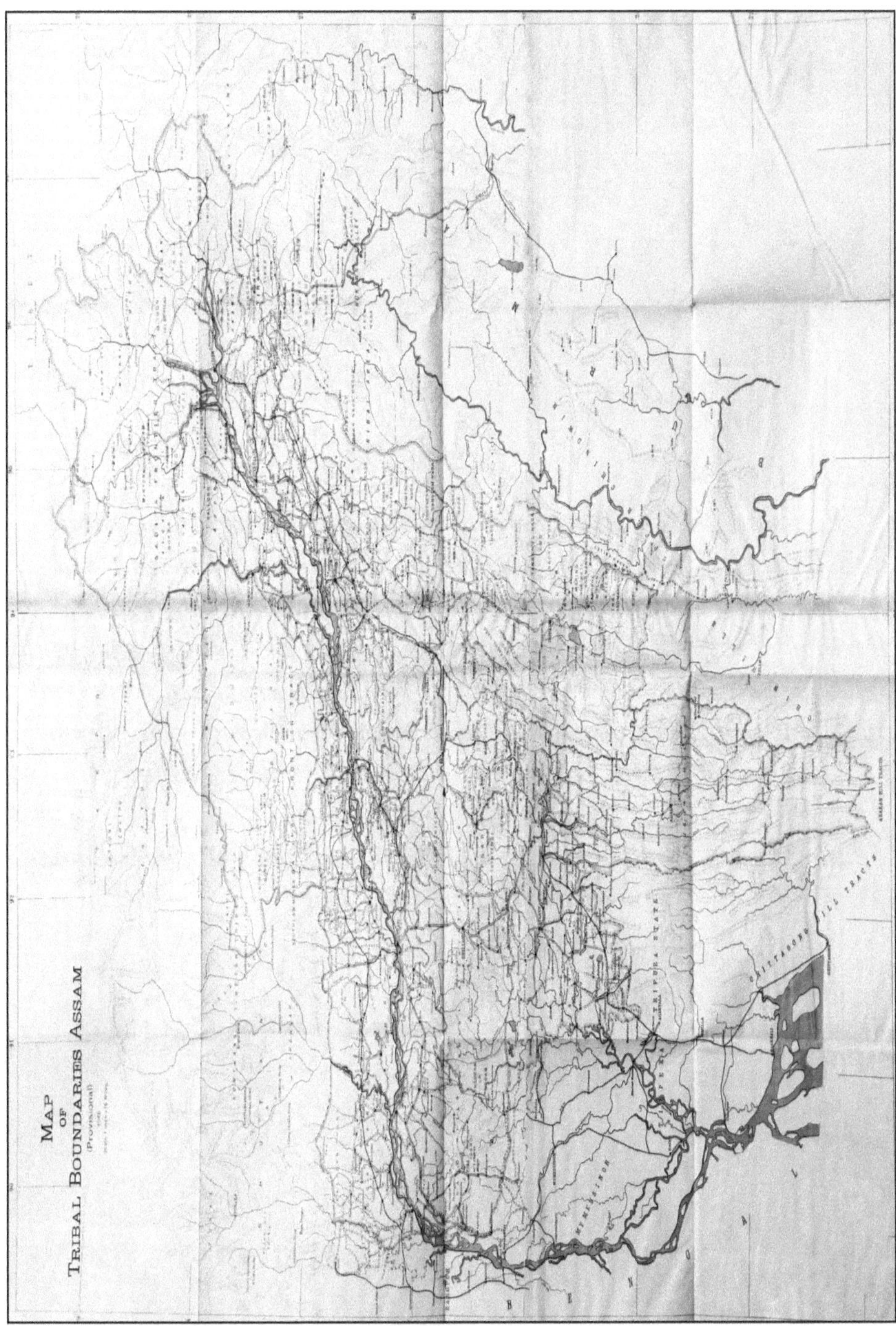

▲ **Map 12:** Tribal Boundaries Map of Assam, including present day Arunachal Pradesh, 1946 (Source: Directorate of Research, Government of Arunachal Pradesh)

Ever since the Dalai Lama entered India at Kanzey Mane, near Chuthangmu, he has experienced in full measure the respect and hospitality extended to him by the people of the Kameng Frontier Division of the North East Frontier Agency and the Dalai Lama would like to state how the Government of India's officers posted there had spared no efforts in making his stay and journey through this extremely well administered part of India as comfortable as possible[151].

Excerpt from the Press Release of His Holiness the 14th Dalai Lama issued from Tezpur, 18th April 1959

7

The Holy Exile – Ancient Indian Wisdom Returns

The late fifties and the early sixties can easily be termed as one of the most difficult times for India. *What's apparent is not real and what's real is not apparent.* The events of 1959 and 1962 and its build up are pivotal in understanding the complex relationship between India and China, particularly in the context of the uprising in Tibet and the later Sino-Indian War. The North Eastern Frontier was at the centre stage and the ground where these two events unfolded, changing forever the world order and its diplomatic landscape. India, a new nation's Diplomats and Military strategists were both outmanoeuvred by the cunningness of the Chinese minds, we will see how.

Two Asian Giants-Freedom & Liberation

As the late forties unfolded, the world, still reeling from the trauma of World War II, watched as two monumental shifts took place in Asia. It was a period marked by significant change and newfound freedom. In 1947, India emerged as a sovereign nation, shedding the chains of British colonial rule. This transition, however, was not without its challenges. India faced the dual trials of a bloody partition and the mammoth task of consolidating its territory into a cohesive national entity.

In the North, another dramatic transformation was taking place. By 1949, China was experiencing its own pivotal moment. The Nationalist

Guomindang party was overthrown, paving the way for the birth of the People's Republic of China (PRC) under the leadership of Mao Zedong. In contrast to India's path led by Mahatma Gandhi's principles of non-violence and civil disobedience, China's journey was carved through the strife of a bloody civil war, further intensified by the aftermath of Japanese occupation[152].

These two Asian giants, India and China, freshly minted as sovereign states, embarked on paths defined by their unique histories and ideologies. The differences in their foundational stories set the stage for the complex and often strained relations that would unfold over the next decade and beyond, particularly between 1950 and 1962. These years were crucial in reinforcing and shaping the current dynamics between the two nations.

The relationship between India and China is complex, shaped by four key factors: deep-seated mutual perceptions, territorial disputes, strategic alignments with global powers, and a significant asymmetry in their power statuses. Historically, the perceptions each country holds of the other have often been negative, with influential Chinese views on India stretching back to the 19th century casting a long shadow over bilateral interactions[153].

The juxtaposition of these two nations, each undergoing significant political and social transformations, set the stage for a complex relationship characterised by both cooperation and conflict. The period following the 1950 earthquake and leading up to the 1962 conflict was marked by a series of diplomatic engagements and military standoffs that highlighted the volatile nature of their interactions. This period is crucial to understanding how historical legacies, territorial ambitions, and the aftermath of pivotal events like the Assam earthquake have shaped the policies and perceptions that continue to influence Sino-Indian relations even today.

Roof of the World-No longer Forbidden

As India and China stepped into new chapters of their histories, the dramatic shift in China's political landscape brought new challenges and opportunities. With the People's Republic of China (PRC) firmly established under the control of the Chinese Communist Party (CCP), the expansionist pursuit swiftly gained momentum. The proclamation of the PRC took place on October 1, 1949, from Tiananmen Square, signifying a profound transformation from the fall of the Guomindang in Nanjing.

In India, the rise of the Communist regime in China sparked a vigorous debate about how to approach this new geopolitical reality. The question of recognizing the new regime and establishing diplomatic relations stirred diverse opinions in Delhi. Some advocated for India to be the first to recognize the PRC, hoping to forge a strong initial bond, while others called for a more cautious approach.

Amid these discussions, concerns about the potential threats posed by the ascendency of the Communists in China were strongly articulated by Sardar Patel. In the far-sighted letter to Nehru in June 1949, Patel highlighted the imperative to reinforce India's position in Sikkim and Tibet, foreseeing the Communist intent to undermine Tibet's autonomy. He advised preparing for such eventualities, emphasising the strategic importance of maintaining a buffer against Communist expansion. He wrote, *"We have to strengthen our position in Sikkim as well as in Tibet. The farther we keep away the Communist forces, the better. Tibet has long been detached from China. I anticipate that as soon as the Communists have established themselves in the rest of China, they will try to destroy its autonomous existence. You have to consider carefully your policy towards Tibet in such a circumstance and prepare from now for that eventuality."*[154]

Counterintuitively, India was among the first nations to recognize the People's Republic of China, a decision which was fraught with implications.

Critics later argued that India's approach lacked a strategic framework and relinquished crucial negotiating leverage, based more on emotionalism and conjecture than on a well-planned strategy[155].

At the time of independence, inheriting from the British, India maintained significant establishments in Tibet, including trade centres in Gyantse, Yatung, Gartok and Lhasa, a telegraph office, and a platoon of the army stationed in Lhasa. These were legacies of the British strategy to establish Tibet as a buffer, initially aimed more against Czarist Russian expansion than against China. Patel's advocacy for preserving this position underscored the broader geopolitical implications for India's northern borders, including Ladakh, Nepal, Sikkim, Bhutan, and NEFA (present-day Arunachal Pradesh).

Prophetic as it may sound, Patel's warning unfolded to reality, and the landscape changed dramatically when Mao's China began its occupation of Tibet on October 7, 1950. By the following year, the *17-point Agreement* between China and Tibet was signed, sealing Tibet's fate and effectively eliminating the buffer that had been a strategic barrier till 1950. India found herself sharing a direct border with China, a development that Major General D.K. Palit later lamented, noting the general lack of awareness about Tibet's strategic importance even among India's external affairs personnel.[156]

This transition marked a critical turning point in regional dynamics, shifting the balance of power and forcing India to reconsider its strategic priorities in the face of a new and formidable neighbour.

Hindi-Chini Bhai Bhai-Five Principles of Deceit

The signing of the 1954 *Agreement on Trade and Intercourse* between the Tibet Region of China and India marked a pivotal moment in Sino-Indian relations. Consequent to the establishment of diplomatic ties with Communist China, this agreement was touted as a significant achievement. However, it soon became evident that it was another instance where the

Chinese delegation managed to outmanoeuvre the Indian side through a mix of deception and strategic engagement.[157]

The Chinese had clear objectives; *de jure* sovereignty over Tibet and to cut the umbilical cord of India's historical extraterritorial influence of India in the region. They embarked on a well calculated calibrated approach-avoid seeking a comprehensive solution, deal piecemeal with India, and advance their goals slowly without overwhelming Indian negotiators.

In this negotiation, India missed a crucial opportunity to resolve the boundary issue. Major concessions were made, including a total withdrawal from Tibet, which swung the advantage decidedly in China's favour. By the end of the agreement, India returned with an unresolved border and lost all her stakes in Tibet. Yet, the agreement was celebrated in India under the banners of *"Hindi-Chini Bhai Bhai"* and praised for its adherence to the Five Principles, or 'Panchsheel'. This optimism masked the underlying strategic setbacks, embodying a classic case of ignoring the harsh realities underfoot.

Almost immediately after the treaty was signed, China began to assert itself more aggressively on the cartographic front. Chinese military garrisons sprang up across Tibet, inching ever closer to the Indian border. Moreover, within just a few months of the agreement, China started to lay claims to areas south of the established boundary, signalling a clear intent to redefine the borders unilaterally[158].

By this time, China had already made significant inroads into the Aksai Chin area. As early as 1952, B.N. Mullick, Head of India's Intelligence Bureau, reported that construction had begun on a major highway linking Tibet with Xinjiang, which cut across Aksai Chin[159], the powers then apparently turned a deaf ear to this vital input, while China was pushing her strategic intent to solidify its presence and control in the region. There is a version which states that the construction of the road began in 1954 and was completed in July of 1957.

During the subsequent visits of Chinese Premier Zhou Enlai to India in 1954 and 1956, these brewing tensions and territorial encroachments were largely brushed aside. The Chinese leadership focused on completing the strategic G-219 National Highway connecting Tibet and Xinjiang within twelve months and downplayed the boundary issues. This strategic highway was critical for China's grand plans in the region, further complicating the already tense relations between the two neighbours.

Thus, the period following the 1954 agreement which saw the initial warmth of "Hindi-Chini Bhai Bhai" give way to a chilling realisation of strategic deception and territorial ambitions, setting the stage for the complex and fraught dynamics that would define Sino-Indian relations for decades to come.

Dalai Lama enters Tawang and brings along Ancient Indian Wisdom

"For one, the moment I was able to cross over from Tibet to India on March 31, 1959, I realised the value of freedom. Since then, I have been the longest-staying guest of the Indian Government, enjoying every possible liberty". -**HH the 14th Dalai Lama**

As the slogans of *"Hindi-Chini Bhai Bhai"* slowly faded into the background, overshadowed by the stark realities of strategic deception and unresolved border disputes, a pivotal event in 1959 added another layer to the complex Sino-Indian relationship. The arrival of the Dalai Lama into Indian territory marked a significant turning point, not for India and China, but also for the small town of Tawang, which found itself at the heart of geopolitical tensions.

In March 1959, a large-scale rebellion erupted in Lhasa as Tibetans rose against the repressive measures imposed by Communist China. The uprising, although fervent, was brutally suppressed by the Chinese military, forcing the Dalai Lama to flee for his safety. His journey led him to the welcoming arms of the Monpas in the Tawang Valley, who were shaking off the chill of winter and the festivities of the Losar celebrations of the Earth Boar Year.

Unbeknownst to the Monpas, their region was about to become the backdrop for a significant chapter in Tibetan, Indian, and Chinese histories. On March 31, 1959, then 23 years old, His Holiness the 14th Dalai Lama crossed into India and was received by the Assam Rifles at Khin-Dza-Mane (Khenzamane), near Tawang. A few days later, on April 3rd, India officially granted him political asylum, a decision that deeply irritated Communist China and added fuel to the already smouldering diplomatic tensions[160].

The 20th April 1959 edition of 'The Time' featured this event as a cover story, depicting the young Dalai Lama in its cover page aptly titled *'The Escape that rocked the Red'*.

The people of Tawang, holding deep reverence for the Dalai Lama as their spiritual leader, were overjoyed at his arrival. The town and its inhabitants turned out en masse to receive their Dharma Guru, showing their deference and support in a tumultuous time. This event not only exhibited the strong cultural and religious ties between Tawang and Tibet but also underscored the strategic importance of Tawang in the broader geopolitical conflicts between India and China. The granting of asylum to the Dalai Lama by India was not a humanitarian gesture alone; it was also a clear stance on the side of what India perceived as the moral high ground.

The book, *Crossing of the Frontier, the exile route of His Holiness, the 14th Dalai Lama-1959* published by an NGO-Losel Nyingje Charitable Society of Tawang, details day wise account of the journey and interview of Harmandar Singh, the then Political Officer at Bomdila. On the D-day, T S Murti, APO, Tawang along with Babu Dawa Tsering and troops of the 5 Assam Rifles received His Holiness along with a small party of eight. A total of 80 Tibetans entered India during the period. Enroute His Holiness consecrated the Gor–sam Chorten, built by Lama Prathar in the 13th Century[161].

Meanwhile, in Delhi, on 3rd April 1959, Prime Minister Nehru made the arrival announcement in the Lok Sabha. It was a hectic day at the Foreign Office; S Dutt, Foreign Secretary handed over a copy of Nehru's speech to the Chinese Ambassador and informed him about the arrival of His Holiness. PN Menon, former Consul General in Lhasa accompanied by Kazi Sonam Tobgyal (Interpreter) and Babu Atruk Tsering (Bodyguard) were dispatched to Bomdila, while Nehru sent a telegram through KL Mehta, Governor of Assam to His Holiness welcoming him to India and reassuring support.

When the news broke, all the media houses rushed to send their correspondents to Tezpur-'*the last outpost of civilisation*' before heading North. The quiet town of Tezpur was suddenly abuzz with hordes of more than two hundred news hunters from about 12 countries and was to break the '*Story of the Century*'[162]. Rene Cutforth, a BBC correspondent, recounts his arrival at Tezpur and the wait for the big news. Received by S Sen, Joint Secretary of External Affairs at Tezpur, His Holiness did not give any interview on reaching Tezpur, but a press statement was issued, which read, *"The Dalai Lama is extremely grateful to the people and Government of India for their spontaneous and generous welcome as well as the asylum granted to him and his followers. India and Tibet have religious, cultural and trade links extending over a thousand of years and for Tibetans it has always been the land of enlightenment, having given birth to Buddha"*[163].

China took total control of Tibet while accusing India of breaking the Panchsheel Agreement, further complicating the intricate dance of diplomacy and power politics in Asia, making the event a turning point in Sino-Indian Relations. Dispassionately assessing the situation, foreign affairs strategists could also argue that in His Holiness, India gained a precious diplomatic tool.

In hindsight, as the Tibetan struggle for '*genuine autonomy*' continues, it can be safely concluded that while the Tibetans lost their country, albeit for now, the exile of His Holiness could save the most precious Indian wisdom, the Buddhism of the Nalanda Tradition (India lost it long back), of which, His Holiness has said, *"Tibetans have been custodians of this tradition for more than 1,000 years. We can say that historically Indians were our teachers, but since then, we the disciples have kept the tradition alive. So, it stirs special feelings in me today to be able to discuss with my Indian brothers and sisters what the Buddha taught."* [164]

It is heartening to learn that in 2023, the foundation stone for the *Dalai Lama Centre for Tibetan and Indian Ancient Wisdom* was laid in Bodhgaya, Bihar. This Centre, when fully functional, will become the epicentre for learning, the almost lost, ancient Indian wisdom of Nalanda University, which was safely preserved by the Tibetan Masters, learnt from Gurus such as Nagarjuna, Aryadeva and Chandrakirti, in the Roof of the world.

———◆———

'The lessons of history teach us the grave potential dangers of an ill-defined and undemarcated frontier'
*– **Henry McMahon**[165]*

"The time may soon come when the North-East Frontier of India will become no less, if it is not more, important for the defence of India than the North-West Frontier of India"
*– **Assam Government to the Simon Commission in 1928**[166]*

"So far as we are concerned, the McMahon Line is the firm frontier by treaty, firm by usage, firm by geography".
*– **Jawaharlal Nehru in the Lok Sabha 13 August, 1959***

8

An Unprovoked War-The Wound that Won't Heal

Five months after India granted asylum to the Dalai Lama, tensions along the Sino-Indian border escalated into a confrontation. On August 7, 1959, an incident occurred at Khinzamane, the same route through which the Dalai Lama had entered India from Tibet. Another encounter between the People's Liberation Army (PLA) and the Indian Army took place in Longju, a small village in the Upper Subansiri District of Arunachal Pradesh, immediate South of Migyitun-the last Tibetan village North of the McMahon Line[167]. This incident marked the first border skirmish in the Sino-Indian conflict.

Following this confrontation, an exchange of heated letters ensued between Premier Zhou Enlai and Prime Minister Nehru, each countering the other's claims about the incident and debating the exact location of Longju (present day Upper Subansiri District) in relation to the McMahon Line. During these exchanges, PLA forces took control of Longju, marking a significant escalation in hostilities which would eventually culminate in full-scale war three years later.[168]

Interestingly, the Panchsheel Agreement, which was supposed to last for eight years, was being tested. The Chinese appeared (or pretended) to be adhering to the agreement while strategically biding their time for an opportune moment. Events during this period only served to further aggravate and sour the relationship between the two nations, seemingly beyond repair.

At a meeting of the Communist Party of China in Shanghai on March 25, Mao Zedong highlighted what he perceived as India's role in the ongoing Tibetan rebellion. From Beijing's perspective, India's actions were seen as a violation of the 1954 Panchsheel Agreement on peaceful coexistence, which included principles such as mutual respect for each other's territorial integrity and sovereignty, mutual non-aggression, mutual non-interference, equality and mutual benefit, and peaceful coexistence. India, in particular, was accused of violating the principle of mutual non-interference.[169]

Indian authorities counted 105 Chinese violations in NEFA and Ladakh's airspace between December 1959 and December 1960[170]. Amid growing domestic pressure, and with the geopolitical stakes rising, Nehru announced *The Forward Policy* in November 1961. This strategy involved the advance of Indian troops and the establishment of posts to exert control over the Indian territories, intensifying the strategic standoff along the border[171].

As it stood then, NEFA had only 300 miles of roads. In May 1960, the central government established a Border Roads Organisation (BRO), to build defensive roads to India's northern borders.[172] A good move but a little late in the day, with the enemies reaching too close to the border, the new organisation could have done only so much. Was it Delhi's late wake up from the slumber or the alleged Elwinian romanticism of letting the frontier communities grow by following their own genius which created this '*void screaming to be filled*'[173].

The Frontier Administration were doing their best but felt the pinch of limited resources to match the Chinese efforts across the borders and were screaming for more resources *so that the border tribals may not look towards the Chinese for their salvation*[174]. The need for more funds for development was, of course, realistic but we will see, later in the chapter, that fears about tribals looking towards Chinese for salvation were absolutely misplaced.

As tensions escalated between India and China over unresolved border disputes, the diplomatic exchanges of early October 1962 set the stage for a significant conflict. When China received India's rejection of Beijing's proposal for border talks on October 3, the path to war became increasingly clear[175]. This decision wasn't made in isolation but was influenced by broader geopolitical dynamics involving the United States and the Soviet Union.

Meanwhile, the Cuban Missile Crisis in October 1962 saw the Soviet Union seeking to consolidate its influence within the socialist world. Despite ideological and strategic rifts that had developed between Moscow and Beijing, the Soviets reached out to support China. On October 14, few days before the conflict erupted, Moscow assured Beijing of its support should a war between India and China occur[176].

Amidst these international manoeuvres, Mao Zedong faced internal pressures. Politically, he needed a clear victory to reaffirm his leadership after recent domestic policy challenges. The perceived slights from India, including the asylum granted to the Dalai Lama, compounded his resolve. The Central Military Commission of China met and, framing their actions as a response to Indian aggression (a clear misrepresentation), formally ordered a 'self-defensive counter-attack.' This directive set the stage for what would transpire on October 20, 1962, at Thagla Ridge-a significant military engagement that marked the beginning of the war[177].

This conflict, just months after the eight-year Panchsheel Agreement lapsed, saw the Chinese People's Liberation Army launch a comprehensive assault against India on October 20, 1962. The war, lasting about a month, resulted in substantial casualties on both sides, with severe losses particularly among Indian forces. This period of conflict deeply scarred the bilateral relations between India and China, leaving a legacy of mistrust and unresolved territorial disputes that continue to affect their interactions to this day.

Unexpected Conflict: A War Without Strategy

As the buildup to the war reached its peak, the war began with the Battle of Namka Chu, at Tawang, on October 20, 1962 in the Kameng Sector. It stands out as a grim testament to the challenges faced by the Indian Army. On that cold winter morning, a significant mismatch in troop numbers set the stage for a daunting conflict: approximately 4,000 Indian soldiers from four battalions faced off against a formidable force of soldiers from two divisions of the People's Liberation Army (PLA).

Barely two weeks before the Chinese assault, the Indian command structure was in total disarray. On October 5, General B.M. Kaul had taken over command from General Umrao Singh[178]. Within a week, his tenure was abruptly cut short due to altitude sickness, and he was replaced by General Gurbaksh Singh on October 17. With so little time and under such challenging conditions, the new command could hardly implement any substantial changes on the ground. The course of the war seemed predetermined from the outset.

The assault commenced with the PLA infantry launching a surprise attack from the southern bank of the Namka Chu River, effectively outflanking the Indian defensive positions. The Indian troops, despite their bravery and determination, were quickly overwhelmed. The battalions of 2 Rajput and 1/9 Gurkhas bore the brunt of the initial onslaught[179]. The Rajputs suffered heavy losses: out of 513 troops, 282 were lost in action, and 171 captured, leaving only 60 survivors. Similarly, 493 Gurkhas were taken as prisoners of war, including their Commanding Officer.

The other two battalions, 4 Grenadiers and 9 Punjab, also faced severe (heavy) casualties but managed to retreat towards Tawang to regroup[180]. However, their movement was disrupted as the PLA pushed them towards Bhutan, effectively neutralising their participation in the conflict.

One of the few highlights for Indian forces was at Bumla Pass, where a platoon of 1 Sikh under Subedar Joginder Singh displayed extraordinary resilience. Despite being heavily outnumbered, they held back a PLA brigade for eight hours, inflicting significant casualties. For his leadership and valour, Subedar Joginder Singh was posthumously awarded the Param Vir Chakra, India's highest military honour[181]. Joginder Singh died in captivity. His ashes were brought back.

Within 12 hours of the battle commencing, the PLA had overrun forward Indian defenses and set their sights on capturing Tawang. By October 23, Indian forces had to vacate Tawang to reinforce and hold positions at the Se La Pass, marking a critical phase in the conflict. This battle not only underscored the strategic missteps but also highlighted the valour of the troops under extreme adversity.

As the Indian troops struggled with the fallout from the Battle of Namka Chu, another critical confrontation unfolded in the Walong sector of Eastern Arunachal Pradesh. On October 22, two days after the devastating events at Namka Chu, the People's Liberation Army initiated an attack in Walong. This area, known for its rugged terrain, saw a fierce response from the Indian forces.

The initial Indian defense in Walong included a platoon of Assam Rifles and battalions from 6 Kumaon and 4 Sikh[182]. This grouping managed to push back the initial Chinese assault, inflicting heavy casualties on the PLA. However, the Chinese were not deterred. They soon brought in reinforcements, intensifying their offensive. Despite the arrival of additional Indian forces, including 4 Dogra and 2/8 Gurkhas, the PLA's enhanced numbers and sustained pressure eventually overcame the stiff resistance they faced.

The battle at Walong was part of a broader series of conflicts that saw all forward defenses in Eastern Arunachal Pradesh collapse under the relentless advance of the PLA. Similarly, in the Western sector of Ladakh, Indian defenses were put to the test until October 27. The PLA's aggressive push through these regions not only overwhelmed Indian positions but also sent shockwaves through India's political leadership, resulting in significant military and political repercussions.

The shock of these defeats had a profound impact back in New Delhi, leading to the dismissal of the then Defence Minister, Krishna Menon. The rapid advance of Chinese forces, culminating in the capture of strategically vital locations like Tawang by October 23, forced a re-evaluation of India's military strategies and defensive postures.

After their initial successes, Chinese forces halted their advance, leading to a three-week period of relative calm. This lull provided a crucial respite, allowing Indian forces and leadership to reassess and plan their next steps in what had rapidly escalated into a full-blown conflict between the two nations. This tactical pause was a pivotal moment, giving both sides a chance to reflect on the initial outcomes of the war and consider their future military and diplomatic strategies.

As the first phase of the conflict wound down, both sides prepared for what seemed an inevitable continuation of hostilities. India moved to bolster its defences, sending reinforcements to strategic locations like Sela and Bomdila, with the command Headquarters stationed back in Tezpur. Meanwhile, China too was not idle; they brought in three divisions, planning a two-pronged assault that aimed to engage Indian forces at Sela and bypass them to strike at Bomdila, thereby positioning themselves within striking distance of Tezpur.

The November Battle of Lagyala remains a solemn chapter marked by both bravery and loss. Led by Colonel Avasthy, the 4th Rajput regiment faced a formidable Chinese force of 500 near the Lagyala Gompa, Kalaktang area of present day West Kameng District. The intense conflict ultimately descended into hand-to-hand combat, resulting in a tragic outcome. The battlefield was strewn with the fallen, with over 200 Chinese soldiers and more than 120 Indian soldiers losing their lives. None of the Indian soldiers survived. The sole witness to this heart breaking event was a young shepherd boy, who later grew up to become the head monk of the Lagyala Monastery, carrying the memories of that fateful day with him for life.

On November 17, the Chinese resumed their offensive, and the Indian defences at Sela were subjected to multiple assaults. The situation grew dire when Indian commanders realised the possibility of being outflanked by the third division at Se La, which led to a decision to retreat to Bomdila. This move, however, resulted in significant casualties, including the loss of their Commander, Brigadier Hoshiyar Singh. By November 19, the PLA had captured Bomdila and was alarmingly close-120 kilometres-from Tezpur.

Historian Roderick MacFarquhar later critiqued the Indian response, suggesting that the early November lull was a missed opportunity to reorient Indian policy. The assumption underlying India's Forward Policy-that China would not escalate the border dispute to full-scale war-had proven disastrously incorrect. The military reality was stark, with PLA forces significantly overpowering Indian troops at the frontier. MacFarquhar argued that Nehru should have suspended offensive operations and sought negotiations, as proposed by Zhou Enlai on October 24, right after the first phase of the Chinese offensive ended. Instead, Indian offensives resumed on November 14, prompting a massive counter-offensive by the Chinese on November 18, which led to a rapid collapse of Indian defences in the East.

The PLA made their assault in Central NEFA in the second phase. The main attacking force was a battalion (approximately 650 men) of the 1st Infantry Regiment ex-Shannan Sub Area under the Regimental Commander, Baiquan and its objective being Limeking in present day Upper Subansiri District. The Chinese commenced their advance on 18 November, which was slowed owing to Indian resistance and difficult terrain. The Chinese managed to outflank Limeking and made contact with the main defences on the morning of 21 November. The Indian troops had already been ordered to withdraw from Limeking during the night of 20/ 21 November to Daporijo. The Chinese were able to secure Limeking early morning on 21 November. The Chinese then advanced towards Daporijo till the last light of 21 November, at which time they received orders to stop and return to Limeking. By then the unilateral ceasefire was announced by the PLA.

When the Army HQ learnt of the withdrawal orders issued by the Brigade, they countermanded the orders and issued instructions for the Brigade to occupy defensive positions in Area Taliha-Daporijo-Ziro. However, it was too late and Limeking had already been lost.[183]

On 16 November in the Siang Sector, the Chinese started their advance from Manigong with the Milin Battalion heading for Tuting and the Independent Battalion going for Menchuka. On 17 November, the troops of Independent Battalion had contact with the Indian defences at Nisangong and a brief firefight ensued. Menchuka was vacated on the night of 18/19 November and the Chinese occupied it by the morning of 19 November. The withdrawal from Menchuka proved disastrous. A small party of 35 led by the Commanding Officer Lieutenant Colonel DA Taylor who ventured out on a 'hunters track' to Tato, got lost. Many, including the Commanding Officer, died of exhaustion. The process of withdrawal proved disastrous with many casualties and several taken as POW. The GOC 2 Infantry Division and the staff were not consulted on withdrawal from Menchuka, indicating chaos written all over the place. On 21 November, the Chinese occupied Gelling. On 22 Nov, when closing up with Tuting, they learnt that the position had already been vacated. As per the higher directions, the troops of Independent Battalion stopped their pursuit in the wake of orders for ceasefire.[184]

This series of events culminated on November 20, when China declared a unilateral ceasefire and announced its troops would withdraw to the Line of Actual Control. This sudden cessation of hostilities left India to reflect on the strategic missteps that led to such dire consequences and the lessons to be learned from the conflict.

Post the ceasefire in November 1962, the aftermath of the war left a significant impact on India's frontier administration and the communities in the affected regions. The return to peacetime was not only about withdrawing Chinese troops but also involved grappling with the deeper consequences of the conflict, especially for the people living in the Frontier.

During the Sino-Indian border war, the People's Liberation Army (PLA) captured over 3,900 Indian military personnel, including a brigadier general and 26 officers[185]. The Indian Red Cross played a vital humanitarian role throughout the conflict. By December 1962, it had successfully facilitated the repatriation of around 600 injured and ill Indian soldiers. In early January 1963, the Red Cross received confirmation of 1,132 prisoners of war (POWs), with 715 wounded soldiers released and 13 bodies returned. However, the status of many POWs remained unaccounted for, and inconsistencies persisted in the repatriation records.

On February 24, 1964, the Permanent Indian Mission in Geneva issued a memorandum highlighting alleged Chinese violations of the Geneva Conventions regarding the treatment of Indian military personnel. The affidavits from repatriated soldiers, detailing the conditions and treatment they endured during captivity, evidenced these findings.

Psychology of the War

The authoritative paper by John Garver, 'China's decision for war with India in 1962', analysing the war through the prism of tools used in psychology summed up that the decision to go for war was a case of *'Fundamental attribution error and projection'*, a very common malady studied by Social Psychologists[186]. He describes two factors in particular:

1. A perceived need to punish and end perceived Indian efforts to undermine Chinese Control of Tibet, Indian efforts which were perceived as having the objective of restoring the pre 1949 *status quo ante of Tibet*,

2. A perceived need to punish and end perceived Indian Aggression against Chinese territory along the border.

The Chinese perception of India's motives were

1. That India was taking forward the British imperial strategy of Tibet as Buffer Zone (*huanzhongguo*). The Chinese attributed this motive to India's Forward Policy,

2. That India felt that control over Tibet would ensure *'Mastery over South Asia'* by Nehru and was *'the most economical method for guaranteeing India's Security'*,

The *'decisive factor'* for the deteriorating Sino-Indian relations, according to Xu Yan was (perceived) Nehru's policy of protecting *'splittist Tibetans'* post March 1959. The subsequent events which reinforced these Chinese mis-perceptions were:

1. That the Dalai Lama was allowed to enter India and the granting of asylum to Tibetan Refugees in India;

2. That the anti-China activities in Kalimpong and Darjeeling continued unabated;

3. The CIA operations with Tibetan resistance groups for Tibet through India during middle of 1957;

4. Nehru's Middle path to Chinese requests to expel the Tibetan Resistance groups from India and finally

5. Nehru's Speeches in the Indian Parliament.

And yet, ironically, India was the first nation to recognise the People's Republic of China and gave up her critical hold in Tibet, inherited from the British, for nothing in return. India was of the view that granting asylum to the Dalai Lama and Tibetans would not be seen as an *unfriendly act*, rather India hoped to facilitate negotiations, and that the Dalai Lama would return to Lhasa, as happened in 1951. India championed the Chinese cause in the United Nations, in the hope that the two leading Asian powers would then create a new axis in world politics, while actively obstructing the Tibetan freedom cause and refused US and UK offers to take up the Tibetan Cause in the United Nations. Nehru believed that India had certain "*cultural*" and "*sentimental*" interests in Tibet by virtue of several thousand years of intimate interaction between Tibet and India and ***that was it.***

The end of hostilities allowed for a period of reflection and mourning for the losses sustained during the war. For the Indian military and civilian populations in the border areas, the return to a peacetime footing involved not only physical rebuilding but also psychological healing. The Government launched efforts to redeem the morale of the troops and the trust of the border population, which included improving logistical support, infrastructure, providing better facilities and reinforcements to the troops stationed at the borders. The seriousness of these efforts remains to be seen and will unfold later in the book.

Tribal Loyalties Unmoved-Chinese Miscalculation

This post-war period was crucial in defining the future course of the region, cementing the national boundaries and the allegiance of the border population. It highlighted the resilience of the local communities and the importance of a well-thought-out frontier policy that respects and incorporates the needs and aspirations of the local population.

One of the notable aspects of the conflict was the loyalty of the tribal communities in India's North Eastern Frontier. Despite the proximity and cultural ties to Tibet, and the Chinese efforts to sway them, these communities remained totally loyal to India. This fidelity was a significant miscalculation on the part of the Chinese, who had hoped to leverage ethnic and cultural ties to their advantage. The strong sense of community and identity among the tribes, coupled with the benevolent governance of the Indian Government through the Frontier Administrators, ensured that their loyalties remained firm.

In the midst of war, when confusion and chaos prevailed, the border population stood steadfast along with the Indian Army. Many enlisted to serve the nation as porters to carry arms, ammunition and even food supplies. While others acted as guides to escort the Army through the village tracks; some towards the borders to fight and others marching southwards to safety. Many villagers nursed the wounded soldiers while providing them food and shelter. Quite a few locals were also taken as POW, and bore the brunt of Chinese torture, some returned while others remain untraceable. This unsung heroism echoes in the vales and mountains even today, when the frontier population render heart touching patriotic songs.

A rare and poignant account of the Chinese aggression of 1962 from the perspective of Monpa eyewitnesses, was compiled into a book, '1962, When the Mountains Cried'-effort of a father-son duo. The book delves deep into the personal stories of individuals from diverse backgrounds, each profoundly impacted by the war. From wood craftsmen to young novice monks, from mothers to elderly villagers, the book captures their harrowing experiences and unsung heroism[187].

Among these accounts, the story of Tashi Gombu, a Brokpa (Yak herder practicing transhumance) from Mirba Village, stands out vividly. Drafted reluctantly as a guide for the Indian Army alongside Sonam of Khrimu, Gombu found himself thrust into a perilous journey from Dirang to Dzela. Despite warnings of Chinese forces already occupying Dzela (Se La), they pressed on until they encountered PLA soldiers at Bagga-Jang. In a fierce skirmish at Nuranang, Gombu was wounded by a bullet and rendered unconscious. Upon regaining consciousness, he witnessed the brutal aftermath as PLA soldiers bayoneted the fallen to ensure no survivors[188]. He was selected by Rinchin Dondup alias Nyerpa Khaw, Political Interpreter, who was assisting the Indian Army.

Subsequently captured and mistaken for an Indian Army or Intelligence operative, Gombu endured torture and forced consumption of human flesh by his captors, who dubbed him 'Hindustan Badmash'. Despite pleas from his family and village, his release was only secured through the intervention of a compassionate stranger who vouched for his innocence. Recognized later for his bravery, Gombu was awarded a government job and retired as an Intelligence agent.[189]

The humane stories from the 1962 war, where NEFA locals went above and beyond to assist the Indian Army, are a powerful testament to how the frontier people identified more closely with India than with communist China. These acts of bravery and compassion illustrate the deep loyalty and love the local populations felt for the Indian administration.[190]

In the Subansiri sector, Tagins played a crucial role in nursing and saving the lives of wounded and frostbitten Indian soldiers. They provided food, guided the troops, and helped carry arms and ammunition, displaying extraordinary dedication. Similarly, in the Mechukha valley, Tinger Komi saved a stranded Indian soldier by providing food and shelter. Disguising him as a Ramo (a local tribe), Komi ensured his safe passage to Along (Aalo), cleverly allowing him to evade the Chinese forces.[191]

At Palin, Dolong Hamar's coordination with the Base Superintendent was instrumental in comforting frightened villagers and ensuring their safe evacuation to Ziro. His efforts exemplified the strong allegiance of the locals to the Indian adminimstration[192].

These stories are not only accounts of heroism but also vivid demonstrations of the frontier people's unwavering support and identification with India during a time of crisis.

When orders for the complete evacuation of the administration were issued, the villagers of Koloriang-comprising the old, young, and even school children-approached the Base Superintendent with a heartfelt plea to stay. They promised to show jungle paths and hide the officials when the Chinese arrived. Though the orders were ultimately followed, upon the administration's return after the ceasefire, the villagers ran to welcome the Frontier Officials, offering voluntary support in their residences[193].

Bob Khathing, then posted as Development Commissioner in Sikkim, was urgently transferred to Tezpur due to the exigencies of the war. Appointed as the Security Commissioner, NEFA, he also took on the roles of Chief Civil Liaison Officer, with the rank of Brigadier attached to the Indian Army's IV Corps, Tezpur, and Divisional Organizer, SSB, North East (Headquarters, Tezpur). His responsibilities included overseeing war efforts, rescue operations, and relief[194].

One can only imagine the profound emotions Bob Khathing must have experienced. He had been instrumental in taking Indian administration to the strategic town of Tawang through sheer grit and hard work, founded and established the town of Bomdila. Seeing both towns slipping into enemy hands would have been a deeply distressing ordeal.

In Shillong, the Headquarters of NEFA, Advisor to the Governor, Rustomji grew restless, unable to remain in the comforts of his home while conflict brewed. Together with Bob Khathing, he left for the frontier, bidding farewell to his aged mother. Upon reaching Tezpur, they discussed civil-military coordination with General Sen, focusing on how the frontier administration could assist the Army in their war efforts. Meanwhile, concerns arose from Bhutan regarding the safety of the young Shabdrung Rimpoche (a reincarnation of the founder of Bhutan), who was with Gompatse Rimpoche in Tawang, fearing the Chinese might exploit him[195].

Rustomji and Bob then travelled to Along (Aalo), Pasighat, and Tezu, meeting with tribal Chiefs to hear their grievances and expectations. Despite the angst over the retreating army, the atmosphere was one of absolute tribal allegiance towards India. Many Chiefs expressed a desire for arms and training to fight the Chinese, leading to the consideration of creating a V Force, although this idea did not come to fruition.[196]

Nari was unstoppable in his efforts, visiting relief camps in Dibrugarh, Nawgaon, and Silghat to meet evacuees from the frontiers. Mrs. Indira Gandhi also visited these camps. At the Silghat camp, Nari was relieved to find Gompatse Rimpoche and the Shabdrung Rimpoche safe and sound. Rustomji then rushed to Daporijo and Ziro, where he was heartened by the strong display of allegiance towards India and disdain for the Chinese.[197]

The widespread loyalty across the Eastern Frontier during wartime can be attributed to the gentle yet effective governance of the frontier administrators, who had earned the trust of the local tribes.

Post war Frontier Administration

After the unilateral ceasefire, the immediate task staring the Administrators was to bring back normalcy by building confidence and convincing people to return from the camps. Their faith in the Army was something which would need a lot of work upon. Rustomji, leading by example, shifted his base to Along (Aalo) with his aged mother. He noted that the tribes were quick in voicing disenchantment but quicker in reposing confidence in India and the Frontier Administration. While the administrative machinery was slowly limping back; the immediate problem of depleted stocks of essentials-salt, food grains were beginning to haunt them. Immediately air drops were organised to address the shortages.

Meanwhile, the Chinese withdrawal from the Lohit, Siang, and Subansiri areas was nearly complete, but they held onto the prestigious Tawang until as late as January 1963. When Nari landed in Tawang after the war, he was struck by the absence of the usual warm reception from the Monpas, and he could empathise with their sorrow and anguish. Later, he learned that due to a communication gap, the Monpas had been waiting at the wrong helipad to offer their customary welcome. A tearful reception followed soon after, accompanied by the traditional chang (local brew) ceremony. Monpas from distant villages gathered to meet Rustomji in an outpouring of respect and affection.[198]

Nari Rustomji unfurled the National Flag, symbolising the region's return to peace and order. A Monpa boy assisted him in overcoming a glitch with the flag, an act that poignantly symbolised the deep patriotism of the frontier population towards India. Rustomji described the occasion as simple yet solemn, highlighting the profound connection and loyalty of the local people to the nation.[199]

Rustomji in his book, 'Enchanted Frontier' sums up so beautifully a befitting tribute to the frontier people that I must quote in full here,

'Tribal people, village people as a whole, are generally conservative and suspicious of change. How is it, then, that this revolution has of a sudden come about in the minds of the people, that within a space of 15 years, a mere flash in time, they have become so awakened to participate in the greater life of the country, of which they knew so little but a few years ago? The foremost reason is, I believe that, we have not forced our wares, we have not imposed ourselves as superior beings, we have tried to work amongst the people as friends and what is no less important, as equal partners. We have respected their institutions, their values, their feelings for their own language and way of life, we have held their hand during the critical period of their coming into closer contact with the wider and often harsher world without, and we have tried, conscientiously, to help them in their adjustment to new and unfamiliar ideas. That they stood by the country so bravely during the Chinese aggression has been their unspoken acknowledgement of our work amongst them since independence. It is the finest, truest and most heartfelt memorial of our achievement.[200]

Looking back, it's worth considering a counterfactual scenario: What if Delhi had accepted Beijing's unofficial 1960 offer[201] to renounce its claim over NEFA in exchange for India's recognition of the PRC's sovereignty over Aksai Chin? Would the 1962 war have been avoided? Could this agreement have led to normalised relations between India and China, with flourishing trade along their extensive shared borders? It's important to note that, despite the war, India has already lost control of Aksai Chin, and the dispute persists. Could a diplomatic settlement in 1960 changed the course of history?

I. Select Photographs from NEFA Period

(Source: DIPR, Government of Arunachal Pradesh, Imperilled Frontiers
by Nari Rustomji, Claude Arpi)

▲ **Figure 1:** Verrier Elwin and Nari K Rustomji with Mishmis of Arunachal Pradesh, 1954

▲ **Figure 2:** Contingent from NEFT participating in the Republic Day Parade in Delhi, 1956

▲ **Figure 3:** Farewell of Shri Jairamdas Daulatram, Governor of Assam at Shillong, 1956

▲ **Figure 4:** His Holiness the Dalai Lama disguised as a layman during his escape from Tibet, 1959

▲ **Figure 5:** Shri P.N. Luthra, IFAS, Adviser to Governor & Brig. Mami, 1962

▲ **Figure 6:** Mr. Luthra and Mrs. Luthra with Rinchin Dondup, Political Interpreter (PI) of Tawang at Shillong, 1962

▲ **Figure 7:** Rinchin Dondup, Political Interpreter (popularly known as Nyerpa Khau) of Tawang praying to Lord Buddha in Shri Luthra's residence in Shillong, 1962

▲ **Figure 8:** Indian Army in the Frontiers during the 1962 War

▲ **Figure 9:** Anini, Headquarter of Dibang Valley, 4 December 1965

▲ **Figure 10:** Smt. Indira Gandhi, Prime Minister at Naharlagun

▲ **Figure 11:** Giani Zail Singh, Union Home Minister at Raj Niwas

▲ **Figure 12:** Mask dance by the Memba Lama at Tuting

▲ **Figure 13:** Shri Yashwantrao Chavan, Union Home Minister at Along (Aalo), 1969

▲ **Figure 14:** Tawang Monastery, 1969

▲ **Figure 15:** Bhalukpong Petrol Pump

▲ **Figure 16:** Governor Shri BK Nehru at Deomali Plywood Factory

▲ **Figure 17:** Governor Shri BK Nehru at Tawang Monastery, 1 May 1969

▲ **Figure 18:** Handmade Paper (Mon-Shug) making in Mukto village, 1969

▲ **Figure 19:** Shri Vidya Charan Shukla, Minister of Information and Broadcasting interacting with locals at Ziro, 11 Febpruary 1970

▲ **Figure 20:** Union Territory Announcement by Smt. Indira Gandhi, Prime Minister, 1972

▲ **Figure 21:** Opening of Pahung Hydel Project by Shri KAA Raja, Chief Commissioner on 28 August 1972

 In Between The Blurry Lines

▲ **Figure 22:** Shri R N Mirdha, Union Home Minister at Deomali, 24 March 1974

▲ **Figure 23:** Assembly House at Itanagar, 19 August 1975

In Between The Blurry Lines

▲ **Figure 24:** Itanagar Bazar in 1976 - 1st Mall of Itanagar

▲ **Figure 25:** Along (Aalo) Hydel Project, 1976

▲ **Figure 26:** New Hayuliang Cooperative Bus, 14 January 1977

▲ **Figure 27:** Silver Jubilee Seminar at Shillong, 7 September 1977

▲ **Figure 28:** Shri Morarji Desai, Prime Minister at Arunachal Pradesh, 3 November 1978

▲ **Figure 29:** Shri Neelam Sanjiva Reddy, President of India at Along (Aalo), 1979

▲ **Figure 30:** Shri KAA Raja demits charge and leaves Arunachal Pradesh, 16 January 1979

▲ **Figure 31:** VV Giri, President of India at Sarada Mission School

▲ **Figure 32:** Visit of His Holiness the 14th Dalai Lama to Itanagar, 1983

▲ **Figure 33:** Laying foundation stone of Centre for Buddhist Studies by His Holiness the 14th Dalai Lama, 5 May 1983 at Itanagar

PART THREE

LOST DECADES & MAKING OF A STATE

The major blow of the Chinese aggression left the entire nation in shock. The Government had to get their act together and immediately. Did we do enough? That is the question we will try and examine here.

The evolution from its early days as a fledgling NEFA to a Union Territory, named Arunachal Pradesh, to full-fledged Statehood represents a journey of both progress and oversight. Initially, this transition was marked by growing pains and a series of missteps, particularly the failure to heed the harsh lessons of past conflicts. Despite the hard-earned experiences of war, the frontier continued to be governed by flawed policies that exacerbated existing issues rather than resolving them.

The maturation from a Union Territory to a State was not merely a change in status but a complex process involving political, social, and economic transformations. Initially, the newfound autonomy was met with optimism, as local leaders and citizens anticipated a future with greater self-governance and more tailored development. However, the initial policy approaches failed to break from past paradigms, resulting in tepidness with inadequate responses to the region's unique challenges. The persistent reliance on outdated strategies, despite clear evidence of their ineffectiveness, only deepened existing socio-economic divides and stymied meaningful progress.

However, the turning point came with a dramatic shift in policy, driven by pressing security concerns. Recognizing the strategic importance of the region and the need to address its long-standing grievances, the Government implemented a comprehensive development plan backed by substantial funding. This massive allocation of resources aimed to overhaul the region's infrastructure, stimulate economic growth, and improve the quality of life for its residents. The ensuing chapters delve into this pivotal phase, exploring the impact of these changes and the renewed hope for a prosperous and secure future for the once-neglected province. The chapters will also probe deeper into these dual facets of policy change, highlighting success stories and ongoing challenges, ultimately painting a picture of a region in the midst of a promising transformation.

'As progress comes to NEFA its ancient model of village authority will need change and reconstruction but it would be well to remember that the change inevitable as indeed it is, should be built on the sure roots of indigenous system and concept of democracy so that the new and imported patterns of local self-Government may not be out of harmony with its past in respect of basic principles'
— P.N. Luthra in his foreword for Democracy in NEFA

9

From NEFA to Arunachal Pradesh; Acronym adopts an *Indic Identity*

Let's take a closer look at how Arunachal Pradesh evolved from being the North-East Frontier Agency (NEFA) to becoming a Union Territory named Arunachal Pradesh, and its administrative journey from Shillong to Itanagar. This journey recounts a story of the coming of age for the North Eastern Frontier.

We have seen that in the early 20th century, the North-East Frontier Tracts (NEFT) was a remote and sparsely populated region under the administrative oversight of the British colonial Government. This area, with its rugged terrain and diverse tribal communities, was totally isolated from the rest of India. After India's independence in 1947, NEFT continued to be a region shrouded in mystery and intrigue, with limited infrastructural development and negligible political engagement.

New Delhi had remained practically unconcerned and took little interest in the affairs of the Frontier and the administration of the Frontier was left to the Governor of Assam and his Adviser as before. Fortunately, both the new Governor Sri Jairamdas Daulatram and the Adviser Nari Rustomji were very sympathetic to the tribal people and discharged indefatigable energy and tact and understanding of the problems in dealing with the tribal affairs.[202]

Under the Regulation of 1954, the administrative units were reconstituted and renamed with redefined boundaries. The administrative picture thus emerged as follows:

Old title	**New title**
1. Balipara Frontier Tract, bifurcated into:	1] Kameng Frontier Division
	2] Subansiri Frontier Division
2. Tirap Frontier Tract	3] Tirap Frontier Division
3. Abor Hills District	4] Siang Frontier Division
4. Mishmi Hills District	5] Lohit Frontier Division
5. Naga Tribal Area Division	6] Tuensang Frontier Division

In 1957, the Tuensang Frontier Division was excluded from the North-East Frontier Agency and included in the newly-constituted Naga Hills-Tuensang Area which now forms the State of Nagaland'. In 1965, the above-mentioned Frontier Divisions of the North-East Frontier Agency were renamed respectively as the Kameng District, Subansiri District, Siang District, Lohit District and Tirap District[203]. The Divisions were further subdivided into Sub-Divisions. These sub-divisions were further sub-divided into a number of Circles and Checkposts. Altogether there were five Divisions, 28 sub-divisions and 81 Circles or Checkposts.[204]

Initially, NEFT was directly under the Union Government of India, with administrative powers exercised by the Ministry of External Affairs through the Governor of Assam, assisted by an Advisor, a very senior Civil Servant.

The Panchsheel Agreement took all eyes and ears away from the frontier. The tempo of development and administration of the frontiers receded from limelight.[205] It was only when the Chinese came down to the Assam Plains that there was renewed interest in NEFA. The Government of India took no time to rectify the past mistakes and integrate the administrative structure of the NEFA administration with that of the state of Assam.

All the territories south of the McMahon Line apportioned into different administrative units and the officers employed in them were renamed following the administrative practice in Assam. The five administrative divisions were now termed Districts which had been split-up into Sub-divisions and the Sub-divisions split-up into Circles and Check-posts. The nomenclatures of the officers were changed to assimilate them with the administrative officers of the Assam Government. The Political Officers and Base Superintendents were now known as Deputy Commissioners and Circles (Officers).[206]

1st August 1965, a significant administrative shift occurred when the control of NEFA underwent a lateral shift from the South Block to the North Block (From the Ministry of External Affairs to the Ministry of Home Affairs). The administration of NEFA was conducted like a Union Territory as per paragraph 18 of the 6th Schedule of our Constitution. This change aimed to streamline governance and focus more on internal development and integration of the region with the rest of India. Despite these efforts, the region remained administratively dependent on Assam, with its headquarters in Shillong, the capital of the then undivided Assam.

Growth of Bureaucracy in NEFA

Initially, there was no special service for the Administration of NEFA. The Officers in the service on the frontier were drawn from the existing All India Service cadres of *Assam*. In a few cases selected Extra Assistant Commissioners of Assam Civil Service were appointed as Political Officers or Assistant Political Officers in the Frontier Service. Thus, the cadres of administration fell under two heads: Frontier Civil Service consisting of posts of Base Superintendents, Assistant Political Officer and Indian Administrative Service personnel in the post like Political Officer. When the Indian Frontier Service was created in 1953 a new cadre of Frontier Administration emerged for the Frontiers[207]. The IFAS was later (in the mid 60s) merged with the IAS.

The genesis of this special Service (for NEFA, Tibet, Sikkim and Bhutan) lies in the philosophy for NEFA expounded by Elwin and anchored by Nehru. Claude Arpi in an article, *'The Indian Frontier Administrative Service-Romanticism and Hostile Borders'* undertook a detailed study of the Service and also interviewed few of the pioneers, most of whom are no longer alive. He listed a non-exhaustive list of the first IFAS officers: Col. P.N. (Pran) Luthra (Indian Army), K.C. Johorey (Indian Army), P.N. Kaul (Indian Army), Har Mander Singh (Indian Army), Major Bob Khathing (Indian Army), R.K. Bharat Singh (Indian Army), Maj. S.M. Krishnatry (Indian Army), Maj. S.L. Chhiber (Indian Army), Lt. Col. Rashid Yusuf Ali (Indian Army), U. Chakma (Indian Army), L.R. Sailo (Indian Army), A.H. Scott Lyndgoh, Hipshon Roy, K.T. Khuma (Indian Army).[208]

On April 4, 1952, Nehru wrote to Jairamdas Doulatram, the Governor of Assam, mentioning a 'special' cadre for the border areas: "I have indicated previously that officers dealing with the tribal people have to be chosen with extreme care; just as the average Assamese officer might not be suitable, the average ICS officer is usually equally unsuitable. In effect, we have to build up some kind of a special cadre. Apart from general policies involved, the approach has to be most sympathetic and friendly. The test of an officer is, how far he gains popularity among the tribes[209].

Three weeks after having written to the Governor of Assam, Nehru sent a note to Subimal Dutt, the Foreign Secretary. The Prime Minister again mentioned the service which two years later would become the Indian Frontier Administrative Service (IFAS): "The real question is of building up a cadre, specially selected and specially trained. Also of giving some measure of training to the local people locally for subordinate types of work. ...I think that Mr. Verrier Elwin could be of great help to us because of his wide knowledge and experience and his human sympathy for these tribal folk."[210]

The first batch of IFAS officers were tasked to administer the Frontiers with instructions "The staff must go along with the flag and the typewriters can follow later on. That is it, physically and literally," In the interview with Arpi, Johorey reminiscing his days in NEFA narrates how the trio of Yusuf Ali, U Chakma and Johorey reached Along (present day Aalo). They were perhaps given the best facilities for accommodation which were really huts made of bamboos, palm leaves and canes, with no mattresses, furnitures and electricity, while taking solace in the fact that the houses were very clean and airy.

The officers of the IFAS were of extraordinary calibre. Take for example, Yusuf Ali who served as Political Officer for 3 years in Bomdila, studied Latin and Greek in England and was son of Adbullah Yusuf Ali, a famous Indian Islamic scholar, known for his translation of Quran into English. He explains to Arpi that though created in 1954, the new cadre was only officialised in 1956, while recollecting the long tours to Daporijo, Along, Seppa; entailing days and weeks of walks.

Most interesting is the story of Maj SM Krishnatry, who along with his wife Geeta undertook an expedition to the Marabai-Tsari area of Tagin land in the present day Upper Subansiri area. They went unarmed and unescorted, which was unique in many ways. Still today, Krishnatry believes that, "this unarmed and unescorted expedition has served to be a watershed in the administrative history of Arunachal Pradesh and has, if it is to be believed by the cynic, set the pace for lasting peace between the tribals and the administration unlike the other tribal communities of the north-east region of India."[211]

Another officer who stood out was Ishwari Prasad Gupta. In his memoir, he recalls, 'I was selected for Indian Frontier Administrative Service in 1961.'[212] In 1966, I was posted as Dy. Commissioner, Dibang Valley whose Headquarter Anini could be reached after 16 days long marches on foot in the difficult terrain.[213] He completed his 3 years tenure working closely for and with the Mishmis and joined headquarters in Shillong. Such was the dedication! Thereafter, he worked as the Chief Secretary of Arunachal Pradesh from 1976 to 1981 and made monumental contributions.

He fondly remembers many officers in his memoirs. There were stalwarts like PN Luthra, KAA Raja, R Khathing, RN Haldipur, HS Dubey, HM Singh, ML Kampani, K Banerjee, SD Lahkar, PP Srivastava, R Yusuf Ali, BS Duggal, S Loveraj, KC Johorey, KB Gurang, SM Krishnatry, LB Thanga, KS Puri, Takap Ringu, Matin Dai, Matin Tangu, Toyi Dai, TS Deori etc to name a few. They all established excellent rapport with the local people. They all made the then NEFA as their home. They lived with families. They thought that their entire career was in NEFA and they never looked towards Delhi like some later officers who left their families back and where to they rushed at the slightest pretext.[214]

Similarly, Ms. Neeru Nanda, an IAS officer from the 1971 batch, is fondly remembered in Tawang for her selfless service. In the early 1970s, she inspired local villagers to help construct a road from Tawang to Lumla, opening up vital connections for the area. She also introduced Himachal Pradesh potatoes, enriching local agriculture. Her dedication to the well-being of the tribal communities was remarkable-a quality that feels rare today.

From Shillong to Itanagar

Shillong, known for its picturesque landscapes and colonial-era charm, served as the administrative Headquarters for NEFA. This choice of administrative centre was driven by historical precedents and logistical considerations. Shillong had been a hub for British administrators, who found its cool climate and strategic location ideal for governing the Northeastern territories.

During the NEFA period, Shillong was more than a picturesque hill station; it was the nerve centre for the region's administrative activities. The *long-distance governance* of NEFA from Shillong involved a complex web of bureaucratic processes and coordination between the central Government and tribal leaders. Shillong housed the offices of various officials who oversaw the implementation of development schemes, maintenance of law and order, and diplomatic engagements with tribal communities.

The officials in Shillong had to navigate the complex social structure of NEFA, marked by multiple tribes, each with its unique culture and traditional governance systems. This required a delicate balance between modern administrative practices and respect for indigenous customs. The interactions between the bureaucrats in Shillong and the tribal leaders often shaped the developmental policies and political landscape of NEFA. Visit of the Parliamentary delegation to NEFA led by the Deputy Speaker in 1966 recommended shifting of headquarters from Shillong to NEFA,[215] distance may have been the determining factor.

In 1972, a transformative milestone was reached when NEFA was granted Union Territory status and renamed '*Arunachal Pradesh*', the acronym, thereby, adopted an Indic Identity, meaning '*The Land of the Rising*

Sun'. The North-East Frontier Agency was renamed Arunachal Pradesh by Bibhabasu Das Shastri, Daya Krishna Goswami and O. P. Upadhya on 20 January 1972.[216] This political-administrative development marked the beginning of a new chapter, aimed at giving the region a distinct political identity and paving the way for greater self-governance. With this new status, the need for a centrally located capital became more evident to better serve the region's administrative needs and people's aspirations.

Efforts to establish a new capital for Arunachal Pradesh began with several possible sites being considered, including Pasighat, Basar, and Yachuli. Not much literature was found on the process of shifting of capital. In an article for a Souvenir[217], J.M. Tangu, IAS (Retd), recounts the pivotal events that led to the selection of Itanagar as the capital. While serving as the Extra Assistant Commissioner (EAC) in Ziro (1970-73) and acting as President of the Anchal Samiti in the region, Tangu visited Doimukh. During one visit, a local gentleman informed him of a potential site west of Doimukh, featuring ruins of forts and no nearby villages except for Gamga/Gangga. After studying the proposed area, Tangu informed his Deputy Commissioner (DC), Shri T.C. Hazarika, about the promising location.

On January 28, 1973, DC Hazarika presented this potential site to the Chief Commissioner, K.A.A. Raja, during his stop at Banderdewa. That same evening, Tangu was summoned to the DC's residence and was instructed to survey the site and build a jeepable road to the location by February 28, 1973-a daunting task given the tight deadline. Unable to sleep that night, Tangu planned the logistics, which involved mobilising manpower, arranging transportation from Ziro to Doimukh, organising food and medical support, and overseeing construction. He enlisted the help of two educated youths, Gyati Taka and Hage Halley, who promised manpower from the Apatani community. A general meeting with the Gaon Burahs resulted in a unanimous agreement to assist, and 5,000 villagers were pledged to help build the road.

The Ziro team was soon joined by people from Raga and Palin, led by Circle Officers Sater Yomdo and Thakjung Shiba, respectively. In a spirit of festivity, the Raga team even brought along a Ponung cultural group. The road construction took on a celebratory atmosphere, with villagers working enthusiastically day and night, using fire for light. While men laboured, women sang and danced, keeping morale high.

Despite the challenges, particularly crossing the Dikrong River, the work was completed on time. On February 28, 1973, K.A.A. Raja inspected the site and expressed his satisfaction, stating, "I am very happy. If it is planned properly and roads and buildings are constructed, it will be one of the most beautiful hill stations in India."

Finally, on March 1, 1973, the Chief Commissioner officially declared Itanagar/Naharlagun as the capital of Arunachal Pradesh at a ceremony in the Doimukh Inspection Bungalow.

After much scouting, Itanagar, centrally located in the then Lower Subansiri district, was chosen for its strategic position and potential for future growth. Many more people have been instrumental in this monumental decision. Nabam Runghi was one such significant contributor to this monumental effort.

The transition from Shillong to Itanagar symbolised a significant step towards local empowerment, with the seat of governance within its own territory. Itanagar's development involved constructing essential infrastructure, including Government buildings, residential quarters for officials, and basic amenities for the populace. Mr. S.D Lahkar and Mr. Tangu were appointed Chief Project Officer (CPO) and Deputy Chief Project Officer (DCPO) respectively for the Capital Project, tasked to make Itanagar ready to function as the capital of Arunachal Pradesh. Meanwhile, the Administration was run from Naharlagun, a small town a few miles east of Itanagar.

The Political Transition

There was almost in every locality or village a local headman either elected by the people themselves or hereditary who performed much useful work, but the people did not enjoy any right of participation in the working of this local self-Government through statutory provisions. Moreover, there was no liaison between the Administration and the people. To remove these Sangs (sic) [pangs] Government of India set-up a committee for Administrative Reforms in NEFA under the Chairmanship of Daying Ering, the nominated member of Parliament from NEFA. The Committee recommended a three-tier system of local self-Government. The Panchayat Raj Regulation of 1967 was drawn up accordingly and promulgated on 2nd October 1969, [218] was the beginning of Local Self Government in NEFA.

This was, sort of, training for the tribals to gradually run their own affairs under statutory provisions within the Constitutional framework. This was to give way to the modern administrative and judicial tenets, sooner than later.

The North-East Frontier did not elect their representative to the Parliament, the representative from the Agency was nominated by the President of India. The Pioneer to walk in the halls of our Parliament was Chow Khamoon Gohain Namshum. In April 1952, Chow Khamoon was nominated as the first Member of Parliament, representing the whole of then NEFA, by the President of India. He was renominated in 1957 for the second term[219]. He resigned in 1960 before completing his second tenure paving way for Daying Ering to be his worthy successor. On demise of Daying Ering, the sitting Member of Parliament, Chow Chandret Gohain Namshum was nominated from NEFA for the 4th Lok Sabha in 1970 and renominated to 5th Lok Sabha in 1971.

On being granted the Union Territory status, Arunachal Pradesh's governance structure underwent change with 30 members in the Legislative Assembly. The Agency Council transitioned from Pradesh Council to Provisional Legislature and the five Councillors to the Chief Commissioner (later designated as Lt. Governor) became Provisional Ministers in 1975 with two seats in Parliament. The first elections to the Parliament and Assembly were held in 1977[220].

The pioneers who wore the political hat for the Frontier included Daying Ering, Wangmai Rajkumar, Khengman Longsam, Mowang Wangham, Hengwang Lowang, Ita Pulu, Chewpak Gohain, Senge Kri,

Gora Pertin, Todak Basar, Kabang Borang, Sutem Tasung, Tamar Karlo, Tapang Gyama, Doni Kunya, Nabam Rungkhi, Gangte Taki, Rinchin Namze, Tsewang Norbu, Prem Dorjee and Naibili Dusisu.[221] They were instrumental in sowing the seeds and nurturing modern democracy in Arunachal Pradesh.

PK Thungon donned the role of the pioneer tribal leader at the helm from 1975-79 as the first Chief Minister of Arunachal Pradesh. Thungon had the onerous task of steering tribal aspirations, building institutions and governance mechanisms. His most difficult task would have been building consensus amongst the various tribes to the myriad demands, each with competitive aspirations. In his interview with the author, he cited lack of precedence as his biggest predicament.

By 1981, the administrative structure of Arunachal Pradesh had expanded significantly. It was managed by a Lt. Governor, a Chief Secretary, a Commissioner, and a Development Commissioner, supported by various secretaries and heads of administrative departments. The territory was divided into districts, sub-divisions, and circles to ensure efficient governance.

As the administrative machinery gradually shifted from Shillong to Itanagar, the new capital began to take shape as the epicentre of governance and development for Arunachal Pradesh. This transition marked a crucial phase in the region's journey from an appendage of Assam towards governance from her own soil, fostering a sense of identity and autonomy among its people.

The formative years from 1972 to 1987 were a period of transformation for Arunachal Pradesh, witnessing the evolution from a territory, remotely administered through the Governor of Assam to a Union Territory with its own administrative capital. The legacy of governance from Shillong laid the groundwork for this transition, highlighting the region's unique challenges and the resilience of its people. This chapter in the history of Arunachal Pradesh encapsulates the spirit of a region striving for democratic governance and integration into the Indian Union, while preserving its rich cultural heritage with an unflinching desire to catch up with the rest of her fellow citizens, eager to make up for the lost opportunities.

A Youthful State is Born, Albeit Prematurely?

A young stenographer was rhythmically tapping away at the old Remington typewriter in Raj Niwas, his fingers dancing over the keys with quiet urgency. It was a cold December evening in 1986, the office was still open. He might miss the evening tea routine with his family. But tonight, an important message needed to be typed and immediately dispatched to Delhi. Something was brewing, definitely a defining moment for Arunachal Pradesh was in the offing.

The journey of Arunachal Pradesh toward statehood was marked by a mix of political manoeuvring, administrative challenges, and contrasting opinions. At the helm of this transition was Lieutenant Governor Shiva Swaroop, an Indian Police Service Officer who had previously served as the Director General of the Central Reserve Police Force. Swaroop's tenure as the Lieutenant Governor of Arunachal Pradesh, from November 1985 to February 1987[222], was a critical period that witnessed significant debates and decisions regarding the future of Arunachal Pradesh.

Lieutenant Governor Shiva Swaroop expressed strong reservations about the move towards statehood. Raj Niwas was not in favour of this transition, citing concerns that it might not be the right step for the region at that time. His apprehensions were rooted in the belief that the region was not yet administratively or politically ready to handle the complexities of full statehood[223].

Swaroop's opposition culminated in a letter addressed to higher authorities, articulating his stance against granting statehood to Arunachal Pradesh. This letter, which his stenographer typed that cold winter evening, highlighted the potential risks and challenges that could arise from such a significant change. His steadfast opposition ultimately led to his resignation when statehood was granted, marking a dramatic exit from the role as he stood by his convictions.

On the other side of the spectrum, the political leadership in Arunachal Pradesh was elated at the prospect of statehood. Leaders saw this as an opportunity to gain greater autonomy, assert their political identity, and drive development in the region. The enthusiasm among the political class was palpable, as they believed that statehood would bring about a new era of growth and integration with the rest of India. Amidst a split opinion on its readiness, a State was born and thus ensued the onerous task of steering its own destiny.

The aspirations of the frontier population for statehood was not new. The seed for the demand was sowed when the first Government was sworn in with Prem Khandu Thungon as the first Chief Minister in 1975. This new Government had many problems headed in top priority as to integrate with stronger emotional feeling among the members of the different communities of Arunachal Pradesh. To achieve the statehood, to conduct peaceful elections, to increase the number of Member of Legislative Assembly, to bring it close[r] to Arunachal Pradesh instead of taking Arunachal Pradesh to Delhi[224].

On 24th March 1977, the Legislative Assembly unanimously adopted a private member resolution for grant of full statehood for Arunachal Pradesh. The main argument was 'If Nagaland could be given Statehood, there is no justification as to why Arunachal Pradesh cannot get the status of a full statehood for the state.'[225] With the popularly elected Government in 1978, the demand for Statehood gained momentum. The Union Home Minister, Shri Brahma Nanda Reddy in his parliamentary deliberations on the 37th Constitutional Amendment Bill[226] providing for Provisional Legislative Assembly and Council of Ministers stated, 'At present the people of the Union Territory are being progressively associated with art (sic) of Administration. He further added, "The Centre is neither reluctant, nor it has lack of confidence in the people of Union Territory in matter of granting them State"[227] When a delegation led by PK Thungon met Morarji Desai, he conveyed to them that the demand was pre-matured (sic) for Statehood of Arunachal Pradesh but he assured the delegation that it would be accepted if the progress in future would be steady and if the Union Territory becomes economically sound.[228]

Notwithstanding, the precondition of Arunachal Pradesh being economically sound set by Prime Minister Morarji Desai, on 20th February 1987, Arunachal Pradesh became the 24th state of the Indian Union.

The public reaction was notably different and mixed. There was a general sense of indifference among the common people in the hinterland, largely because many did not fully grasp the implications of statehood. For the average citizen, the concept of becoming a full-fledged state within the Indian Union seemed distant and abstract. The disconnect between the political leadership's excitement and the public's indifference arising out of ignorance highlighted a gap in communication and understanding about the benefits and challenges of statehood. Gegong Apang, the man of the moment, held celebrations in all the District Headquarters and also to educate the people on what statehood entails and how the region will see more development.[229]

Following the resignation of Shiv Swaroop, the administrative reins were temporarily taken over by the Governor of Assam. This interim period was crucial as it provided a buffer for the central Government to manage the transition smoothly. Eventually, RD Pradhan, a former Home Secretary of the Union, took over the responsibility, steering Arunachal Pradesh through the final phases of its transition to statehood.

The contrasting views on statehood underscore the complexities involved in such a significant administrative change. While political leaders celebrated the newfound status, the reservations of experienced administrators like Shiv Swaroop remind us of the importance of readiness and preparedness in governance. Their concerns, though overridden, highlight the need for a balanced approach that considers both the aspirations and the ground realities of the region.

With administration yet to take firm roots, limited education levels of the tribes, scarce fund generation within the State, Gegong Apang, Chief Minister since 1980, was up for a herculean task of steering the fate of the multitude of aspirations of the population.

In retrospect, the journey to statehood for Arunachal Pradesh was not only a political milestone but also a testament to the debates and decisions that shape the destiny of a region. It is a story of visionaries who dreamt of a brighter future and cautious administrators who urged for a measured approach, together weaving the complex narrative of Arunachal Pradesh's path to becoming the 24th state of India.

The era from 1987 to 2008 was a pivotal period for Arunachal Pradesh, marked by significant strides in development, institution-building, and profound social change. As Arunachal Pradesh navigated its newly acquired statehood, the need to preserve its indigenous culture against the encroachment of outside influences became paramount. The Donyi Polo movement played a crucial role in this cultural renaissance, reaffirming traditional beliefs and practices amidst the rising tide of alien cultural forces. This movement not only reinforced the spiritual and cultural identity of the Arunachali people but also served as a bulwark against the erosion of indigenous values in a rapidly modernising world.

Simultaneously, the State embarked on the complex task of institution-building. With statehood came the responsibility of creating robust governance structures capable of addressing the unique challenges of the region. During this time, efforts were made to establish institutions that could lay the foundation for long-term development. Schools, healthcare facilities, and administrative frameworks were put in place, setting the stage for a more organised and responsive government. These efforts were crucial in enabling the State to transition from a largely remote and disconnected region to one that was increasingly integrated into the national framework, all while maintaining its distinct identity.

Perhaps one of the most significant achievements of this era was the stitching together of a collective identity among the diverse tribes of Arunachal Pradesh. The idea of "*Arunachal*" as a unified entity took root, fostering a sense of brotherhood and shared purpose among all communities. This period saw the consolidation of a common identity that transcended tribal lines, helping forge a sense of unity and belonging among the people. It was a time of social churning, where the seeds of a cohesive Arunachali identity were sown, laying the groundwork for the State's future as a harmonious and integrated society.

The period was also marked by the establishment of several key institutions aimed at driving economic development and self-sufficiency in

Arunachal Pradesh. Among these were the Arunachal Pradesh Industrial Development and Finance Corporation (APIDFC), Apex Bank, Aruntron (an electronics company known for manufacturing televisions), Tezu Cements, and Nigmoi fruit processing enterprise of *Aap Ase* fame, focusing on pineapples and oranges. These institutions were envisioned as pillars of the State's burgeoning economy, providing essential services, employment opportunities, and a foundation for future industrial growth.

However, over the years, many of these institutions began to falter, moving towards decadence rather than fulfilling their initial promise. Factors such as mismanagement, lack of sustained investment, and the challenges of operating in a remote and difficult terrain contributed to their decline. What started as ambitious ventures aimed at transforming the State's economic landscape eventually struggled to adapt to changing market conditions and the evolving needs of the population.

The decline of these institutions is a poignant reminder of the complexities involved in state-building and economic development in a region as unique as Arunachal Pradesh. While their establishment was a testament to the vision and aspirations of the time, their downfall underscores the need for continuous support, innovation, and adaptation to sustain progress.

As Arunachal Pradesh moved beyond its formative years, the next phase in its journey commenced with achieving statehood in 1987. This new status brought with it the challenge of navigating political and administrative complexities while empowering its citizens with the responsibility of self-governance. Subsequent chapters delve into the post-statehood era, examining key military and diplomatic events, including the Sumdorong Chu Standoff and high-profile visits by Indian leaders. It explores the region's evolving political landscape, significant developmental initiatives, and the dynamic interplay between local aspirations and national policies. Let's explore how Arunachal Pradesh continued to shape its identity and governance in the face of new challenges and opportunities.

Interview with Shri Prem Khandu Thungon Ji, First Chief Minister of Arunachal Pradesh

1. From a Bureaucrat to becoming the First Chief Minister; indeed a long journey of unparalleled success. Can you share your educational journey?

I was first admitted to school in Rupa sometime in 1948-49. Our Sherdukpen people are very proud people. They think themselves to be a superior tribe or superior mankind. They were hesitant to send their children to school because the teacher is not a Sherdukpen. Because they used to say that their children should not get beaten by **Muchhteqpa (Non Local)**.

At that time, my father was a Political Interpreter, well known as PI. So, my father was asked by the administration to bring children to school, otherwise the school teacher (Master Ji) would go back. He was a propagator of modern education and very supportive of the school. He sent me and Tsering Thungon, a cousin several years older than me, to school to show an example to the community that he is sending his own son to school, and they should also send their children. I was hardly of school going age at that time. So, if you see the first school register of Rupa school, you will find, first name Tsering Thungon, and second Prem Khandu Thungon. At that time, we used to hear ABCD *sikhna chahiye.* Then, in the same year or the next year, in my own village, Shergaon, a school was also opened. So, I studied in Shergaon up to class three.

There was only one middle school in the whole Kameng district at that time at Rupa. I went there. After that, it was shifted to Bomdila when it was made district headquarters in 1952. Balipara Frontiers Tract headquarters actually was Charduar earlier. The district headquarters was shifted to Bomdila. The PO, Political Officer at that time, or people used to call Borsheb, used to be at Charduar earlier. From 1952, they shifted the headquarters there. By 1953-54, M.E. school was shifted from Rupa to Bomdila and I did my education up to class 10 from Bomdila School. Class 10 at that time, used to be called matriculation and the exam used to be conducted by Guwahati University. After that, I went to study pre-university science at Shillong under Guwahati University. Then I went to Jorhat Engineering College. After that, I appeared for a competitive examination for selection of Circle Officers in NEFA, I got selected and was posted to Along, now Aalo. That is how my bureaucratic career started.

2.   What was the impact of pioneer Officers like Nari RustomJi, KAA Raja, PN Luthra, Akbar Hydari and others in shaping your career and many other pioneers of our state?

I met Rustom ji personally several times, who was Advisor to the Governor of Assam for administering the then NEFA. Akbar Hydari, I have heard his name, but I have never met him. Mr. P. N. Luthra and Mr. K. A. A. Raja were two of the administrators I worked closely with. I have seen, rather, I drew inspiration from officers like Rustom Ji, who was an old ICS officer. These 2-3 officers were directly in contact with the then NEFA almost every day. They were the real well-wishers of the people of Arunachal Pradesh, particularly the tribals, and committed to do their duty very, very well. They knew very well that tribals are to be brought up to the same level as the rest of the people in the country, in all respects, in administration, economy, communication and socio-political development.

This was the main inspiration I got from them. When I was a college student, I started understanding India and its society. From them, I got the feeling that they are from far-off places but are still working so hard, so sincerely – this means we will have to work more sincerely and more devotedly than them to come at par with the rest of the country. That is how I got inspiration from them through personal contact.

They were old timers who influenced Delhi to adopt the tribal policy enunciated by Dr. Verrier Elwin and they adopted the same policy for NEFA. That is how we started to have facilities to develop ourselves and various tribes.

3.   One important milestone was getting our Union Territory status. How was the Union Territory status for Arunachal Pradesh granted? How was the name Arunachal Pradesh selected? What was our people's reaction to the grant of UT status?

Arunachal Pradesh was known as North East Frontier Agency (NEFA). Even before that NEFA was known by different names for different regions such as Balipara Frontier Tract, Se La Sub Agency, Lakhimpur Frontier Tract, Subansiri Frontier Tract, Sadiya Frontier Tract and Tirap Frontier Tract. We didn't have one name. During Smt. Indira Gandhi's tenure, she said we have to make one unified unit, and a name has to be given. She was the main force behind this.

There were few names floated like Arun Uday, Arunachal Pradesh and a few others. Citizens were asked what name they preferred from the above choices. We chose Arunachal Pradesh. The Agency Council also approved and that is how the name Arunachal Pradesh was unanimously adopted.

Arunachal Pradesh was administered by the Governor of Assam as the direct agent of the President of India. Before that, it was also under Assam administration, but for a short time. The Governor administered on the advice of the Adviser, like Rustom Ji, P N Luthra, KAA Raja etc. Therefore, there was a bureaucratic administration in NEFA.

This was also felt by Daying Ering Ji, our first Minister under Nehru Ji, who felt we should be at par with the rest of the country as far as democracy, administration and governance are concerned. So, the Agency Council was formed to advise the Governor of Assam and the Adviser of NEFA. The Agency Council operated and functioned quite well. Then Indira Gandhi Ji, the Prime Minister of India, thought that democratisation should take place as soon as possible. So, she announced Arunachal Pradesh as a Union Territory in 1972, with a Chief Commissioner. After 1972, the Agency Council was named as Pradesh Council and elections to the Pradesh Council were held in the same year. After the Pradesh Council elections, five councillors were appointed by the Chief Commissioner, and the Council became the first kind of Assembly. Then, on 15th August 1975, the Pradesh Council was converted into a full-fledged Assembly. People of Arunachal Pradesh were very happy as they could participate fully in a democratic government. I am thankful to my colleagues for electing me as the first Chief Minister of the new Government.

4. **Another milestone was a grant of statehood. How did we get our statehood? People's reaction? Some say it was premature. Who was against the grant of statehood? What were your views?**

After grant of UT status, the people of Arunachal Pradesh wanted statehood. A very, very miniscule minority was opposed to it. Naturally, any important decision has certain criticisms or reactions. We found that for speedy development, we should have a little more power, a little freer hand from the Centre, because a UT is directly controlled by the Home Ministry. Even today, you hear a lot of similar *jhagda* going on in Delhi. We also faced that a little bit but solved it amicably. As in the case of a Union Territory with a full-fledged Assembly, I was an active worker for grant of statehood, with the blessings of the people of Arunachal Pradesh. We had to convince the Central Government during Shri Rajiv Gandhi's tenure that we should be given statehood soon.

I decided to go to Delhi as an MP in around December 1979 or early 1980. Shri Gegong Apang, who was the Agriculture and PWD Minister in my Government, became the Chief Minister.

Those days, there were a lot of insurgency activities in Mizoram, under the leadership of Mr. Laldenga. Mr. Laldenga was in a foreign country. Rajiv Ji decided to bring him back, and after long discussions, it was decided that Mizoram will be converted from a Union Territory to a State, and Mr. Laldenga would be made the Chief Minister of Mizoram. I was Rajiv Ji's colleague at that time, colleague as in his MP and Minister for some time. I decided to take a chance and told Rajiv Ji that we were given Union Territory status at the same time. Now if you are going to give statehood to Mizoram and if you don't give us, you will be giving a bonus to insurgency and violence and because we didn't raise arms, the message will go to the people of the country and the whole world that if you don't raise arms, you don't get. This went very well in his mind (laughs) and he immediately decided to agree.

I contacted Shri Gegong Apang and asked him to grab this opportunity and prepare for submitting all papers. We had some meetings in the Prime Minister's residence with the Prime Minister, and our representatives, Chief Minister was there. Omem Moyong Deori was PCC President at that time. Dulom Saab (Tadak Dulom) was Senior Minister. And we had a meeting with Rajiv Gandhi. Very soon, in the same year, at the same time, a Bill was passed in Parliament for grant of statehood to Mizoram and Arunachal Pradesh.

So I can claim I contributed in this way, and this is my humble contribution to the people of Arunachal Pradesh who gave me so much love, affection and respect. Now people may say the Union Territory and statehood was premature; I don't think it was premature, we are running well efficiently.

Who was against the grant of Statehood?

I don't want to name the leaders, many of them were very good leaders of the people of Arunachal Pradesh. These *chutput* statements will always be there in democracy and politics. If you do something, someone will always criticise you or oppose you, that is the beauty of democracy.

5.   How easy or difficult was being the first CM of state?

I must say I enjoyed the journey as the first Chief Minister of the State. As far as the difficult part is concerned, we had no precedence, no predecessors, no guide on whom to rely. We had no Ministers when I became the Chief Minister. Since we had demanded and achieved statehood, we had to handle it. The difficulties we knew and had to overcome. That was the romance in my mind.

We used to have CRPF or central Government police personnel, no State police. So, one of the first things I did was to start the process of creation of Arunachal State Police. There was no PWD, we had to depend on the Central Public Works Department, which is directly controlled by the Central Government. This overdependence on the Central Government was not in consonance with the emotions of the people, it was not congruent with the vision of the elected Government; we had to create new Departments.

So, I created APWD in place of CPWD. Mr. Tenzin Norbu, who retired as Chief Engineer, was earlier in CPWD. He was absorbed as assistant engineer in PWD. I told him that if you join PWD, a new Department, you will get quick promotions, and really, he got promotions quickly. Now, we have several zones and several Chief Engineers. So, the first foundation of PWD was also laid by me. There was no tourism department, that was also opened by me. I don't remember now, but if someone looks through old records, they will find so many Departments I opened at that time as the first Chief Minister. These were the operational and functional difficulties I faced; I enjoyed those difficulties also. I enjoyed every step of the process. I enjoyed it more because I created my own. Now, in Arunachal Pradesh, whoever becomes Chief Minister, the basic road is laid, the track is laid, you can drive on that track.

The people of Arunachal Pradesh were completely aware of our commitment and dedication. They have given me so much love and respect and elected me four times to the Lok Sabha and twice unopposed to the Assembly. In return, I also did not deceive people's desire, will and trust.

6. Your journey to Parliament and how did our state benefit from your presence in Delhi?

We were a Union Territory till we got our statehood in 1987. I was the Chief Minister from 1975 onwards and I had to run to Delhi at least twice a month, sometimes four-five times as well. For every small matter, finance, administrative decisions, policy matters, approvals had to be obtained from Delhi. At that time, we had no source of revenue in Arunachal Pradesh. We depended entirely on the Central Government's grants, assistance and share. The annual budget when I became the Chief Minister was just Rs. 28 Crore. Today, even a small contractor will have that in his pocket (laughs). We have a vast area. As Chief Minister, you have to show your presence right from Longding till Bumla. You have to do development work everywhere. For development works, again you need Central Government funding and Central Government approval. If you want to develop the State, you have to run to Delhi again and again.

I had my colleagues, they were quite co-operative, but as I said earlier, we had neither elders nor seniors to guide us. My colleagues had no experience of Delhi, no experience of running the Department, no experience of administration. Thank God I was a Circle Officer, so I had a little administrative knowledge.

I told myself that if you are a real well-wisher of Arunachal, you must see it develop. I felt it is not possible for one man to work in both Delhi and Arunachal Pradesh. That means I alone cannot develop it. I had a discussion with Mr. Gegong Apang that he become the Chief Minister, and I go to Delhi to assist him in getting more funds and early approvals. I resigned as the Chief Minister and Mr. Gegong Apang's name was put forward as CM. In the meantime, Mr. Tomo Riba, who was older to me in age and very willing to become the Chief Minister, defected with several MLAs and got the majority. He was sworn in instead of Mr. Gegong Apang and ran the Government for 44-45 days.

Then, Apang told me *Migom usko todna hai toh aap hi leadership aur le lo*. I said alright, after that again you'll become the CM. I again become the Congress legislative leader. 6 MLAs came back, we got back the majority and Mr. Riba resigned. To form the Government, Tadar Tang Sahab, 3-4 of us and I went to New Delhi to seek the President's approval for forming the new Government. At that time, Morarji Desai was the Prime Minister. A lot of *tolmol* was there in the country. Around 7 o'clock in the evening when I landed in Delhi, All India Radio announced that the Home Minister Mr. YB Chavan had made a statement while visiting Shillong that day that Arunachal would be under President's rule and fresh Assembly elections would be conducted simultaneously with the Lok Sabha polls. So for a while, Arunachal was placed under President's rule.

Then came the 1980 elections, when Indira Gandhi came back to power. We contested the MP and MLA elections together under my leadership. We prepared the list of candidates; I put my name on the list for MPs, not MLAs. This list was placed before Indira Ji who crossed my name from the MP list and placed it on the MLAs list. I had requested to contest as MP and Madam was giving me MLA's seat. So "madam I want to come here", "no no you remain there." I straight away went to Pranab Mukherjee and requested him because the next day the names would be announced. So, at around 10-10:30 at night, I took Pranab Mukherjee along with me and requested Madam that I want to contest as MP. She said, "and then who'll become CM. You go back to run the state." I told "I have promised, I have a very efficient colleague Gegong Apang, he will be able to run." And she said "if there's some *gadbad* you'll be held responsible." I said "yes Madam." Pranab Ji agreed.

We had election for a 30 member assembly. By that time, PPA was formed by Bakin Pertin and Tomo Riba. We got 13 members and PPA got 13 members – so we were 50-50. 4 people were independent MLAs. Out of that, 3 were from Kameng District. One was Apa Tashi Khandu, second was Sinam Dususow, one was I think, Wangnam Wangshu. When results were being announced, I had taken my MP victory results from Along and was on the way to Delhi. I had halted that evening at Tezpur Circuit house. Only radio was there at that time, there was no mobile phone. The quickest method of communication was wireless telegram. At Parvati Nagar, Tezpur, we used to have a SSB unit which had wireless facilities. I postponed my journey to Delhi and was stationed at Tezpur with the sole purpose of getting independent MLAs to support us. This means to join Congress, to support Congress, to make Gegong Apang Chief Minister. Gegong was stationed at Itanagar. That evening, two MLAs came. I got written support for Gegong Apang from Sinam Dususow and Apa Tashi Khandu. So we became 15; they were 13. Rest 1 we got somehow. When we became 15, few more MLAs were willing to join.

That is how we got a majority and Apang was elected as CLP leader. On the 3rd day, I reached Delhi and went to Yashpal Kapur, who was political secretary to Indira ji. He said "Where were you? Madam was looking for you."

I said, "I was making our own Government", he said "Okay, you have to explain to madam", I said, "yes."

Next day morning, I went to meet her around 9-9.30, because she used to meet 8-9/9.30 am, *"Public darshan me hi chalagaya!"*

Indira Gandhi: "Where were you?"

PK Thungon Ji: "I was making my government, our Government"

Mrs. Gandhi: "Oh good, good. Done?"

PK Thungon Ji: "Yes madam"

Indira Gandhi: "Next expansion, you will be taking oath as Minister"

I was making a Government in the state, and they were looking for me at the centre to make me a Minister.

This was in the initial months of the year. By June, the Council of Ministers was expanded, and I became a Minister. This is the story of how I went to Delhi and how I was able to benefit the people of Arunachal Pradesh.

Once I went there, I was in touch constantly with the Home Ministry. Most of the officers, JS or above in the Ministry, were UT cadre officers. Many of them had also served in Arunachal. I also worked with two officers who would later become Chief Secretaries of Arunachal, ML Kampani and IP Gupta. It was not difficult for me to contact them and work for Arunachal Pradesh. Whatever points or subjects were raised or discussed upon therefore were brought to my knowledge. I was also in constant touch with the then Planning Commission and managed to get our allocations doubled. I was in constant touch with other Ministers and particularly the Prime Minister, which helped accelerate the grant of statehood to Arunachal Pradesh. Thus, I feel I did not go to Delhi in vain. I tried my level best to serve Arunachal Pradesh in whatever way I could. Not only Arunachal, I served the nation in whatever way I could. For example, the Panchayati Raj system was introduced during Rajiv Ji's time on the recommendations of my committee.

The Indira Gandhi National Open University was also introduced by me when I was working as Deputy Minister in the Education Ministry. This project also has a story behind it. During the Assam agitation, Assamese students lost 2 years as universities were closed. I used to say, "we cannot afford to lose any time." I had one college in Pasighat and a night college in Itanagar, now Dera Natung Government college. With blessings of Indira Gandhi Ji, I affiliated Pasighat college and night college in Itanagar to Punjab University. Therefore, our children never lost 2 years like the children of Assam.

I had said that a similar situation may arise in any part of the country, and even internationally. If a university is closed and the college cannot be affiliated to any other university, then the students would lose their time. I wanted to affiliate Pasighat and Itanagar colleges to Delhi University, but they refused since their territorial jurisdiction is within Delhi only. In the entire country, there were only a few universities which could affiliate colleges from other states and areas. Therefore, I proposed the creation of a National Open University to Indira Ji. She agreed, and I entrusted Mr. Kireet Joshi, who was the Additional Secretary in the Ministry to work out the details. I also engaged with one Father Kunan, an educationist to start and activate this open school system. Now, children of India are getting advantage of the IGNOU system. You can study under IGNOU sitting in Itanagar.

I also convinced Indira Ji and with her help, I was able to bring a University to Arunachal Pradesh, now Rajiv Gandhi University. Indira Ji's last visit to Arunachal Pradesh was in January 1984 to lay the foundation stone of Arunachal University at Doimukh. Indira Ji supported me a lot in my efforts since I was very sincere. Indira Ji used to appreciate this, whatever proposals I gave, she usually accepted it.

I remember telling the Governor of Assam at that time, Shri LP Singh, that I don't have an engineering college, I don't have IIT, I don't have ITI – I want to produce mechanics, engineers and research scholars in one institution. That is how NERIST was concieved. Captain Williamson Sangma was at that time a very senior and influential Chief Minister in the North East. I had to take special interest and convince NEC to sanction NERIST in Arunachal Pradesh. Someone had told me Madhya Pradesh may have a similar institution. I went to Bhopal but did not find a similar institution. There was no such institution in India. So, the curriculum and syllabus had to be created afresh. I established NERIST and later went to Delhi as Deputy Education Minister under Smt. Indira Gandhi Ji. I started engaging within the Ministry, with other universities, with University Grants Commission and scholars from other universities to create the syllabus for an institution with ITI courses, full-fledged engineering courses and higher-level research scholars in one place. I got support from Dr. Kireet Joshi and other educationalists. The Director of NERIST at that time, Professor PR Sengupta – I also asked him to come to Delhi 2-3 times to discuss. Therefore, I established and then created the syllabus of NERIST. I am very happy that it is running successfully now.

Another thing. Who started Navodaya Vidyalayas? I started it during Indira Gandhi's time. I had given the name Special Central Schools. I wanted Central Schools to be a kind of nation-building effort and foster unity and integrity of the country. Because the central school syllabus is from the Centre, i.e., NCERT, it is one syllabus, whether it is a school in Tamil Nadu or Himachal Pradesh, Saurashtra or Arunachal Pradesh. That means your knowledge and Saurashtra or Madras' students' knowledge, will be the same, in congruence, along the same lines. That creates the fabric of the nation stronger in the minds of the young people. Today's young people will become tomorrow's administrators, tomorrow's politicians, they will have the responsibility of holding the country together, not divided. But if your views are not the same, there may be problems for unity and integrity, that was my intention and feeling. That is required.

Indira Ji was assassinated in 1984, and Rajiv Ji became the Prime Minister. By this time, I had become the Chairman of the Panchayati Raj committee and was no longer in the Education Ministry. Mr. KC Pant, who was the education minister at that time, felt that there are already some special Tibetan Central Schools, and therefore rightly gave the name Navodaya Vidyalaya. My thought was that every district should have one such school. Today, one Navodaya Vidyalaya is running in almost all districts of the country and contributing to the unity and integrity of the nation. This was my brainchild, my vision.

The National Open University was also renamed as Indira Gandhi National Open University in 1985.

This is all I can remember for now. My major contributions to the nation are the Panchayati Raj system, IGNOU, Navodaya Vidyalayas and open schools. Besides my own State of Arunachal Pradesh, at the national level also, I tried to contribute whatever was possible, whatever I could. This is why I am a happy person who earned no material wealth, does not have many properties or anything. I am now just an ordinary citizen. I am happy because I rendered whatever service I could for Arunachal Pradesh and India during my tenure.

7. What according to you are the Differences/similarities of today's Arunachal and then?

I should say there is no difference in spirit. In our generation, we used to feel we should progress, we should go further. Today also, there is the same spirit, same intention to progress. But materially, there is a difference in quality of life. Earlier, when I used to go to Bomdila from here, it used to take two days, now it takes 5-6 hours. However, I don't think there is much difference between those days and now, as far as intention, spirit and efforts are concerned.

Development is not fixed. One kind of development is not the only development. It has to be developed in all aspects to become an effective, energetic and thoughtful human being. This spirit is the same even now.

I can see a slight difference in the approach of people today compared to the beginning of my career in Arunachal Pradesh. I have gone to all parts of Arunachal and met almost all tribes and all sections of people. One difference I can see is that emotionally and morally, people used to be more straightforward and honest and take pride in themselves, their tribes, customs, culture and languages. These days there are differences. In 1968 when I stayed in an interior place in the Adi area for a few days and while going back to headquarters I offered some tips to the chowkidar, a local man as *baksheesh*. He said *humko dena chahiye aapko aap humare yaha aya hain, humara pani kheti hai, humko zaroorat nahi hai.* He was proud of his *pani kheti* and he will not take tips, and he is rather prepared to give you if he can give something. After 28 years, in 1996, I again went there for a meeting and lunch. While I was about to leave, there was a line of chowkidar, peon, cook, safaiwala – I could see they were lining up for tips. I gave Rs. 500 and they were not satisfied with Rs. 500. There are 2-3 such instances I keep citing.

So, this is the difference in material progress. But this is quite normal in any progressive society. Changes take place but the spirit and intention of the people remains the same. These days also, our youngsters want to progress. We had our own vision and achieved many things. Many things remain to be achieved by the younger generation. The progress of society, the progress of the country goes on like this. There is no difference. I say this because our spirit is the same.

I have also seen the rest of the country. As far as Arunachal is concerned, I feel Arunachal has made significant progress because our people are sincere and to a great extent, still honest. This is why progress becomes easier and development takes place in the right direction. I don't see much difference in spirit and action. As far as the new generation is concerned, I see in them the same spirit we had in our younger days. It should continue in the same way and I think Arunachal will progress quite fast.

8.   What was people's and administration's reaction to 1962 war?

In 1962, I was a young student. I was in Shillong when my hometown, Bomdila, fell to Chinese aggressors. As soon as I heard, I moved towards Bomdila.

The day, I met the political officer at Tezpur and came to know my parents were also coming down. I met my parents later on; we were refugees in Assam for some time.

As far as the reaction of the people is concerned, I think people were totally against Chinese aggression. Our disliking for China increased. This was, in one way, a blessing in disguise for India, our country. It became a kind of shield for India, because after 1962, almost everybody in Arunachal started talking against China. After that, they could not even imagine such aggression. That was my feeling, and it was the feeling of all Arunachal brothers and sisters. Moreover, our affiliation to the teachings of the Dalai Lama, that means, Buddhist preachings, also gave courage to the people of Arunachal, particularly the Buddhist community in the border areas to stand against the Chinese.

Our administration was very sincere, but we can't blame the administration since we had a very scantily administered area. Wherever they were, they did their very best. I have seen in my own Kameng District, due to heavy incursion, many of our administrative officers also lost their lives. I knew one young Circle Officer who was killed between Dirang and Bomdila. Since I knew him, I felt very bad. These things increased the *aakrosh* of the people against China.

9. What according to you were the biggest achievements in 30 years (1980, 1990, 2000)?

I can't remember everything but I can say one of the major achievements in 30 years is statehood. After achieving statehood, the pace of progress in Arunachal increased. The development that has taken place till now is the result of the smooth functioning of the State, legislatively, administratively and economically. I think this progress will keep on improving.

10. What according to you is the biggest threat and strength for Arunachal's future?

If we are not united, if we don't know how to live together and respect each other, this will create problems. This is more dangerous than external problems or differences. Arunachal Pradesh has more than 26 major tribes and different cultures, traditions and languages. Sometimes, I feel the younger generation has yet to learn how to live together with unity in diversity.

The other threat, particularly for the new generation, is the use of drugs etc. I have seen some students, young students, getting addicted to drugs, which will prove to be very dangerous.

Economically, if we exploit our hydropower potential, this alone can create good revenue for Arunachal Pradesh. Likewise, we have plains, mountains, alpine areas, dense forest area, virgin forest area so we have enough flora and fauna. If we harness this economically, we can be very prosperous. These are certain resources which create strength for Arunachal Pradesh.

Human resources are the biggest strength of any society. The people of Arunachal Pradesh are very hard working, honest and devoted by nature. They are one of our greatest strengths. There are so many other things which I can't explain within a few words. All I want to say is that the strength of Arunachal is very good economically, politically and administratively.

11. Have you met Bob? Your reminiscences of Bob Khathing?

Bob Khathing used to be very popular when we were in school and college. Right from school, I think, class 6 onwards, I have heard his name. And later on, I met him in Shillong when I was in college. He was an additional advisor to the Governor of Assam. He was the gentleman who first established Bomdila Headquarters. My father was a Political Interpreter and was a friend of Bob Khathing right from his tenure at Charduar Headquarters. They were the people who fell the first tree in the jungles of Bomdila to establish Bomdila headquarters. That is how I remember him. The other part of the story I heard about his contribution is that he travelled on foot from Charduar to Tawang to establish the Administrative Centre in Pung Teng in Tawang.

He had a lot of contribution so far as tribal areas development is concerned. That is why I remember him. I know he was a friend of my father, but I have met him only once at Shillong, when I was a student in college.

12. During your time 'The Arunachal Pradesh Freedom of Religion Act, 1978' was enacted. What circumstances prompted this move? What is its relevance in today's context?

When I became Chief Minister, one of the biggest problems I faced was that people from outside used to come and exploit, mislead our people. Particularly, in areas on the Assam-Arunachal border, a lot of disturbances used to occur, even killings took place. This was not just for one or two days but lasted almost 12 months.

I started studying the reasons behind this. Our people are simple, honest and hardworking. But some people from outside used to come inside Arunachal Pradesh and try to denigrate our traditions and cultures and get people converted. This was one of the reasons, apart from the land, for all the *jhagdas*, killings, *Marpeet*.

In the Assembly also, we discussed at length. One of the very progressive MLAs, Mr. Akan Lego, brought a resolution in the Assembly that our culture, religions and traditions should be protected, otherwise a lot of such *gadbad* will take place. The resolution was unanimously passed by the Assembly and the Government and Chief Minister were asked by the Assembly to take some legislative measures. Thus, the Freedom of Religion Bill was passed by the Assembly and approved by the President of India. It has now been named The Arunachal Pradesh Freedom of Religion Act, 1978. Thus, there were two reasons for bringing the Bill. In those days, there was a lot of misguidances, disturbance and a bill was needed for protection of law and order in the State. Second, was the unanimous resolution passed by the Assembly.

The Bill was not against one or two religions or one or two cultures. If a Christian is converted, we can't blame Christians. If Muslim conversion takes place, we can't blame Muslims only. Likewise if a Buddhist conversion takes place, we can't blame Buddhists only. In our democracy, with a secular Constitution, you are free to practise any religion, but that does not mean you disturb other religions. Therefore, the provision in the Bill is that once one gets converted, one should report to the district authority. If someone harasses a person who has converted, the DC can immediately arrange for his protection.

If his name is not registered, the DC will be helpless. Actually, the Bill was not against any religion; rather it is in favour of every religion. In some cases, people interpreted wrongly and my name went up to the Pope at that time (1975-76) saying I was against Christians. I was blamed in the whole North East at that time and all Christians were against me, including Captain Sangma, but later they realised. So as far as relevance is concerned, the Bill has eternal relevance – it was relevant at that time, it is relevant today and it will remain relevant in future as well.

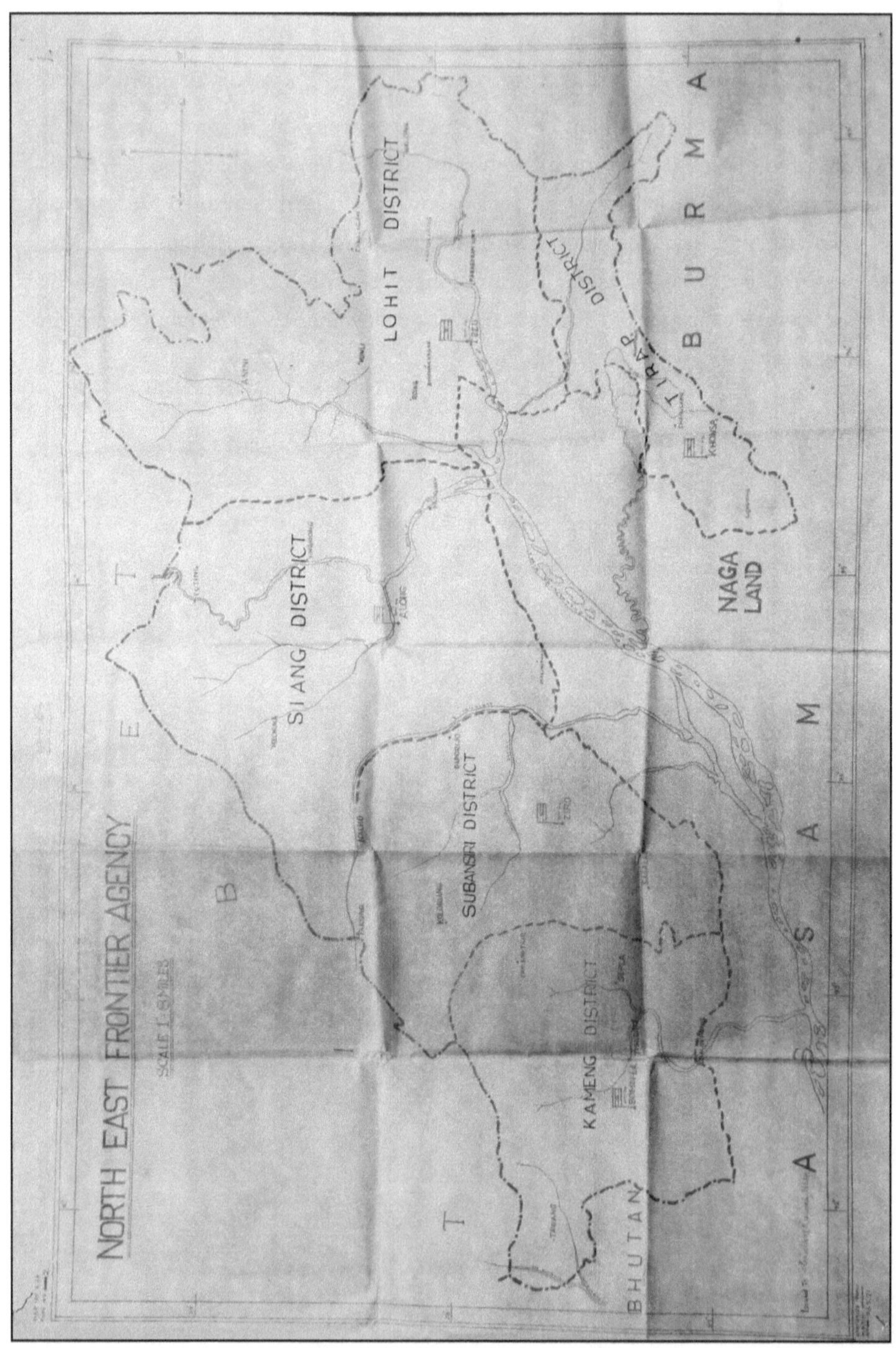

▲ **Map 13:** Map showing NEFA Administrative Divisions, 1971
(Source: Directorate of Research, Government of Arunachal Pradesh)

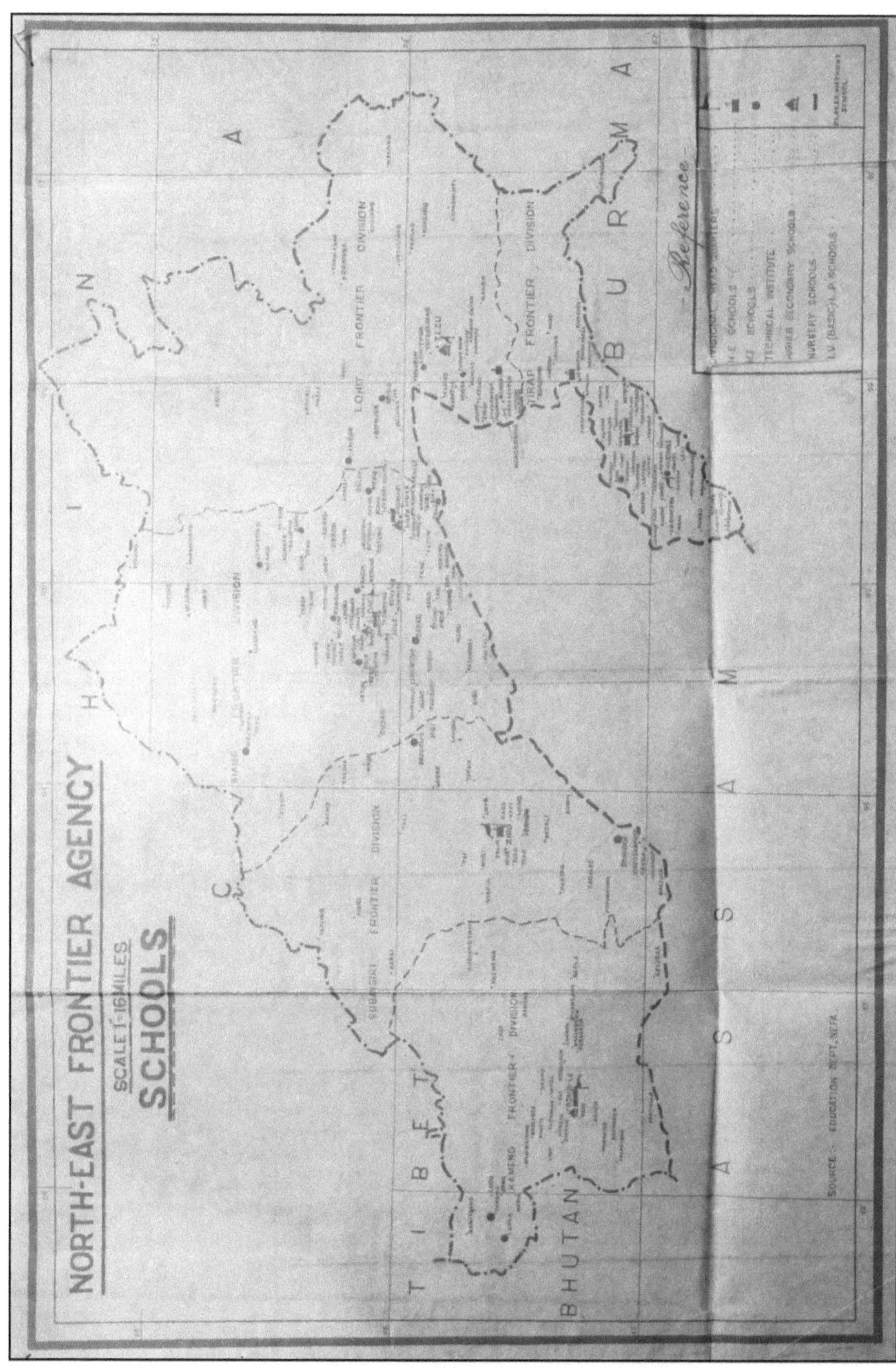

▲ **Map 14:** Map showing Schools in NEFA, 1971
(Source: Directorate of Research, Government of Arunachal Pradesh)

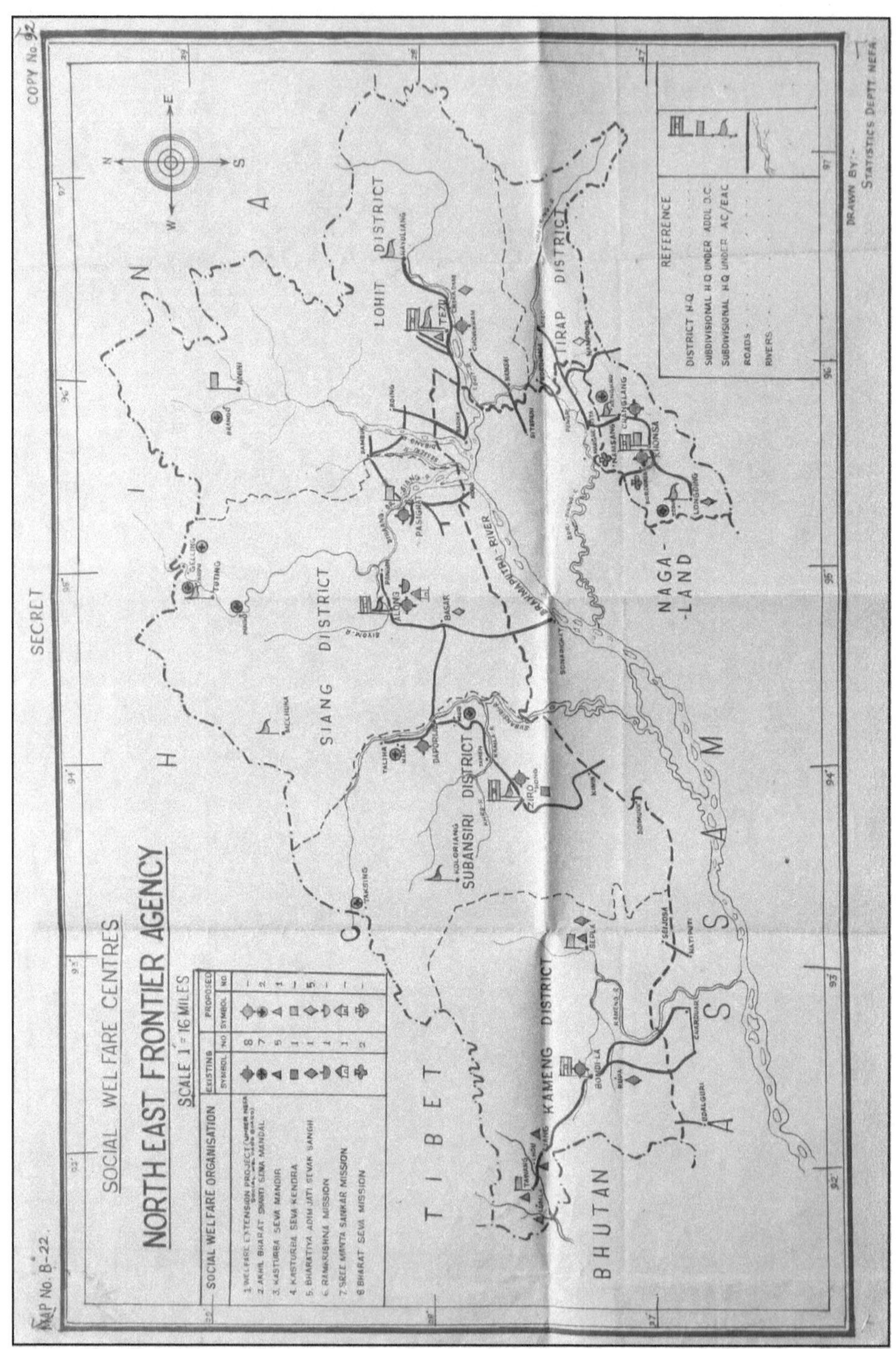

▲ **Map 15:** Map showing Social Welfare Centres in NEFA, 1971
(Source: Directorate of Research, Government of Arunachal Pradesh)

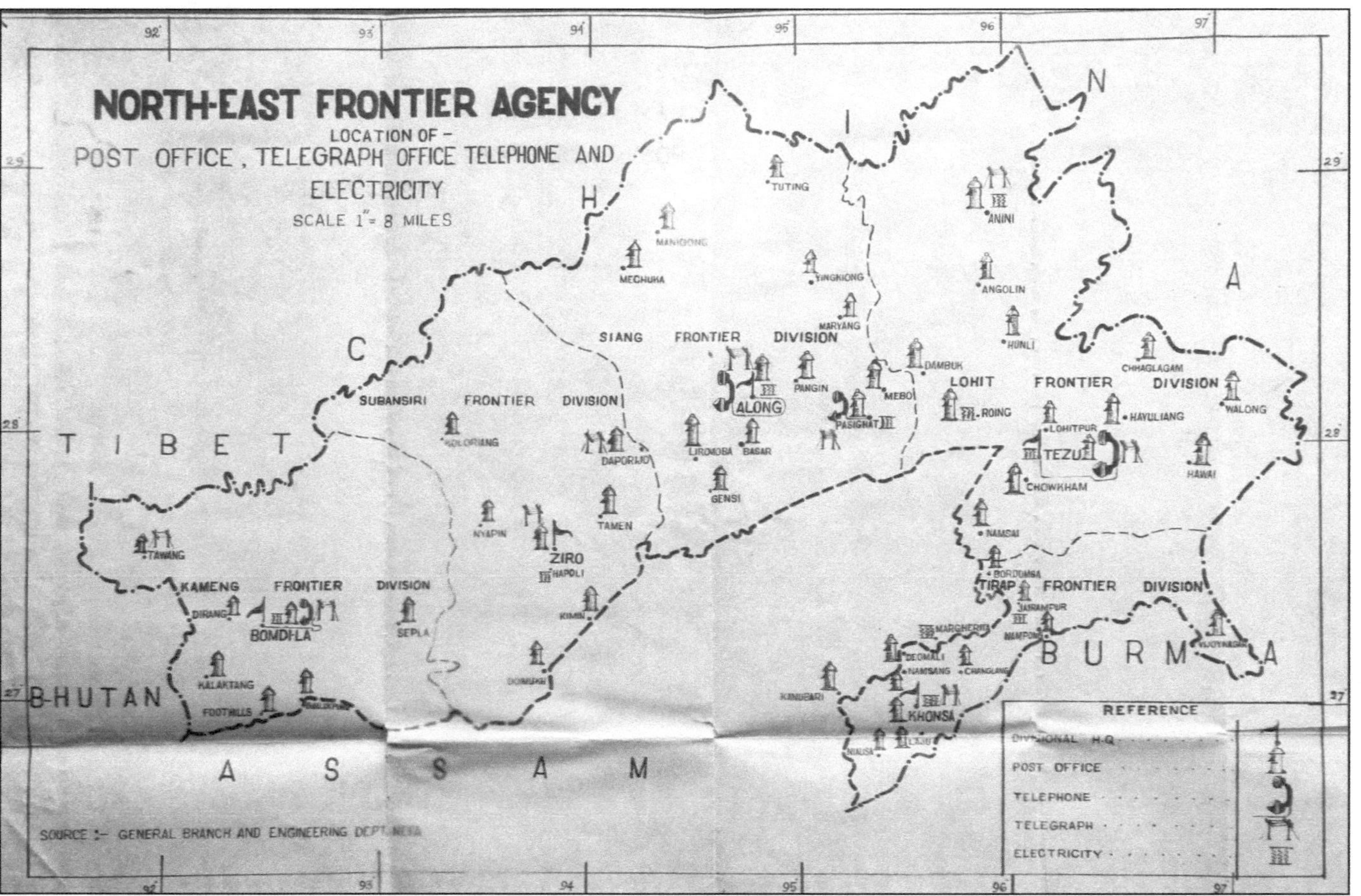

▲ **Map 16:** Map showing Post Offices, Telegraph Offices, Telephone and Electricity Lines in NEFA, 1971 (Source: Directorate of Research, Government of Arunachal Pradesh)

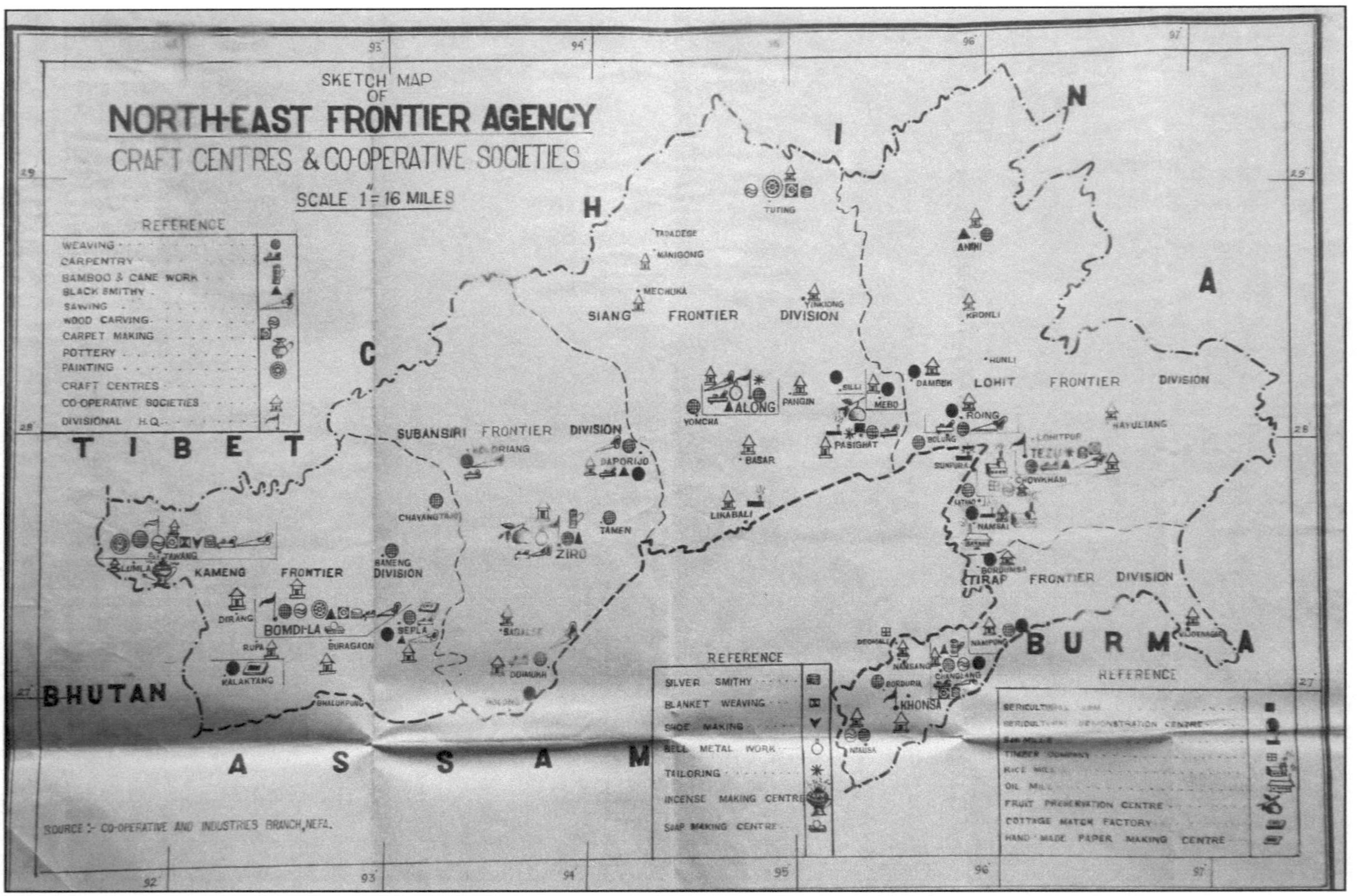

▲ **Map 17:** Map showing Craft Centres and Cooperative Societies in NEFA, 1971
(Source: Directorate of Research, Government of Arunachal Pradesh)

'Language, any language, has a dual character: it is both a means of
communication and a carrier of culture.'
— **Ngũgĩ wa Thiong'o**

10

Tongues of Harmony: The Quest for a Common Voice

In today's world of LOLs, emojis, and memes, communication across cultures happens in seconds, often without a single spoken word. But imagine a time when even neighbouring villages couldn't understand each other because they spoke entirely different languages. That was the reality in Arunachal Pradesh, where 26 major tribes and over 100 sub-tribes each with distinct dialects, mutually unintelligible, with no common language to unite them. The state, rich in culture and diversity, faced immense challenges due to this linguistic diversities, making communication between communities and even governance incredibly difficult. Without a shared tongue, the unity of this newly formed territory was at stake, pushing the need for a common voice to the forefront.

Historically, there was no common *lingua franca*, which created significant communication barriers. Each tribe spoke a different dialect, making inter-tribal communication challenging. Notwithstanding the lack of intelligibility among the different language groups, the Mutual Intelligibility (MI) factor even among intra-group is very less in some cases. The diversity of language and culture and its impact can be understood from the fact that Arunachal Pradesh does not have an 'indigenous' language as a lingua franca.[230]

There are two languages (sic) and sixty dialects spoken in the state. With the exception of two scripts, Bhoti and Tai-Khampti, no other tribes have a written script. These two languages have been introduced in the primary classes in their respective area of domicile[231].

The lack of a unified language underscored its implications for the state's social and administrative complexities. The *linguistic barrier* that the newly created Union Territory inherited, if not overcome timely, had the potential to disintegrate the fragile unity with disparate tribes stitched together into a single Territory. It was imperative that this essential void was filled up, urgently.

There (were) only eleven schools in NEFA in the pre-independence period' (Begi, 2007: 29). Schools in right earnest were started in the late 1940s only, with Assamese as medium of instruction in both pre-primary and primary classes. It remained so until 1974, when it was switched to English in response to demands made by the then NEFA Students' Union. Since then, English has been the medium of instruction at all levels of education with Hindi as second language and Assamese/Sanskrit as the third language in middle level (class VI-VIII).[232] In fact, a lot of credit is due to Indira Mili[233], who was the Chief Education Officer of NEFA for ten years from 1947 in bringing modern education in the Agency. Equipped with a Master's Degree from University of Edinburgh and trained from Oxford University, her pioneering works in sowing the seeds of modern education and working closely with the NEFA tribals are truly exemplary.

A significant policy shift towards national integration and mainstreaming was on the anvil. The foremost step included adopting English and Hindi as the primary medium of instruction in schools, replacing Assamese,[234]much to the chagrin of Assam, which had been used earlier as a medium of instruction. This change was driven by the need to foster a sense of national identity and facilitate better communication across the diverse linguistic landscape of the Frontier. The shift had profound implications, including improved accessibility to national educational resources and better opportunities for higher education and employment for the local populace.

NEFAMESE: A Pidgin Language[235]

Before the formal adoption of Hindi and English, a pidgin language known as NEFAMESE emerged. This language was a blend of Assamese and local dialects, predominantly spoken in the foothills adjoining Assam. NEFAMESE served as a practical solution for basic communication among people from different linguistic backgrounds within the region. However, it did not have the reach or formal recognition to serve as a medium of instruction or in administration. Its usage was confined to the foothills and even today, serves in colloquial interactions.

Linguistic transition in Arunachal Pradesh

Analysis of census data[236] from 1961 to 2011 reveals a gradual but significant shift in language use in Arunachal Pradesh. Initially, Assamese and local dialects dominated. However, post-1972, there was a noticeable increase in the use of Hindi and English. By 2011, Hindi had become widely spoken, particularly in urban areas and among the younger generation. The education policy, Government employment and inter-tribal communication needs contributed to Hindi filling the void of the common language,

Unlike other North-Eastern states, Arunachal Pradesh embraced Hindi more readily. Several factors contributed to this unique trend. During the 1962 Sino-Indian War, local tribes were actively involved as porters and guides, necessitating the use of Hindi to communicate with Indian soldiers. This exposure laid the groundwork for Hindi's acceptance. Additionally, Government employment often involved a mix of North Indian and local staff, making Hindi a practical choice for daily communication.

Interestingly, there has been no significant conflict between the local dialects and Hindi in Arunachal Pradesh. They have coexisted harmoniously, with Hindi often serving as a bridge language. The early exposure during the 1962 war and subsequent reinforcement through education and Government employment cemented Hindi's role in the region.

The policy shift in 1972 to use English and Hindi as medium of instruction had an immediate impact. With many teachers from North India joining as teachers, educational institutions, especially primary schools, began using Hindi. This influx of Hindi-speaking teachers and the use of Hindi in education led to the emergence of a distinct version of Hindi in Arunachal Pradesh. This localised Hindi incorporated elements from English and local dialects, creating a unique linguistic blend that is distinct to the state.

Organisations like the Ramakrishna Mission and Vivekananda Kendra Vidyalayas played significant roles in reinforcing the use of Hindi and English through their educational initiatives. Furthermore, trade interactions also promoted the use of Hindi. Marwari traders, who were prominent in the region, used Hindi for business, which further encouraged its adoption among the local population.

The Ramakrishna Mission began its work in Arunachal Pradesh in the 1960s. The Mission made significant contributions to education and healthcare in the state. The Mission established its first school in Aalo in 1966, followed by another centre in Narottam Nagar, Deomali, in 1971. These two Institutions were the harbinger in laying a strong foundation and have been instrumental in shaping the educational landscape of Arunachal Pradesh. In 1979, the Ramakrishna Mission established a multidisciplinary hospital in Itanagar, which became a crucial healthcare provider for the people of Arunachal Pradesh. The hospital offered various medical services and remains a lifeline for the local population. It was after 46 years, in 2017, that the third RK Mission school was opened in Lumdung, East Kameng.

Similarly, Vivekananda Kendra Vidyalayas, inspired by Swami Vivekananda's ideals, have played a pivotal role in the education sector of Arunachal Pradesh. VKVs have established numerous schools across the state, providing quality education with a focus on holistic development. These schools emphasise moral and spiritual education alongside academic learning, fostering a sense of national integration and cultural pride among students.

VKVs have also been involved in community development activities, promoting literacy, health, and social awareness in rural areas. Their initiatives have contributed significantly to the upliftment of various communities in Arunachal Pradesh.

In the heart of Arunachal Pradesh, the Vivekananda Kendra's journey began at the invitation of the then Lieutenant Governor, K.A.A. Raja. This journey, initiated in 1975, marked the beginning of a transformative era in the region's education system. The Kendra first deployed teachers in Government schools to understand and connect with the community they aimed to serve. By 1977, the Vivekananda Kendra had established seven schools across the state in locations such as Balijan, Jairampur, Kharsang, Oyan, Roing, Seijosa, and Sher. These schools were strategically spread across the five districts of Tirap, Lohit, Siang, Subansiri, and Kameng.

The first school dedicated to girls was opened in 1978 at Tafrogam in Lohit district, emphasising the Kendra's commitment to gender-inclusive education. Over the years, the Vivekananda Kendra Vidyalayas Arunachal Pradesh Trust has grown exponentially, managing 41 Vidyalayas, 2 Kasturba Gandhi Balika Vidyalayas, 2 Eklavya Model Residential Schools, and a College of Teacher Education.

The Sharada Missions have also made valuable contributions to education and health in Arunachal Pradesh. Sharada Missions have been particularly focused on the education of girls, providing them with opportunities to receive quality education in a supportive environment. This emphasis has helped in improving the educational status of women in the region.

Fusion and some Confusion

Adopting a new language was not without its challenges. The population faced predicament on two fronts; one was from the teacher, unaware of the local circumstances and the other was from the locals who could not place themselves in context of the new languages-both Hindi and English.

These teachers were mostly from northern India with strong Hindi background. Significant numbers were from neighbouring Assam and from southern India too. Most had little or no exposure to English culture. The teacher's cultural limitations have led to many wrongly spelt native names and surnames. These teachers also carried with them their own personal cultural experiences and linguistic prejudices which they transmitted to their students unwittingly. To cite a few examples, Yazalyii became Yazali,

Yochulyii to Yachuli, Aalo to Along, Cher to Sher, Lyichii to Lichi and so on.[237]

The efficiency of learners was doubly incapacitated by their own native linguistic restrictions/shortcomings and unwitting transmission of inappropriate sounds by their teachers, tradesman and Government employees in the initial years of the State building process. Some of the typical vernacular sounds were 'chuha' (mouse) as 'suha', kacha (raw) as 'kasa', Very as 'bhery' by our Assamese teachers; station as 'istation', school as 'ischool', blood as 'balad' by the north Indian teachers and yal, yum and yan for L, M, and N respectively by the southerners. There are examples are galore of natives' phonological *faux pas* as many of the tribal dialects do not have all the corresponding sound system of English, Hindi and many other languages. One can hear a Nyishi speaker (Tani) asking for 'kana' and 'hana' (Khana), rice in Hindi, khabar, news 'kabar', thanda (cool) as 'tanda'. In Apatani tribe, where 'h', 'r' and 'l' is mildly pronounced, Naharlagun turns into 'Nuanagun' and Bus becomes 'Bans'. The sound 'f' 'v' and 'ph' is absent in most tribes except in some sections of the Nyishi and Tangsa tribe where it is strongly accented. So, in case of the former, telephone becomes 'telipoon', office, 'oppice', fifty 'pipti', valley is 'balley', phase and face becomes 'pace'. In the latter office is 'ophice' and valley becomes 'phalley'. Raasta, (road), is 'daasta' among the Noctes of eastern Arunachal.[238]

The linguistic impact, primarily because of three competing languages of Assamese, Hindi and English on the frontier population was visible in a way that '…the popularity of Hindi and Assamese has not only impeded the learning of English but made quite an inroad into local tongues. The former by virtue of being the national language and the latter because of its status as medium of instruction up to 1973 in the state and also as third language too. The influence of Hindi is such that many of the second and third generation children do not speak their own mother tongue. It was a fashion in the 60s and 70s to teach Assamese to one's children rather than own mother tongue by the 'educated' people. It progressed to Hindi in the late 80s and 90s and the trend is still own……It has been clearly and firmly echoed by many experts in the field that language cannot be taught outside a social context. Learning of language (sic) is an individual act but it occurs in the society (sic). The social context include (sic) components such as the sociolinguistic situation, the general exposure of learners to other languages, the roles of the target language and other languages in the outside community and in the home, and the general perception of values of the target language'.[239]

As a consequence, Hindi became the predominant language and served as the single *lingua franca* of Arunachal Pradesh, albeit with a tinge of native flavour, devoid of grammar and lack of gender. The adoption of Hindi was so acute that the Government had to devise programs to promote mother tongues. It is the only State in the Northeast where Hindi is spoken with such ease; even the Legislative proceedings in the Assembly are conducted in Hindi. In fact, speeches by some legislators would put many from the Hindi speaking states to shame!

As we look back, Arunachal Pradesh, moving away from the shadows of isolation, was undergoing a massive churning. The eagerness of young girls and boys and their excitement to unshackle themselves were evident in the large enrolments in these schools. Perhaps, finally we were waking up from the deep slumber of seclusion.

In summary, Government efforts were reinforced by the contributions of organisations like the Ramakrishna Mission, Vivekananda Kendra Vidyalayas, and Sharada Missions. They have been instrumental in the development of education and health sectors of Arunachal Pradesh. These monumental strides have played a significant role in the state's integration into the national framework while addressing local needs and challenges.

What the state got in the process was a bridge to intermingle and connect. Hindi became more than a language, it cemented people and bolstered the idea of Arunachal Pradesh. It shaped a unified identity by bringing together each tribe and, in doing so, helped shape an identity for Arunachal Pradesh that honoured its diversity while reinforcing its shared values.

"There's no wrong time to make the right decision."
– Dalton McGuinty

11

Development is the Best Defence;
Ushering a *New Dawn*

The 1962 Chinese aggression left an indelible mark on India's strategic thinking, especially concerning its North eastern borders. The brief but intense conflict, which lasted a month (from October 20th to November 21st of 1962), exposed several vulnerabilities-military, diplomatic, political, and administrative. It revealed the stark reality that the northern borders of Northeast India, particularly Arunachal Pradesh, were woefully underprepared. At the time, the gaps were so significant that the Indian Government learned of the Chinese unilateral ceasefire and their retreat through media reports. This was a wake-up call, highlighting the urgent need to strengthen these frontier regions.

However, the post-war years saw a missed opportunity. Despite the clear lessons of 1962, efforts to rectify these deficiencies were slow. The dominant narrative in strategic circles was to leave the region undeveloped, fearing that any infrastructure could be advantageous to an invading force. This policy, whatever might have been the intention, proved to be a strategic blunder, leaving Arunachal Pradesh's Northern borders largely untouched and vulnerable.

Genuine Development Suffers; Victim of a Flawed Policy

It is often said that those who forget history are condemned to repeat it. Despite the humiliating defeat in 1962, the *'forgetfulness'* of Delhi was a recipe for history repeating in the North Eastern Frontier. The physical distance of Arunachal Pradesh was accentuated by the mental distance from Delhi. The ghost of the Northern borders lingered while the policy of *'leave it as it is'* and the *'Strategy of denial*[240]*'* continued. The flawed policy of keeping Arunachal Pradesh infrastructurally deficient, reasoning that it would deter quick entry of enemies from the North, if not stupid, was definitely the laziest proposition for a national strategy to tackle her most formidable enemy. The lessons from the episode of 1962 were not learnt with seriousness and earnestness. Was there a thinking, as many discuss privately, that the *Chicken's Neck* would be the last of the concessions, in case of an eventuality? Was the policy driven by this thought? Perhaps, we will never know.

As we kept ourselves engrossed in deliberating on the pros and cons of granting statehood, something else was brewing in the North. While Delhi was confused and disoriented on how to handle the turbulent neighbour, China was already making in roads and encroaching southwards. Again.

The Sumdorong Chu Standoff[241]

Immediately after Arunachal Pradesh attained statehood in 1987, it was immediately thrust into a geopolitical spotlight, again, testing the resilience and strategic acumen of India's leadership. The Sumdorong Chu standoff of 1988 marked one of the most significant post-statehood challenges faced by the fledgling state. This confrontation occurred in Tawang district, a region already fraught with historical tensions due to its proximity to the contentious McMahon Line.

The issue began when Indian troops discovered Chinese forces setting up a post at Sumdorong Chu, an area India considered its own. This move by China was perceived as an attempt to change the status quo along the Line of Actual Control (LAC) (Line of Actual Control-Notional demarcation line between Chinese controlled and Indian controlled territories, first espoused by Zhou Enlai, subsequently came into currency post 1962 war). The Indian Government, under Prime Minister Rajiv

Gandhi, responded with a measured but firm military buildup, making it clear that any infringement on its territory would not be tolerated.

Since the 1962 conflict, India had avoided returning to Namka Chu, the site of a major defeat. The Namka Chu stream separates the Thag La ridge in the North from Hathung La ridge in the South. India's attempt to occupy the Thag La ridge had been the trigger for the 1962 Chinese attack. Given the lack of defensible positions north of Tawang, the erstwhile Indian strategy had been to prepare for battle at the Se La pass to the South. However, after a review in 1980, military strategists emphasised the importance of defending Tawang, identifying the Hathung La ridge as the only viable line of defence.

In 1983, an Intelligence Bureau team began annual visits to the Sumdorong Chu pasturage, Northeast of the Namka Chu and Nyamjang Chu confluence. This continued until 1986 when the team found Chinese forces had set up semi-permanent structures and refused to leave.

Under General Sundarji's orders, and codenamed Operation Falcon, India airlifted troops and vehicles to Zemithang area from October 18 to 20, 1986. Indian forces strategically occupied high ground near Sumdorong Chu, including the Hathung La ridge, leading to further mobilisation on both sides. China called for a flag meeting on November 15, but the standoff continued until May 1987.

Recognizing the risk of inadvertent conflict, both India and China decided to de-escalate. This standoff led to a resumption of dialogue, which had been dormant since the 1962 war. After Rajiv Gandhi's 1988 visit, political turmoil in India caused a hiatus, but in 1993, the two countries signed an agreement to ensure peace along the LAC.

The agreement introduced the concept of "mutual and equal security," envisioning a thinning of forces based on geographical and logistical considerations. Crucially, it aimed for both sides to agree on a mutually acceptable LAC. However, each side still has its own version of the line, with disputed points remaining, particularly in the Sikkim-Bhutan-India trijunction and the Sumdorong Chu area.

Prime Minister's Visit to China

In the midst of this tense standoff, Prime Minister Rajiv Gandhi made a historic visit to China in December 1988. This visit was significant not just for the bilateral relations between the two countries but also for its potential impact on the situation in Sumdorong Chu. The visit aimed to open a new chapter in Sino-Indian relations, focusing on building trust and resolving long standing issues through dialogue and cooperation.

During his visit, Prime Minister Gandhi engaged in extensive discussions with the Chinese leadership, including Deng Xiaoping. The talks were aimed at reducing tensions and finding a peaceful resolution to the border disputes. This high-level engagement was a strategic move to calm the situation at Sumdorong Chu and to lay the groundwork for future cooperation between India and China.

The outcome of the visit was a mutual agreement to maintain peace and tranquillity along the LAC, marking a significant step towards stabilising the border regions. The dialogue also led to the establishment of joint working groups to address the boundary issues, reflecting a commitment from both sides to resolve disputes through negotiation rather than confrontation.

The Sumdorong Chu standoff and the subsequent diplomatic efforts underscored the complexities faced by Arunachal Pradesh in its early years as a state. The incident served as a stark reminder of the geopolitical challenges inherent to the region. It also demonstrated the critical role of strong political leadership and diplomacy in navigating these challenges.

Prime Minister Rajiv Gandhi's visit to China was a pivotal moment that helped de-escalate a potentially volatile situation. It showcased the importance of high-level diplomatic engagement in addressing security concerns and maintaining regional stability. The experience gained from managing the Sumdorong Chu standoff contributed to shaping India's broader strategic approach to its Northeastern frontier and relations with China.

In summary, the post-statehood period of Arunachal Pradesh was marked by significant geopolitical challenges, with the Sumdorong Chu standoff highlighting the need for vigilant border management and proactive diplomacy. The successful resolution of this standoff, facilitated by Prime Minister Gandhi's timely visit to China, set a precedent for future conflict resolution and underscored the importance of sustained diplomatic efforts in maintaining peace and stability in the region. Most importantly, this was a stark reminder that Delhi needs to keep her ears on the grounds of the Eastern Frontier while the hands must move to strategically strengthen the vulnerable region.

Fast forward to 2003, LK Advani, then Deputy Prime Minister, visited Arunachal Pradesh. During his visit, Advani candidly admitted to the media that the policy of neglecting infrastructure development in the region after the 1962 war was a mistake. He acknowledged that this decision, motivated by fear of benefiting the neighbour in case of another conflict, was a *historical blunder.*[242] This admission brought to light the misplaced strategic thinking that had persisted for decades and underscored the need for a significant policy shift. It took us four decades to realise that neglect was not the strategy to counter China. Too Little, Too Late, critics would say. Hopefully, this realisation would foster a new era for Arunachal Pradesh and enhance India's strategic manoeuvring capabilities, many thought at the time.

By 2003, there was a noticeable shift in strategic thinking within the corridors of power in Delhi, emphasising the development of the Northeast region. This shift was, perhaps, facilitated by the fiscal benefits of liberalisation and globalisation, giving the Government more resources to invest in infrastructure. The planning and policy work on the Special Accelerated Road Development Program for the Northeast (SARDP-NE)[243] had already commenced, further reinforcing this new approach. Something was in the offing.

Special Package Announcements of 2008: The Turning Point

While Delhi was mooting a decisive policy turnaround for Arunachal Pradesh, a significant political shift occurred on April 9, 2007, when Dorjee Khandu was sworn in as the 6th Chief Minister of Arunachal Pradesh. Khandu's leadership marked a proactive approach towards the state's development. Three days into his tenure, Khandu initiated efforts to secure a special development package for Arunachal Pradesh. A young IAS officer was tasked with formulating a comprehensive development proposal aimed at attracting the Prime Minister's attention.

The proactive role of the Planning Commission and political manoeuvring by the Chief Minister played crucial roles in driving this mega proposal forward. The young officer recalled presenting the package proposal to a group of senior officers led by Cabinet Secretary TS Chandrashekhar. Positive feedback and the support of key figures like Montek Singh Ahluwalia facilitated the approval process.

The Push for Development: The PM's Special Package

The efforts culminated on January 31, 2008, when Prime Minister Dr Manmohan Singh visited Itanagar and announced a significant economic package for Arunachal Pradesh. Known as the *PM's Special Economic Package for Arunachal Pradesh* 2008, it was a landmark moment for the state. The package included a massive Rs. 10,000 crore (in 2008; which increased manifold on execution) allocation for various developmental projects, including the 3,000 MW Dibang Multipurpose Project, new Legislative Assembly Building and State Civil Secretariat, and extensive road network improvements such as the 1,600 KM Trans-Arunachal Highway, Greenfield Airport, Railway line to Itanagar, 10 Advanced Landing Grounds, 110 MW Pare Hydro power Project, Drinking Water Facilities among others.

This package was not simply about infrastructure but also aimed at integrating Arunachal Pradesh more closely with the rest of India, promoting economic development, and enhancing the quality of life for its residents. Singh's announcement was met with widespread acclaim and marked a watershed year for the state. The Prime Minister's visit, his first to the easternmost state in 2008 was a significant political event attended by around 50,000 locals in tribal attire, symbolising the long yearning of the region for development.

The visits by LK Advani and Dr. Manmohan Singh, coupled with the special economic packages, highlighted the tectonic shift in India's approach towards Arunachal Pradesh. These initiatives underscored a renewed commitment to rectifying past neglect and investing in the state's future. The policy changes and developmental efforts initiated in the early 2000s have since laid the groundwork for more robust infrastructure and economic growth in Arunachal Pradesh.

As the state continues to evolve, these moments of political recognition and strategic investment serve as stark reminders of the importance of learning from the past and adapting to ensure a secure and prosperous future for Arunachal Pradesh and its people.

The Strategic Shift and Confident Leadership

Reflecting on the transformative years post-statehood, the officer, now a Joint Secretary to the Government of India, reminisced about the substantial confidence the Government of India placed in the state leadership on the judicious utilisation of funds allocated through the Special Package. He opined that there appeared to be no deep strategic thought at the highest levels behind the announcement of the package, though I would maintain that strategic interest was definitely a pivotal consideration. Nonetheless, this marked a significant policy turnaround, driven by the recognition of previous strategic missteps and the urgent need to correct them.

He further recalled, before the announcement of the package, the proposal was vetted by the National Security Advisor (NSA). Both the Governor and Chief Minister personally briefed TKA Nair, the Principal

Secretary to the Prime Minister. During UPA-I (United Progressive Alliance-Congress led coalition Government), Prime Minister Dr Manmohan Singh and the positive roles played by the Planning Commission-especially by Montek Singh Ahluwalia, BK Chaturvedi, and SN Brahma-were instrumental in accomplishment of this defining milestone in the state's history.

The Implementation Challenge: Turning Vision into Reality

The announcement of a Special Economic Package for Arunachal Pradesh marked a pivotal moment for the state, but it quickly became evident that the true challenge lay not in the promise of funds, but in how those funds would be put to use. Obviously, Arunachal had neither prior experience nor capacity to handle such a huge development package. The creation of a Project Monitoring Unit (PMU) within the Planning Department of the State Government in 2010 was the first critical step toward transforming policy into tangible development. Tasked with overseeing the projects under the Prime Minister's package, the PMU had to be built from the ground up, ensuring rigorous coordination between departments and constant monitoring.

To provide high-level oversight, a PM Package Monitoring Committee, chaired by the Chief Secretary, was established. This committee, with the Director of the PMU acting as its Member Secretary, conducted regular reviews. Meetings were held weekly and fortnightly at the PMU level, and monthly at the Committee level, pushing a steady progress. The committee's role was to break down inter-departmental silos, resolve execution bottlenecks, and keep projects moving forward.

Yet, as with any major infrastructure initiative, obstacles arose. Securing clearances under environmental regulations was one of the toughest challenges. Permissions were needed for the diversion of forest land, compensatory afforestation, and payment of net present value, not to mention plans for disposing of muck. Several proposals had to pass through Wildlife Boards and ultimately gain approval from the Ministry of Environment and Forests. These bureaucratic layers caused frustrating delays, often leaving the PMU with little recourse to accelerate progress.

Another persistent hurdle was land acquisition. Arunachal Pradesh, with its entirely tribal population and community land system, lacked formal land records, further complicating the process. Governed by the Jhum Land Regulation, compensation for land acquisition sometimes invited unethical practices. More informed individuals would purchase land from unsuspecting villagers around project sites, seeking to claim higher compensation once the projects commenced. This exploitation not only sowed mistrust but also caused significant delays in the implementation of many projects.

Despite these obstacles, the creation of the PMU and its diligent monitoring efforts represented a vital first step. However, the road to successful implementation required more than just administrative oversight- it called for a delicate balance between development, environmental stewardship, and the fair treatment of local communities. The success of this ambitious package lay not just in the hands of policy-makers, but in the ability to navigate the unique challenges of the region.

Despite the challenges, significant progress was made. However, some projects remain incomplete due to persistent issues with land acquisition and environmental clearances. Moving forward, the need to streamline these processes and ensure that all stakeholders work collaboratively to overcome these hurdles were felt. The state continued to build on the momentum generated by the Special Economic Package, leveraging its strategic importance to foster sustainable development and regional stability.

The Special Economic Package for Arunachal Pradesh was a landmark initiative that promised to transform the state's infrastructure and economic landscape. The implementation journey, while fraught with challenges, demonstrated the importance of strategic planning, political will, and effective coordination in realising such ambitious projects.

The 1,600 KM Trans-Arunachal Highway connecting the state from East to West is not just a road, but a line of interaction and integration between tribes; a line of confluence and development of the pan Arunachal identity. The majestic State Civil Secretariat, Legislative Assembly are some of the icons which came out of the package. These are not merely structures and symbols of governance; they are sanctuaries where citizens place their trust and hopes, seeking support for a better future.

As the state continues to navigate its developmental journey, the lessons learned from this path breaking experience will undoubtedly shape its future endeavours. Some other announcements, as we will see later, such as the 2,880 MW Dibang Multipurpose Project and the Greenfield airport would take shape subsequently.

The fruits of development were tangible and resonated deeply with the spirit of Arunachal Pradesh, embodying its relentless pursuit of progress and self-reliance. As the state continues to navigate its future, the lessons from its past will serve as a guiding light, ensuring that Arunachal Pradesh not only preserves its rich cultural heritage but also thrives as a dynamic and integral part of the Indian Union.

In conclusion, this major development package was indeed a landmark and a defining moment for the State. It has achieved remarkable success, transforming the landscape with significant advancements in road, rail, and administrative infrastructure. The project has not only delivered tangible improvements but has also faced and overcome numerous challenges along the way. These experiences have imparted valuable lessons that will guide future initiatives. The people have witnessed first-hand the benefits of true development, experiencing enhanced connectivity and efficiency. As we look forward, the way ahead involves building on these successes, addressing any remaining issues, and continuously striving for greater progress and innovation in our development efforts.

This was just the beginning! Arunachal Pradesh was on the brink of riding a powerful wave of development. But, as with any great journey, there was a momentary storm-a political upheaval that tested the very fabric of the State. Whether fair or unjust, this period of churning was something the people of Arunachal Pradesh had to endure. Yet, the indomitable spirit of the Arunachalee people-resilient, unyielding-would not be subdued. They brushed off the challenges and pressed forward, driven by an insatiable desire to achieve greatness. It was this very spirit that ignited an unstoppable force of progress, unleashing the animal spirits of development across the State. Let's see how this unfolds.

PART FOUR

THE GOLDEN DECADE

The period of 2014 to 2024 could easily be termed as the Golden Decade for Arunachal Pradesh. It was during this phase that the State witnessed an unprecedented jump in the share of central taxes, devolved through the recommendations of both the 14th Finance Commission (FC) and the 15th Finance Commission; while the 14th FC was the watershed paving way for the increased share, the 15th FC consolidated and enhanced Arunachal's share of taxes. It was during this period that Arunachal's most valuable asset was taken cognizance of and duly rewarded.

Increased Devolution meant more funds for development. Hence the state could take up more infrastructure projects, while many new social welfare and self-employment schemes were also conceived for the benefit of the people.

During the same period, the Northeast Region as a whole and Arunachal Pradesh in particular received special attention from the Central Government led by the Prime Minister himself. From 2014 to 2024, India's North-eastern region saw significant transformation driven by Prime Minister Narendra Modi's focused initiatives. This part explores the strategic shift from promises to concrete actions, emphasising the central Government's commitment to the Region's development.

Many important projects announced in 2008, which were incomplete because of various reasons, got a major fillip. The Trans Arunachal Highway neared completion, the Railway line to Naharlagun was commissioned, the Airport at Itanagar was made operational, 3,000 MW Dibang Multipurpose Project made major strides with all clearances in place and ready for on-site works.

Psychologically, the call for the First Village instead of the Last border village, had a very positive impact. The Vibrant Village Program, a programme for developing the border villages was a big boost to the Border Villagers, the first sentinels. Let's see how the development landscape of Arunachal Pradesh in particular and the region in general transformed during this decade.

*"The impediment to action advances action.
What stands in the way becomes the way."*
– Marcus Aurelius

12

From Trees to Treasure: *The Green Boost*

On 12.12.1996, the Supreme Court of India delivered a landmark judgement. The *Godavarman Case*[244] was more than a legal battle-it was a turning point in protection of forests from wanton exploitation. It began as one man's plea to save the Nilgiri forest and transformed into a nationwide movement, reshaping views on preservation of our natural heritage. This landmark case with the full weight of the Supreme Court reoriented the modus of conservation of forests across the country. It wasn't about saving trees; it was about redefining our relationship with nature and ensuring that future generations inherit a world still rich in wilderness. Arunachal was to be impacted by this judgement, as the decision stopped all felling in Arunachal too. The many thriving plywood and associated factories were closed overnight. None would have predicted that this judgement, which then was an impactful decision for Arunachal Pradesh, would turn out to be a blessing in disguise. Let's see, how?

Arunachal Pradesh, the largest state in Northeast India, is a land of stark contrasts. It is vast and rugged, yet sparsely populated and landlocked, making development a challenging endeavour. The state's terrain is a tapestry of dense forests, towering mountains, and winding rivers, but these natural wonders also create formidable barriers to progress. The scattered population, spread across isolated villages and hamlets, only adds to the complexity, making the task of development akin to piecing together a sprawling, intricate puzzle.

One of the most daunting challenges is the region's monsoon season. For 7 to 8 months each year, Arunachal Pradesh is drenched in heavy rains, transforming its roads into rivers and its fields into swamps. The monsoon is not only an inconvenience; it is a force of nature that disrupts life and development in profound ways. The rains don't slow down progress-they actively undo it, washing away roads, damaging bridges, and eroding hillsides. The cost of maintaining infrastructure in such a climate is staggering, with each year bringing new repairs and rebuilding efforts. It's as if the state is locked in an endless struggle with nature, fighting to keep what it has built from being swept away.

Yet, amid these challenges lies a treasure of unimaginable value. Arunachal Pradesh is home to some of the richest forests in the world, a veritable Eden teeming with life. These forests are more than a backdrop to the state's natural beauty-they are a biodiversity hotspot, filled with countless species of plants and animals, many of which are still undiscovered. This ecological wealth is an unparalleled asset, a green treasure trove that could be the state's greatest boon or its biggest burden.

This delicate balance was recognized in 1996, when the landmark judgement put a halt to unchecked logging, ensuring that Arunachal Pradesh's forests would not fall victim to the chainsaw. Since then, the state's forest cover has only grown, untouched by the rampant deforestation that has plagued other parts of the world. The time had come to cash in on this green dollar. Could the Finance Commissions help in yielding this aspiration?

One of the primary financial sources for the state is the allocation of grants through the Finance Commissions[245], which are mandated under Article 280 of the Indian Constitution. The Finance Commission devises a formula for the vertical devolution of taxes collected by the central Government and recommends a formula for horizontal inter-se distribution among the states based on criteria like population, area, income distance, tax effort, and fiscal discipline.

Until the 13th Finance Commission,[246]Arunachal Pradesh received fewer grants due to its small population and the state's inability to effectively present its unique challenges. For Arunachal Pradesh, the 13th Finance Commission recommended a share of 0.328% of the aggregate central taxes devolved to all states, which was inadequate given the state's unique geographical and economic conditions. These challenges included recognizing the forest as both an ecological resource and a development obstacle, the high per capita cost of delivering public services, and the general cost disabilities faced by the state. Historically, Finance Commissions have used various criteria for distributing central taxes among states.

The following table outlines the criteria used by previous commissions:

Criteria	Ninth	Tenth	Eleventh	Twelfth	Thirteenth
Contribution	10%	-	-	-	-
Distance of per capita income	45%	33.50%	60%	60%	62.5%
Population	22.5%	25%	20%	20%	10%
Backwardness	11.25%	12.50%	-	-	-
Inverse of per capita income	11.25%	12.50%	-	-	-
Area	-	-	5%	5%	7.5%
Infrastructure	-	-	5%	5%	5%
Tax effort	-	-	10%	-	7.5%
Fiscal discipline/Self reliance	-	16.5%	-	10%	7.5%

This table shows that the last several Finance Commissions have placed greater weight on the "Income" and "Population" criteria, with lesser weight on factors like "Geographical Area" and "Fiscal Discipline." Importantly, factors such as "Environment and Forest Conservation" and "Backwardness" have not been given any weightage, resulting in a low percentage share for states like Arunachal Pradesh in the overall distribution of central taxes. As a consequence, Arunachal Pradesh was perpetually in a vicious cycle of juggling its meagre resources between revenue and capital expenditure; revenue temporarily eroding the capital funds. Frequently, the State would be compelled to resort to Ways and Means Advances (WMA)[247] of the Reserve Bank of India to finance the day to day running of the Government. This would obviously impact the critical development needs of the State.

14th Finance Commission-The Game Changer?

The 14[248] Finance Commission, chaired by Dr. Y V Reddy[248] was a ray of hope for the turnaround. Under the Presidential order dated January 2, 2013, the Fourteenth Finance Commission was tasked with recommending the distribution of tax proceeds between the Union and the States. This distribution is essential because there is often a mismatch between the responsibilities of the states and their ability to raise adequate revenues. Additionally, it aims to reduce inequalities among states vis-a-vis their revenue capacities and the cost of providing goods and services. It also recommends fiscal transfers from the centre to the states to address both vertical and horizontal imbalances.

The Fourteenth Finance Commission had several critical tasks, crucial being the following:

1. Determine the proportion of central taxes shared between the Centre and the States.
2. Specify criteria for the distribution of these taxes among the states.
3. Determine the weights attached to different allocation criteria.

Presenting a Convincing Case

Chief Minister Nabam Tuki gave a single instruction to the bureaucracy to present a strong case with the mandate to keep the State's interest paramount. Led by Chief Secretary Ramesh Negi, the Planning Department initiated extensive preparatory work to present a compelling case to the Commission. This involved gathering and integrating extensive data and inputs for the report and holding regular brainstorming sessions and making multiple trips to Delhi to meet with the Secretary to the 14[248] Finance Commission, A N Jha to present our case. It was the foresight of the State administration to make our forest cover the rallying point and present a compelling case before the Commission. Through several rounds of meetings and deliberations, the state crystallised its arguments on two specific points:

- The devolution formula should give significant weight to forest cover, initially considering it on the lines of Carbon Credit.
- More weight should be placed on the area and less on tax efforts.

As per tradition, the Commission visits each state to hear their cases firsthand. For Arunachal Pradesh, the visit was scheduled for June 23rd 2014. Given the peak monsoon season, the helicopter stationed at Guwahati for the Commission to travel to Itanagar had to be cancelled due to inclement weather. The Commission was compelled to travel by road, a journey fraught with floods and detours through village roads. This would normally mean a difficult start and the Commission's perception may not have been in the State's favour. Such a scenario would have huge implications. After all, the Commission would decide on how much grant Arunachal receives for the next five years. Despite these apprehensions, the state officials remained hopeful but anxious about the impression this arduous journey would leave on the Commission members. In fact, much to our relief, we learnt later that it was this journey which was an eye-opener for the Commission, which laid bare the inherent difficulties of the region, incomprehensible from the cosy rooms of Delhi.

The Commission faced numerous hurdles during the journey, including floods and a delayed arrival. Despite their visibly tired and weary appearance, the state officials did their best to present their case convincingly. Would it result in a favourable recommendation?

Argument for a New Formula

We strongly argued that transfers must aim to correct imbalances in overall resource flows and support the development of peripheral and backward regions. Special Category States like Arunachal Pradesh face unique challenges, including adverse credit-deposit ratios, unattractive investment climates due to geographical and climatic conditions, and underdeveloped infrastructure. Therefore, any formula for resource sharing must seek to reduce inequities among states regarding their revenue-raising capacity and public service standards.

The State Government thus urged the Fourteenth Finance Commission to:

1.	Increase the state's share of central taxes from the current 32% to 50% and include surcharges, cess, and service tax in the shared resources.

2.	Adequately increase Arunachal Pradesh's inter-se share in the divisible pool.

3.	Provide appropriate financial provisions for conserving forests and maintaining ecological balance, suggesting at least a 10% weightage for "Environment and Forest Conservation" in the tax allocation formula.

4.	Consider the state's topography, harsh climate, long international border, higher cost of service provisioning, large geographical area, infrastructural deficits, remoteness from markets, and dispersed population when determining the state's share in central taxes.

These were our main submissions before the Commission. We had made our points. All we could do was anxiously wait, like a young scholar awaiting her exam results.

Final Recommendations and Arunachal Pradesh

YV Reddy, a seasoned administrator was quick to read the issues of the State. The comprehensive preparation and the compelling presentation of our case paid off, as the Commission recognized the unique challenges faced by Arunachal Pradesh. As Arunachal Pradesh's convincing arguments found resonance with the 14th Finance Commission, for the first time in the history, forest as a wealth was rewarded.

Accordingly, 'Keeping in view the ecological benefits and the need to support States in shouldering the responsibility of managing the environment, we have decided to consider area covered by forests as one of the important criteria for horizontal devolution. The devolution formula, thus, captures both revenue and cost disability and also enables the States to consider forests as a national treasure that needs to be protected'.[249]

A weightage of 7.5% was given to areas under forest cover, which was never considered by all previous Commissions. The overall percentage of devolution from the divisible pool was also enhanced to 42%. Another major shift was the weightage given to area from 10% in the 13th Finance Commission to 15%[250]. Arunachal Pradesh would be the biggest beneficiary of these pathbreaking recommendations. Our inter-se share (Arunachal's share amongst states) of central taxes jumped from a mere 0.328% to 1.370%.[251] This was an unprecedented jump, perhaps the highest amongst any other state of India.

Criteria	Weight (%)
1. Income Distance	50
2. Population (1971)	17.5
3. Area	15
4. Demographic Change (2011)	10
5. Forest Cover	**7.5**

There were speculations that the recommendations of the Commission were too heavily tilted in favour of the States, leaving less resources for the Union Government, and therefore, the same may not be accepted. The new NDA Government (National Democratic Alliance- Coalition Govt led by Bharatiya Janata Party) accepted the recommendations in toto in the true spirit of cooperative federalism and to quote Prime Minister Modi, *"We want to promote cooperative federalism in the country. At the same time, we want a competitive element among the states. I call this new form of federalism Cooperative and Competitive Federalism"*[252] This gave unprecedented fiscal elbow room to the State to undertake developmental activities. In effect 'the benefits of FFC transfers are highest ......for states like Arunachal Pradesh....among the SCS (Special Category States)'[253].

The tentative devolution during the five-year period of 2015-16 to 2020-21 was estimated at Rs. 55,000 Crores, which was indeed a huge jump from the 13th FC devolution of Rs. 9,103.80 Crores. This huge resource base now available with the state, provided the Government with huge room for manoeuvring the felt needs of development in the state.

Hence, the 14th FC recommendations are by far one of the most significant events in shaping today's Arunachal Pradesh.

15th FC: Consolidating the formula of 14th FC

The 15th Finance Commission was constituted to recommend the devolution formula for the period of 2020-21 to 2025-26, NK Singh was appointed as Chairman with AN Jha as Member amongst others. It is pertinent to note that AN Jha was the Secretary of the 14th FC. The recommendation for vertical devolution was increased from 40% to 41%[254]. The Commission added a new dimension to the forest criteria by naming it forest and ecology and increasing the weightage from 7.5% to 10%[255]. With this, the inter se state share for Arunachal Pradesh increased further to 1.760% for the period 2020-21 to 2025-26. Consolidating on the 14th FC, the 15th FC provided for more devolution, which would provide sufficient resources to steer the felt needs of the State and aspirations of the people.

The forest cover of Arunachal Pradesh remained the single most important determinant in the massive jump in share of devolution of tax revenue in both the 14th FC and the 15th FC. The calculation by the 15th FC on inter-se weightage on forest and ecology reveals that Arunachal Pradesh has the highest share at 13.302 followed by Madhya Pradesh with 10.563[256]. Once a debilitating factor towards 'development', these trees actually turned out to be treasures, one of immense value in enhancing the quality of life of the population and development index of Arunachal Pradesh. However, it is imperative to realise that this *green boost* is a factor of the cover of forest, and therefore, an added responsibility upon policy makers and citizens alike that this 'golden goose' needs our utmost care.

Between both the Commissions, the 10 years from 2015 to 2025, Arunachal Pradesh would be amongst the states receiving highest percentage increase in share of tax devolutions in the country, and certainly the highest amongst the smaller states. In this context the decade could be easily called the Golden Decade for Arunachal Pradesh.

In a twist of fate, the very obstacle that once threatened to stall progress became the catalyst for an unprecedented surge in development. What seemed like an insurmountable challenge-a state starved of funds and struggling to meet the aspirations of its people-transformed into an opportunity that brought unexpected prosperity. The influx of funds, sparked by the obstacle itself, not only fuelled long-awaited projects but also rekindled hope and ambition among the people. This turn of events underscored a timeless truth: sometimes, the greatest sources of growth and change emerge from the very challenges we fear the most. The state's journey from scarcity to abundance is a testament to the power of resilience, proving that what stands in the way can indeed become the way, a reward for the tribal way of life; living close and with nature.

It must be borne in mind that a Commission's recommendation is one aspect and accepting the recommendations by the Union Government is the crucial factor. When the 14th FC recommendations were submitted, the National Democratic Alliance (NDA) Government was in place, after a resounding victory. The leader of the Alliance and Prime Minister, Narendra Modi had been Chief Minister for twelve and half years. He was fully acquainted with the aspirations of States and the fiscal constraints they faced. Despite the recommendation devolving a substantial share of central taxes, the Government accepted the recommendation in toto. Indeed, cooperative federalism was displayed in letter and spirit. After all, if the states grow, the nation grows.

With the 15th Finance Commission period coming to an end, the 16th Finance Commission has been constituted with Dr. Arvind Panagariya as Chairman for recommending devolution of share of taxes from the divisible pool for the period 2026-31. Considering the importance of their recommendations, Arunachal Pradesh would be keenly watching the developments. All we can do is keep our fingers crossed and make our case heard, and heard well.

"For me, every village at the border is the first village of the country. The people living at the border make for the country's strong guard"
– Prime Minister Shri Narendra Modi

13

Touchdown in the Frontier: *Giving Wings to Tribal Aspirations*

The '*Iron Bird*' was nothing new for the frontier population. Right from the 1940s, during World War II- because of the '*Hump Mission*', tribes would be witness to the numerous 'loud sounding' Iron Birds flying over them, all heading to China, many crashing enroute. Post-Independence, the Indian Air Force and more so, the Kalinga Airlines serviced the frontier region. Most remote Assam Rifles positions were air maintained, because of lack of surface communication.

'*Wangnyum, the younger son of Chowphaa Wanglin III, was inducted into the NEFA Administration as a Village Level Worker (VLW) in 1954 along with Wangdong Medam and Jaliam Medam of Borduria Village. In the early 50s. The three were sent to Pasighat for basic training on the latest agricultural technology. The 20 minute flight to Pasighat was operated by Kalinga Airlines, owned by Biju Patnaik. It was a World War II vintage Dakota aircraft.*'[257] Looks like some Frontier people flew long before they ever travelled by motor vehicle.

Kalinga Airlines was a private airline based in Calcutta, India. It was founded in 1947 by aviator and politician Biju Patnaik, who was also the airline's chief pilot. The airline was nationalised and merged into Indian Airlines in 1953.[258] Biju Babu has entered the Hall of Fame of Pilots for flying improvised aircrafts in the "Hump" operations to supply the Chinese nationalists- one of the most challenging air operations in World War II.[259] Hence, he was familiar with the NEFA skies. The Kalinga Airlines have (had) a contract with the NEFA Administration for airlift of stores.[260]

NEFA was well serviced in the 1960s and 70s by Air. Ziro, Daporijo, Walong, Aalo, Tuting, Vijaynagar, Alinye, Mechukha, Pasighat (Paglek, PI Line)[261] all had landing grounds serviced by Otter, Caribou, Douglas aircrafts. Anecdotes suggest that for retailers at Aalo, it was cheaper to charter a plane to bring their merchandise from Dibrugarh than by roads! However, over time during the 1980s, air service declined and most of these Landing Grounds fell into disuse.

With central Government's changed outlook towards Arunachal Pradesh, as part of the 2008 development package, all these ALGs were also to be revived. Today, Mechukha, Ziro, Aalo, Walong, Tuting, Vijaynagar, Pasighat ALGs are operational landing grounds. Yet because of the limited runway length, their usage is limited.

An airport for the state capital, which was conceptualised in 2005, was also announced in 2008. Yet, the airport could not make any headway owing to a plethora of reasons- site selection, litigation, land compensation issues. As such, Arunachal Pradesh remained the only State in India with no airport in its Capital, till recently.

Things were to change when Prime Minister Modi laid the foundation stone for the Greenfield Airport at Itanagar, the State Capital on February 9th of 2019. Despite COVID pandemic, within a record time, the airport was inaugurated by Prime Minister Modi on November 19th of 2022 with much fanfare. This was perhaps the biggest infrastructural achievement of Arunachal in recent times. Giving wings to the frontier had the power to unleash the untapped potential of the state. It was aptly named *'Donyi Polo Airport'*, which literally means 'Sun and Moon', representing the indigenous faith of the state.

This was the 3rd Airport in Arunachal Pradesh after Tezu and Pasighat and the 16th in Northeast India. But this one was special; it has capabilities to cater to large commercial aircrafts with night landing facilities; a true link to the rest of India and the world. *"Today is a joyous and historic day for the people of Arunachal Pradesh. Three years ago, Prime Minister Modi came to lay the foundation stone of the greenfield airport.*

Though the COVID pandemic created havoc, within a span of three years, the Prime Minister himself has flown from Delhi and inaugurated the Donyi Polo airport. It's a proud moment for every Arunachali," said Chief Minister Pema Khandu in his address.[262]

LK Advani during his visit to Arunachal Pradesh had said in 2003, *"Arunachal Delhi se door hey, par dil se nahin."*[263] With the Donyi Polo Airport, Delhi is now two hours away, bridging the physical distance too.

Since 2014, India's Northeast in general and Arunachal Pradesh in particular has become a focus area with the Prime Minister re-imagining and expanding the Look East Policy initiative to the "Act East" Policy. Prime Minister Modi's dedication to the development of the Region is underscored by his frequent visits. Between 2014 and 2023, Modi visited the Northeast approximately 60 times, a record number that surpasses the combined visits of all his predecessors. These visits were instrumental in launching and overseeing various development projects, ensuring that the central Government's initiatives were effectively implemented on ground. Modi's visits were not just ceremonial; they were strategic, aimed at fostering economic growth, improving infrastructure, and integrating the region more closely with the rest of the country.

Policy of Regular Ministerial Visits

To further accelerate the region's development, a policy was institutionalised where a Union Minister visited each Northeastern state every 15 days. This initiative, coordinated by the Ministry of Development of North Eastern Region (MDoNER), aimed to maximise the efficacy of projects and schemes implemented by the Government. By 2023, 74 Union Ministers had made over 148 visits to the Northeast, leave alone the numerous visits of senior Government functionaries. These visits were crucial in mapping the aspirations and sentiments of the local population, ensuring that the projects were aligned with the needs of the people. To put this in context, earlier visits to Delhi for each and every aspiration of the Region was the norm. Now Delhi came to the Region to give the much needed impetus for development.

These visits facilitated announcement and monitoring of substantial infrastructure projects. Projects worth Rs. 1,34,200 crores were announced, including 4,000 km of roads, 20 railway projects covering 2,011 km, and 15 air connectivity projects. The development of national waterways on the Brahmaputra and Barak rivers further improved connectivity, leveraging the cost-effective riverine systems of India and Bangladesh. These projects are part of a broader strategy to enhance the region's infrastructure, making it more accessible and economically vibrant. Road Connectivity got a major boost with the total length of National Highways in the region increasing from 8,480 km in 2013-14 to 15,735 km in 2022-23, showcasing a remarkable growth of 85.55%. Arunachal has been a major beneficiary with 64% growth in road length since 2016 with about 20,000 KM of road built during this period, which includes about 2,500 KM of National Highways. 4G telecom, railways and airways further cemented the region with the mainstream during this period.

To streamline and enhance the monitoring of these visits, MDoNER launched the "Poorvottar Sampark Setu" portal. This portal provides valuable insights and graphical information about state-wise and district-wise visits of Union Ministers. It helps generate summary reports on the progress of various projects, making it easier to track and manage the implementation of development initiatives. The portal is a powerful tool designed to ensure transparency and accountability in the execution of government schemes.

PM Modi's and Union Ministers' frequent visits to India's Northeast ensured effective implementation of development projects, leading to significant infrastructural and economic improvements in the region. These efforts exemplify the central Government's commitment to integrating the Northeast into the national growth narrative. The strategic focus on infrastructure, connectivity, and regional integration has transformed the Northeast, making it a vital part of India's development story. Arunachal Pradesh stood as the biggest beneficiary of the eager indulgence of the Centre.

Digital Governance: Connecting the Unconnected

Digital India was another initiative that brought profound change to the region. Before this push, large parts of Arunachal Pradesh were digitally disconnected, existing in a kind of technological isolation. The introduction of improved digital infrastructure changed this dramatically.

Suddenly, what was once out of reach became accessible. Students could access educational resources from across the globe, farmers could get real-time information about markets, and ordinary citizens could avail Government services without having to make long, arduous journeys. The digital divide that had long kept Arunachal Pradesh on the fringes was beginning to close, and with it, new opportunities for growth and development were opening up. With about 1,500 more 4G towers under execution, connectivity in the Vibrant Border villages will get massive boost.

This wasn't just about the internet-it was about connection in the broader sense. It was about ensuring that the people of Arunachal Pradesh were not left behind in the digital revolution, that they too could participate fully in the nation's progress.

Political Participation at the National Level

If political representation is any yardstick for a state's importance to be measured in the national context, the case of Arunachal Pradesh is a curious one! Out of 543 Members of Parliament in Lok Sabha, Arunachal Pradesh has only 2 Members. That would translate to a bare 0.37%. In an electoral democracy, what are the odds that from the 0.37%, one can hope for a Ministerial berth in the Centre? According to the Constitution of India, the total number of Ministers in the Council of Ministers must not exceed 15% of the total number of members of the Lok Sabha. Looks like a very long shot by any stretch of imagination. Here comes Kiren Rijiju, representing the Western Parliamentary Constituency. Incidentally, he represents my Constituency. Since 2014, Rijiju has been tasked with some of the most important Ministerial assignments. He began as Minister of State for Home Affairs from 2014 to 2019, Minister of State for Minority Affairs from 2019 to 2021, Minister of State (Independent Charge) for Sports and Youth Affairs from 2019 to 2021. He held the prestigious portfolio of Law from 2021 to 2023 and was moved as the Cabinet Minister of Earth Sciences and Food Processing Industries in the Government of India from 2023 till June 2024. Currently, he is serving as the 28th Minister of Parliamentary Affairs and 7th Minister of Minority Affairs.

Looking back in time, Daying Ering served as Parliamentary Secretary in the Ministry of Home Affairs in the first Indira Gandhi ministry from 15 February 1966 to 13 March 1967[264]. He again served as Deputy Minister in the Ministry of Food, Agriculture, Community Development and Cooperation in Second Indira Gandhi Ministry from 18 March 1967 to 21 June 1970. Further, PK Thungon served as Deputy Minister for Supply and Rehabilitation (1980-1982) and Deputy Minister in the Ministry of Education, Culture and Social Welfare (1982-1984) in Third Indira Gandhi Ministry. Then he served as Minister of State in the Ministry of Commerce and Industry (1991-1992), Ministry of Industry- Department of Heavy Industry and Public Enterprises (1992-1993), Ministry of Urban Affairs and Employment in (1993-1995) in P. V. Narasimha Rao Ministry.

The political history of Arunachal Pradesh at the national level has come full circle. With Kiren holding some really prestigious portfolios in the Modi Cabinet, it is made amply clear that national Interests don't always work according to electoral numbers. Calibre and credibility far outweigh a state's numerical representation when answering the call of duty for the nation.

Frontier Villages as first Villages of the Country

The Prime Minister's seemingly straightforward statement carried profound implications, marking a significant shift in how both the Government and the public perceive border villages. These remote outposts, long viewed as mere dots on a map, are now recognized as the true guardians of our frontier. In April 2023, Union Home Minister Amit Shah made a landmark visit to Kibithoo in Arunachal Pradesh and chose to launch the National Vibrant Villages Programme (VVP) from this border village. His presence underscored the Government's dedication to elevating these distant outposts into the vanguard of India's progress, highlighting their strategic and cultural importance.

The Vibrant Villages Programme has already begun to reshape Arunachal Pradesh. This ambitious initiative is designed to turn border villages into bustling centres of development, curbing migration and weaving these communities into the fabric of national life. In the first phase, the programme had earmarked 455 villages in Arunachal Pradesh for this transformative effort.

Strategically, the programme is pivotal for bolstering India's border security. By enhancing living conditions and economic prospects in these remote areas, the Government aims to stem out-migration and fortify its presence and vigilance along the frontier.

Beyond its strategic and economic goals, the VVP also celebrates and preserves local culture. Through the organisation of local fairs, the promotion of traditional cuisines, and the support of community-led tourism ventures, the programme seeks to highlight the rich cultural heritage of Arunachal Pradesh. This not only attracts tourism but also fosters a sense of pride and identity within local communities.

In essence, the Vibrant Villages Programme represents a comprehensive strategy for developing Arunachal Pradesh's border villages. By focusing on holistic development and national integration, the programme aims to build sustainable, thriving communities that contribute to both India's security and its cultural wealth. The success of this initiative will lie in how these villages are made into economic hubs; mostly centring around tourism and not looking only through strategic imperatives. This will bring in the vibrancy which has been envisioned through the programme.

Viksit Arunachal key to Viksit Bharat

Prime Minister Modi's vision for India's development was inclusive, emphasising that the country's progress was intrinsically linked to the development of India's Northeast. This perspective was reflected in substantial investments in infrastructure, healthcare, education, and connectivity. Within the Northeast, development of Arunachal assumes special imperative, considering the remoteness and its strategic location.

Since 2016, Arunachal Pradesh has made remarkable strides in both economic stability and infrastructure development, reflecting a period of significant transformation. The state's economic landscape has seen impressive growth. The Gross State Domestic Product (GSDP) has more than doubled, rising from ₹20,373 crore in 2016 to ₹48,028 crore in 2023. Similarly, the state budget has grown substantially, from ₹12,533 crore to ₹29,657 crore. This financial growth has been accompanied by a sharp increase in per capita income, which has more than doubled over the same period. GST collections and the number of taxpayers have both surged dramatically, indicating a robust improvement in fiscal health and revenue generation.

The advancements in infrastructure have been equally striking. The average annual road construction has seen an eightfold increase, significantly enhancing connectivity across the state. Rural roads have expanded more than threefold, vastly improving accessibility in remote areas. National Highways have also seen considerable growth, contributing to better transportation networks. Electrification efforts have successfully brought power to more households, and the availability of drinking water connections has increased dramatically, ensuring widespread access to clean water.

During the same period, the Northeast region experienced remarkable improvements in infrastructure, particularly with a substantial expansion of its National Highway network. Over this period, the length of National Highways in the Northeast grew by an impressive 4,950 kilometres. This ambitious project involved an investment of ₹41,459 crore, reflecting a significant commitment to enhancing connectivity and supporting regional development. From 2014 to 2023, the Northeast region saw major upgrades to its rail network. 1,618 kilometres of new railway sections were introduced, which was 170% more than the average Kms added each year from 2009 to 2014. This included the creation of new rail lines, conversion of existing tracks to a broader gauge, and doubling of tracks.

This comprehensive growth in the highway and rail network not only improved transportation efficiency across other parts of the country but also played a crucial role in boosting economic activities and accessibility within the Northeast, bridging gaps between remote areas and major urban centres.

These infrastructure improvements have had a profound impact on the socio-economic landscape of Arunachal Pradesh. Enhanced connectivity has facilitated the faster movement of goods and people, which is crucial for economic activities and integration with the national market. Improved roads and railways have boosted tourism, agriculture, and local industries providing new employment opportunities and fostering regional development.

The boost in connectivity and infrastructure has played a key role in fostering peace and reducing violence in the region. Reports indicate a 73% decrease in violent incidents from 2014 to 2023, reflecting the broader stability that accompanies economic progress. Prime Minister Modi's emphasis on the Northeast, with significant infrastructure investments, has notably transformed the region and Arunachal Pradesh.

Overall, these developments reflect a period of dynamic progress, with substantial improvements in both economic stability and infrastructure that are transforming the state's landscape and quality of life for its residents.

In the evolving landscape of Indian governance, the 'Double Engine Sarkar' model emerges as a game-changer, propelling regional development through a dynamic partnership between the central and state governments.

Through this model, the joint efforts of both levels of Government have revolutionised Arunachal Pradesh. This dynamic synergy has led to remarkable advancements in infrastructure, economic growth, and regional security. By further focusing strategically on connectivity and regional integration, the Northeast can become a cornerstone of India's broader development story. Much more remains to be done to fully realise the immense potential of these *Ashtalakshmi* States.

In effect, the vast resource base of North East India and more so of Arunachal Pradesh, if sustainably harnessed, the region can be a major contributor to the long-cherished dream of every Indian to see India as a developed nation. Large mineral deposits, abundant water, beautiful landscape, unparalleled biodiversity and a very talented pool of human resource bring an unimpeachable offer on the table, that the region wants to play a pivotal role in India's growth story. Only a platform with sincere intent is what is required. Not a big ask!

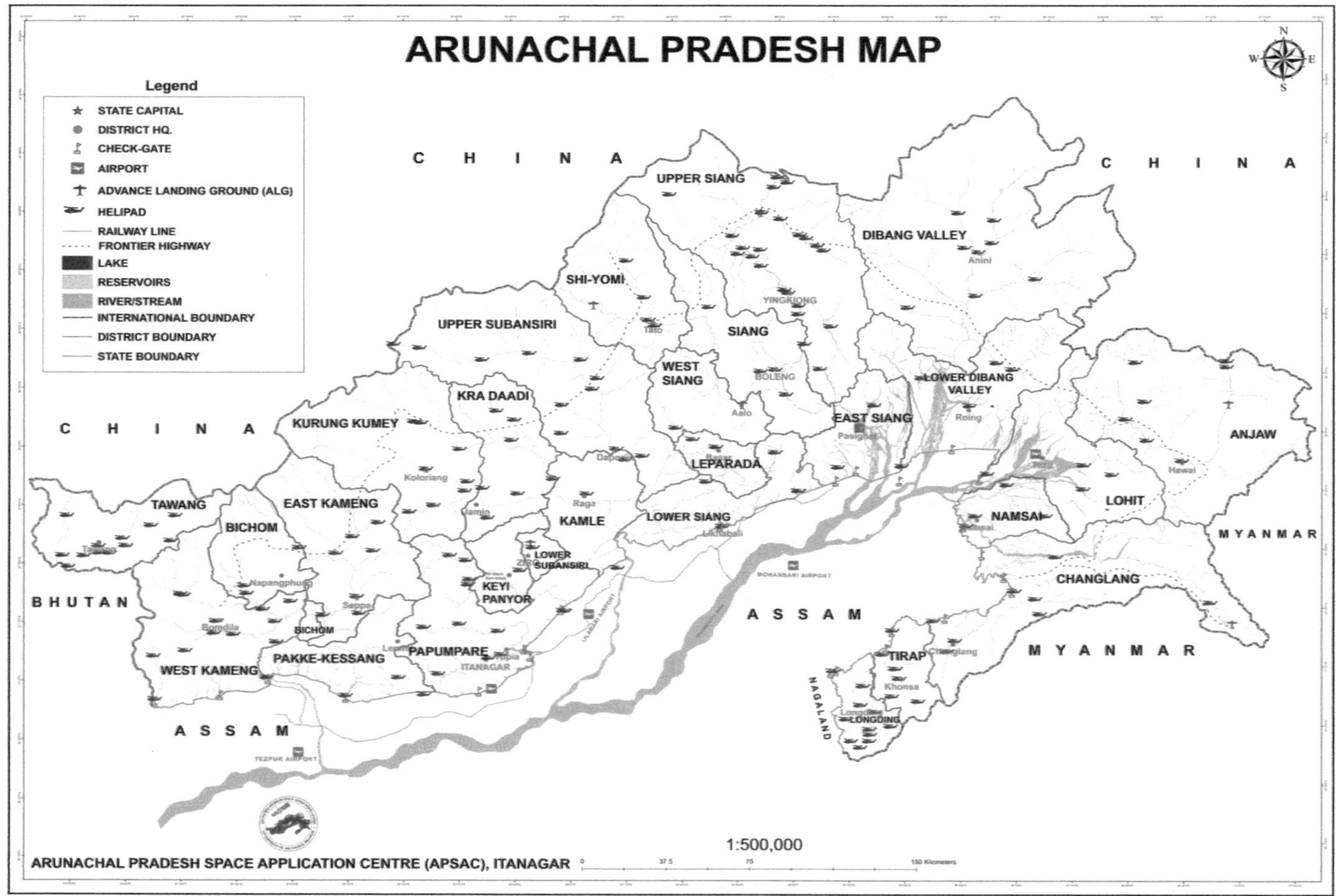

▲ **Map 18:** Map of Airports, Advanced Landing Grounds and Helipads in Arunachal Pradesh, 2024
(Source: Arunachal Pradesh Space Application Centre)

"Reform is not about the status quo. It's about creating a new vision for a better future."
– Unknown

14

Championing Change: *Political Will* for Transforming Lives

While the Union Government displayed sincere commitments towards the development of Northeast India in the last ten years, the State political leadership of Arunachal Pradesh went the extra mile to ride on the reassuring support of the Union Government and embarked on the toughest of reforms in the State. The political will exhibited was no lip service, there was no mincing of words. Public interest was the mantra and would override all other considerations.

Amongst many, the creation of the Arunachal Pradesh Staff Selection Board would perhaps stand out. Earlier, other than group A jobs, a not so transparent system of employment was prevailing. There was a general tendency to fill up these vacancies on political considerations or by relatives of persons involved in the decision-making process. Some vacancies were also up for grabs for extraneous considerations.

Now, this practice led to a vicious cycle where politicians were under immense pressure to oblige their constituents. Every election would be a bargain on how many government job promises would be made. In the process, merit took the biggest toll. Eligible youth with no political connections, no relatives in bureaucracy and no resources to 'buy' jobs reeled under extreme frustration. The net result was a pool of inefficient manpower in the government adversely hampering public service delivery.

To break this 'convenient arrangement' was an uphill task and an unpopular one, politically. This would, therefore, require huge political capital to be invested. The Leadership and Government intention was amply clear and thus by an Act of the Assembly the Arunachal Pradesh Staff Selection Board was constituted. Merit was to be the only consideration for getting into Government Service. This unruffled many vested interests but was very well received by the people of Arunachal, especially the youth. Despite some teething problems and initial hiccups, owing to prompt and exemplary action, the Board could plug the deficiencies and is now a thriving example of transparency in recruitment. As many as 27 APSSB Examinations have been conducted successfully since 2018, wherein about 3.5 Lakh candidates applied and almost 3,200 recommended for Government employment in various categories.

Another malaise plaquing the State was the utter disregard for rule of law and the consequent misappropriations. Stringent action, unheard of earlier, against corrupt practices was undertaken. Many systemic changes were also taken simultaneously to plug the loopholes. Going paperless was the game changer. Arunachal Pradesh was amongst the leading states in migrating to electronic files. This ushered in transparency and eliminated the issues of tampering of files, which the hard files were prone to. With 40 lakh+ files handled online, Arunachal is now the 1st in e-office implementation in North East Region.

The transformations in governance and giving a ray of hope amongst the citizens, that the system will be run on transparency, was perhaps the biggest task. Gaining trust and aligning minds towards a single purpose takes a lot of time. The diversity of Arunachal Pradesh makes the task even more arduous. Yet during the last ten years, the frontier population, especially the youth, rallied behind the thought of a developed and merit-oriented society, ready to embrace the boons of modern development. A lot of this has to do with the honest intention of the leadership to lead the state towards unprecedented development, where every single citizen is an active participant in this journey.

Between 2016 and 2024, the social sector also witnessed incredible improvements. The institutional deliveries went up by 27% and teachers' postings as per norms shot to 90% from meagre 24% in 2016. School dropouts saw an impressive decline from 9% to 2.30% and infant mortality saw a 10% point dip. Moving towards saturation of targeted intervention,

Arunachal Pradesh displayed professionalism and was the first state in Northeast India to achieve 100% saturation in taking piped drinking water to the villages. In the housing schemes, the target achieved was 93% and 96% for urban and rural areas respectively. For farmers, 99% disbursement of PM Kisan Samman Nidhi, 100% Soil Health Card and 99.9% Kisan Credit Card was made possible during the period.[265]

Significant initiatives in these years include the launch of Asia's first Healthcare Drone Network 'Medicine from the Sky,' delivering medicines and diagnostic samples to hitherto unconnected villages. Right from 2016, Arunachal Pradesh has undertaken a massive healthcare infrastructure, manpower and quality upgradation drive to achieve affordable, accessible, equitable and quality healthcare to all citizens. The results of these sustained efforts were seen during the COVID 19 pandemic, where Arunachal Pradesh achieved an astounding recovery rate of over 99%.

Similarly, Arunachal Pradesh stands today as one of the pioneer States moving towards fledged implementation of the National Education Policy, 2020 aiming to provide universal access to education, improve learning outcomes and develop 21st century skills amongst all students and youth. Today, from humble beginnings, Arunachal has achieved a literacy rate well above the national average and reached a 100% Adjusted Net Enrolment Rate in elementary education, a nearly 30% rise since 2015-16. Upgradation of schools and associated infrastructure has also been one of the State's priorities. With an increased network of Schools, India's first 3D printed classrooms and the first State University, significant progress has been made in ensuring accessibility, equity and quality of education at all levels. Lot is yet to be done, especially in improving learning outcomes.

We also witnessed the launch of 5G services in Itanagar and 2,583 villages with 4G connectivity. Kibithoo on the Indo-Tibet border, India's First village, now has 4G connectivity. All this resulted in a 148.6% increase in tourist footfall-36% in foreign tourists and 151.8% in domestic tourists. The State's journey from limited healthcare facilities to doctors passing out from the first medical college of the State is a milestone. The number of medical seats has now increased from fifty to hundred. Impressive assurance scheme of Rs. 5 Lakhs per family has been a boon for many poor families to afford quality healthcare anywhere in India.

While these reforms were reshaping the economic and social landscape, another significant issue was being addressed-the Assam-Arunachal Pradesh boundary dispute. This dispute, which had simmered for decades, was more than just a border issue; it was a source of tension and uncertainty for the people living along the boundary.

The *Namsai Declaration* in 2022 marked the beginning of a new era. By agreeing on the status of the disputed villages, the states took a significant step toward resolving their differences. But it was the Memorandum of Understanding (MoU) in 2023, signed in North Block in presence of the Union Home Minister that truly marked a turning point.

The decades old boundary dispute between Assam and Arunachal Pradesh, which saw bitter litigation, was brought to the negotiating table. The foresight of the leaders both the States of Assam and Arunachal Pradesh brought to closure this dispute. What remains now is delineation on the ground.

For the people living in these disputed areas, this resolution meant a return to peace and normalcy. It meant that they could go about their lives without the fear of conflict, that their homes and livelihoods were no longer in a state of limbo. The resolution of the boundary dispute was not just about drawing lines on a map-it was about healing wounds and building a future where cooperation and development could thrive.

To my mind, the most striking transformation in the State over the last decade has been the shift in attitude. As the saying goes, *"A nation is not defined by its borders or the boundaries of its land, but by the character of its people."* Arunachal Pradesh is no exception-its strength lies in the resolve of its citizens. The real challenge was not merely charting a clear course of action at the leadership level, but instilling that vision into the hearts and minds of every individual. Remarkably, the State has made considerable success in this endeavour. The ripple effect of positive leadership has become contagious, fostering a powerful coalition of goodwill. Unifying diverse aspirations, dismantling vested interests, and rallying the entire State around a common cause is no small feat, yet it has been achieved with remarkable resolve and success. Indeed, the nexus of good is infectious!

The positive momentum is clearly evident in the impressive array of medals won by our sportspersons over the past decade. In recent years, Arunachal Pradesh has also witnessed an inspiring array of success stories that showcase the state's vibrant talent and innovative spirit. Naara Aaba Winery has made a name for itself with its unique Kiwi wine, while Aroty Panyang has brought attention to bamboo architecture with her groundbreaking designs. Many Padma Shris have been awarded to remarkable individuals who exemplify excellence. The music scene has also flourished with talents like Taba Chake, Nabam Takar, Chorun Mugli, Phil Jamja, Dobom Doji and David Angu, who have enriched the cultural landscape. In the field of acting, Riken Ngomle, Chum Darang and Paalin Kabak have captured audiences with their compelling performances. Tourism has also thrived with Oken Tayeng in his pioneering role, and has highlighted the State's unique attractions. Additionally, Lobsang Phuntso of Jamtse Gatsal has gained acclaim for its contribution towards education. These diverse achievements collectively illustrate the State's dynamic growth and the extraordinary potential of its people.

There was, in a sense, an explosion of creativity and entrepreneurial exploration, a development which was received with a mix of enthusiasm, disbelief and sometimes scepticism. A conducive ecosystem for all these to thrive was the quintessential driving force. Overall, there was a visible detonation of pent-up energy in diverse fields such as sports, entrepreneurship and creativity. These remarkable achievements not only underscore individual dedication and skill but also reflect a collective spirit of determination and progress. The growing commitment to nurturing talent and honouring merit vividly demonstrates how optimism and hard work can translate into tangible, proud accomplishments. This thriving ecosystem, however, is one that requires ongoing support and facilitation from the Government to sustain and enhance its success.

Interview of Shri Pema Khandu Ji, Chief Minister of Arunachal Pradesh

1.   From Reluctance to Leadership

You once described yourself as a reluctant politician. Now you are the second longest serving CM of Arunachal Pradesh. How did you come to embrace this path, and how has your journey evolved since becoming Chief Minister?

Although I come from a political family, I never had the ambition or dream to enter politics-it was destiny, I suppose. Once I stepped into political life, I made it a point to always remember that the position I hold is a public responsibility, not something to be treated as a family inheritance. After becoming Chief Minister in 2016, I had the opportunity to implement several reforms in sectors that were holding back the state's progress and address key developmental gaps. Since then, I have been doing my best to serve the public effectively.

2.   Steering through Uncertainty

Arunachal Pradesh has had a history of political instability, with many short-tenured Chief Ministers. What were the biggest challenges you faced in bringing stability to the state, and how did you overcome them?

- Regarding instability, I believe, steps from the numerous challenges related to development and the high aspirations of the people, where expectations often surpass what can realistically be delivered. Arunachal Pradesh is one of the most diverse states in the country, home to many distinct tribes, and geographically, it is the largest state in the Northeast, with a challenging terrain.

- Bringing development to a low-revenue-generating state like Arunachal is indeed a significant challenge. However, I consider myself fortunate that the Union Government, under the leadership of Honourable Prime Minister Shri Narendra Modi, has been supporting the state across all sectors. As a result, visible progress can be seen throughout the entire state.

3. Personal Fulfilment

After almost nine years as Chief Minister, what moment or accomplishment gives you the greatest sense of satisfaction?

- It is all for you to witness for yourself. Key indicators speaks in volume of our accomplishment in the past nine years and it is still ongoing. The fiscal prudence of the state has gained a massive uplift as the GSDP has seen increase of 136% while the state budget has seen an increase of 186% since 2016.

- State own resources soared to 172% in comparison to 2016. We recorded 800% increase in road construction. Our electrification has also seen rise of 104%.

- Health institutional deliveries has seen a rise of 26.7% while education sector has witnessed a quantum leap in terms of infrastructure and enrolment.

- Gearing up to be the future power house of the nation, our installed hydro power capacity has increased to 213% since 2016.

- Beneficiary oriented schemes, be it National Flagship Schemes or State Flagship Schemes, we are doing good in all parameters.

- Around 2,700 border villages have 4G network connectivity now

- The first Medical College started and the MBBS seats in TRIHMS increased from 50 to 100.

- India's first 3D printed classrooms completed in the twin capital city of Itanagar- Naharlagun

- Sela Tunnel inaugurated providing all-weather road connectivity to Tawang, featuring a 2,598-meter tunnel situated at an altitude of over 13,700 feet, with an 8.63 km approach road

- The 500-meter Nechiphu Tunnel inaugurated, located at an altitude of 5,700 feet, unique D-shaped tunnel connecting the Balipara-Charduar-Tawang Road in West Kameng district. It Reduces the distance by 6 km.

- Greenfield Airport- Donyi Polo at Itanagar has connected Arunachal to the National Aviation Map. Donyi Polo Airport has recently received its all-weather license

- Functional Household Tap Connection has been done to all 2,28,926 households. 1st State in North East to declare Har Ghar Jal.

- Our youths are doing wonders in sports as close to 1,100 medals won by sportspersons in various Zonal, National and International Sports Event.

- Sports Policy of Arunachal Pradesh gives 5% reservation in recruitment in State Government jobs and 10% reservation in Police Department

- We have established State Sports Academy in Miao, Changlang and National Center for Sports Science Research which is one out of six in India.

- Sangey Lhaden Sports Academy has been declared as the Khelo India State Center of Excellence for Archery, Hockey, Wushu, Boxing, and Weightlifting

- Massive sports infrastructure is being built to encourage sporting activities in the state.

The list of accomplishment and achievements continues. I have highlighted just a few.

4. The Heart of Arunachal

In your opinion, what is the biggest strength of Arunachal Pradesh and its people? How does this strength shape the state's future?

- As I mentioned earlier, while we face unparalleled challenges, Arunachal Pradesh is also blessed with immense natural resources. The state government has already begun implementing policies to convert these resources into revenue, particularly in the hydropower sector. The day is not far when the state will be generating thousands of crores in revenue.

In addition to natural resources, our human resource holds tremendous potential, especially the youth across every tribe. They simply need guidance and support, and with that, the sky is the limit for what they can achieve.

5. Facing Imminent Challenges

What do you see as the most pressing challenge or danger facing the state today, and what steps should be taken to prepare for it?

Arunachal Pradesh is home to numerous tribal communities, and in the olden days, despite the lack of development, the happiness index was remarkably high among these groups. However, with the passage of time and the influence of modernity, many tribal people have started moving away from their traditional way of life, posing a significant threat to the age-old indigenous culture.

While development is important, it is equally crucial that we remain deeply rooted in our traditions and culture. To address this concern, a special department has been established to preserve and promote the original indigenous culture and traditions among the tribal communities. This initiative aims to ensure that progress and cultural heritage go hand in hand.

6.   Connecting with the People

You've visited all parts of the State, including some of the most remote and inaccessible areas of Arunachal Pradesh. Perhaps the only CM to do so. When you meet people in these distant locations, what is the first thought or feeling that comes to your mind?

Meeting people in the most remote and inaccessible areas of Arunachal Pradesh elicits a profound sense of connection and respect. The first thought or feeling that often comes to my mind is one of deep admiration for their resilience and the strong sense of community they maintain despite the challenges posed by isolation and limited resources. Their unique cultural heritage, traditions, and the warmth with which they greet visitors further evoke a feeling of gratitude and a renewed commitment to addressing their needs and bringing development to these areas. Witnessing their way of life firsthand reminds me of the diverse and rich tapestry that constitutes Arunachal Pradesh and reinforces my dedication to inclusivity and holistic development.

7.   Making Bold Decisions

You've made several bold decisions in the interest of the state, even when they might have been politically risky. How do you find the courage to make such decisions, and what goes through your mind when you know they could affect your political position?

As I mentioned earlier, the position I hold is a public responsibility, and every day I start with the understanding that I must work for the greater good of my state, my nation and the people. When decisions need to be made, they must be made. I don't worry about losing my position for taking tough decisions, as avoiding them would be a waste of both my time and the public's time.

Governments will come and go-that is the nature of our great democracy-but difficult decisions must be made whenever necessary to ensure progress and the well-being of the state

8. Bonding with the Armed Forces

You often make it a point to interact with the Army and Central Armed Police Forces (CAPF) during your visits to border areas. How do these interactions impact you emotionally, and what message do you take away from these meetings?

- The Indian Army and CAPF especially stationed in border areas are not only special to me but to the people of my state and the country. They are standing guard at extreme conditions for our safety and territorial integrity. We cannot forget 1962 and we also know that India and our armed forces are not stuck in 1962. We have moved forward. Under Prime Minister Narendra Modi, India has transformed into a world power. Meeting our armed forces in border outposts swells me with pride as an Indian. I always come back with pleasant memories and try every time to make them feel how special they are and how much the people owe to them.

9. Reform and Legacy

Many refer to you as the "Reform CM" due to the transformative changes you've introduced. Which reform or initiative stands out to you as your personal favourite, and why?

- From day one, I have made it crystal clear that corruption in all forms will be fought tooth and nail. My aim was and will be to bring a visible change in government functioning. This called for a paradigm shift in the work culture, especially of the government employees, starting from the top. Before me, all decisions on policy matters including annual budget formulations were an inhouse matter. We changed it with people's participation. Every policy related decisions were taken after due consultations with all stakeholders including community based organizations, women's organizations, student organizations and all political parties. Before every budget preparation, extensive consultations were made with all stakeholders. Even individuals were invited to give their suggestions online, best of which are awarded and incorporated in our final budget.

To bring in responsibility, accountability and transparency, we adopted the Digital Arunachal venture in line with the Digital India Mission and incorporated e-office for all official transactions as well as communications.

Realizing that the root cause of corruption stems from recruitment of government employees, particularly in Group C and D posts through unethical means, we established the Arunachal Pradesh Staff Selection Board (APSSB). We adopted the zero-tolerance policy towards corruption and even arrested people, irrespective of their position, caught in the act.

Winning back the confidence of people was a major challenge and with cooperation of my colleagues in the government, we could do it. The process though is an ongoing one.

We corrected the recruitment system, improved the health service delivery, enhanced accountability and trust, uplifted the education system, developed robust infrastructure, adopted inclusive policies, aligned technological advances to ease access to public services. By doing so, I can say that we could establish a more robust, just, and progressive society, improving the overall quality of life for our citizens.

Naming a particular reform as my favourite would be improper and unjustified as each reform, we brought in were for the good to our people.

10. Vision for Arunachal's Future

Looking ahead to 2047, when India celebrates 100 years of independence, how do you envision the future of Arunachal Pradesh? What kind of state do you hope to leave behind for the next generation?

When we celebrate 100 years of Independence, I wish to see the parameters we have set in all sectors are achieved. The happiness index of the state increased. We have surplus power, foodgrains and we become the fruit bowl of the country. Our natural resources are sustainably tapped without creating ecological disbalance. Robust infrastructure is built for the convenience of our citizen but the magnificent and rich tapestry of wildlife in Arunachal Pradesh is equally conserved and preserved.

I wish to see no youth is without work, and everybody is contributing their bit for the development of the state. I also wish to see the sports persons from our state representing in Olympics and bringing medals for the country. Sustainable economic growth is visible while we become the most sought after tourist destination in the world.

To sum up it all, we are a happy and prosperous state.

Epilogue

'What is honoured in a Country will be cultivated there'
— **Plato**

Towards the Future

Reflecting on Arunachal Pradesh's complex past, we see a state shaped by strategic and political decisions that drew lines-*Inner, Outer, and McMahon*-marking significant shifts in its destiny. These demarcations, initially meant for administrative ease and colonial control, became defining moments that left indelible marks on the region's social, political, and economic landscape.

These lines had their genesis in the British colonial desire to protect their frontiers from perceived threats. *The McMahon Line* was formalised in the 1914 Simla Agreement that ultimately led to the modern state boundaries for Arunachal Pradesh, separa ting it from the lands to its North. Yet, that line – traced out by the bureaucrats in faraway offices – was just a boundary, a cartographic designation and lines on maps. It would take the trappings of sovereignty for protecting tribal lands from the outside world and redefining decades of relationships between Arunachal Pradesh and its neighbours.

Culturally, these lines preserved the natural insularity of the tribes, protecting their rich cultural fabric from becoming overwhelmed by outside influences. Yet, as far as economic development was concerned, the restrictions meant that Arunachal Pradesh remained backward and peripheral to the rest of India. Staking economic development for cultural authenticity became a trade-off. A smart deal, when we look back now!

Geo-politically, the lines have been a focus of constant contestation and strife, particularly in the case of the McMahon Line, which China has lately refused to accept. Arunachal Pradesh's security is still affected by this dispute, as residents' identities and modes of governance are wrongly being questioned. From the very beginning, the 'lines of cut-off' also imposed a cultural separation between the tribes and that of mainland India. It meant that policies were administered differently between these parts, and with different attitudes by 'the outside', which in many ways was the centre of empire, on 'the inside'.

In social terms, the boundaries helped maintain the distinctive cultural identities of Arunachal Pradesh's tribes, but in the process, their isolation became protracted, hampering social development and integration in terms of social trends in India. The advantage was that we maintained our exceptional identities, languages and customs, but at the expense of slower social development and lesser exposure to the diverse, varied India.

Finally, the historical lines around Arunachal Pradesh have affected every facet of life in the state, protecting its demographic and cultural homogeneity, but also restricting its economic and social development, a tussle between protection and isolation. The lines of Arunachal Pradesh continue to govern the future of the state, caught between the desire to preserve its past and to step into its future.

I feel this balance will be crucial as we move into a discussion of the challenges and opportunities that Arunachal Pradesh is faced with today. The state is challenged by the twin goals of overcoming historical infrastructural deficits and taking advantage of its strategic location and rich natural resources. Opportunities exist in areas of tourism, natural farming and hydroelectric power, each of which has the potential to transform the economic landscape, but each also comes with its own set of associated challenges, from environmental sustainability and cultural protection to planning and implementation. The way the state engages these opportunities will decide the path of its more integrated and prosperous future.

Current Challenges and Opportunities in Arunachal Pradesh

Arunachal Pradesh, today, is at a crucial crossroads, where the push for modernity is putting traditional values to the test. Its governance structure and the community settings present a complex mix of challenges and opportunities that demand thoughtful consideration. Here are a few of those challenges for you to reflect on.

1. Governance: A Struggle for Stability

Governance in Arunachal Pradesh has long been a delicate balancing act, and it remains one of the state's most significant challenges. Unlike other States, Arunachal doesn't have its own cadre of officers. Instead, it relies on officers from the AGMUT cadre-a system which succeeded the special cadre of Indian Frontier Administrative Service (IFAS) in the late 1960s. Though these officers, being the brightest, bring their expertise and dedication, their brief tenures in a place as complex as Arunachal Pradesh doesn't do justice to their enthusiasm.

The state's terrain is some of the most challenging in the Himalayas, demanding not only skill but also deep, sustained commitment. Unfortunately, short postings make it difficult for these officers to launch and follow through on long-term projects. The result is often a reliance on ad hoc decisions, with little room for the kind of institutional memory that builds lasting solutions.

In contrast, the Indian Frontier Administrative Service (IFAS) officers of 1953 were specifically trained to manage frontier regions like Arunachal. They approached their roles with a genuine sense of empathy, understanding the people they were sent to serve, rather than governing from a distance. This historical approach offers valuable lessons for today. The challenge isn't a lack of vision-many officers truly care about Arunachal's future, and some continue to advocate for the state even after their postings end. It is the short tenures which don't do justice to their vision and intent.

The current structure of governance in Arunachal Pradesh needs an urgent rethink. There's a pressing need to find a middle ground-a solution that allows for continuity and long-term planning, ensuring that the state's development isn't hindered by constant turnover. This is not about administrative efficiency, alone; it's about creating a governance system that truly understands and serves the unique needs of Arunachal Pradesh.

Finding this balance won't be easy, but it's essential if the state is to overcome its governance struggles and achieve lasting stability.

2. Land Resource and Equity?

In Arunachal Pradesh, land is more than property; it's a vital part of the community's identity, closely tied to their spiritual and cultural traditions. Unlike many other states in India, Arunachal doesn't have formal land records or detailed cadastral surveys. This means that land is often seen as a community resource, owned collectively by the people rather than by individuals. However, this age-old system is facing new challenges.

Recently, a worrying trend towards elite capture is emerging. Those in positions of power are increasingly claiming large areas of land, including rivers and mountains, for themselves. This shift has sparked numerous controversies, particularly when it comes to land acquisition for development projects. Disputes over who actually owns the land, combined with inflated land valuations, have led to significant delays. These delays, in turn, hold back the progress of critical infrastructure projects, which the state desperately needs. Recently, a worrying trend of public sentiment towards elite capture also seems to be emerging.

The situation is becoming more urgent. If these issues aren't addressed soon, the consequences could be far-reaching, both for the people of Arunachal Pradesh and for the state's future development. The subtle conflict between age-old traditional community land ownership vs the modern concept of private property is something which will require gentle reconciliation. Systems which have served the community for generations, need to be protected from exploitation, especially from the *nouveau riche*. At the same time, the available clear and fair processes must be adhered to for resolving disputes and ensuring that development can move forward without trampling on the rights and traditions of the local people.

In short, safeguarding the integrity of Arunachal's land ownership system while addressing the challenges of modern development is crucial. It's a delicate balance, but one that must be struck to ensure that the state's progress is not compromised by the interests of a few.

3. Dependence on Government and Investment Barriers

Arunachal Pradesh's economy faces unique challenges, shaped by its geographical isolation and limited trade with neighbouring countries. Being a landlocked state, it doesn't have the kind of trade opportunities that might fuel a more diverse economy. As a result, people are heavily reliant on government jobs and petty contracts, which have become the primary source of income for most residents. In many ways, the state Government functions as the main "industry" in Arunachal Pradesh, providing employment, business opportunities, and contracts that drive the local economy.

However, this dependence on government support has its drawbacks. The lack of industries means there are few alternatives for employment or economic growth. For most people, securing a government job is seen as the only viable option. This reliance on the state creates a cycle where economic activity is limited, and the potential for broader development remains untapped.

Adding to these is the Inner Line Permit (ILP), which, while essential for preserving the cultural identity of Arunachal Pradesh, also acts as a barrier to outside investment. The restrictions on land purchases by non-residents further limit economic opportunities, making it difficult for the state to attract the kind of investment that could spur growth.

This situation presents a difficult dilemma. On one hand, there's a need to protect the unique cultural heritage of Arunachal Pradesh. On the other, the economic constraints posed by the entry and other restrictions are holding back the state's development potential. It's a complex issue that will require thoughtful consideration in the coming years.

Finding a way to balance the preservation of cultural identity with the need for economic growth is crucial. Arunachal Pradesh has enormous potential but realising it will require addressing these barriers to investment while still maintaining the values and traditions that make the state unique. We must look for a middle path, perhaps. This will be a key challenge as the state looks to build a more resilient and diversified economy for the future.

4. Agriculture and Market

Agriculture in Arunachal Pradesh faces a unique set of challenges, largely driven by the state's low population density. With a limited local market, farmers often find little motivation to produce more than what they need for their own subsistence. This situation is further complicated by the strong presence of external suppliers, which makes it difficult for local farmers to compete and gain a foothold in the market. As a result, many farmers struggle to see the value in expanding their production beyond basic needs.

However, there's a glimmer of hope on the horizon. Improvements in connectivity have started to open up new opportunities for agricultural production. Initiatives like *Mission Krishi Veer*[266] are particularly promising. By focusing on the state's large military and paramilitary population as a ready-made market, these programs aim to create a more stable and reliable demand for locally grown produce. This approach could provide the much-needed incentive for farmers to increase their output and engage more actively in the agricultural economy.

Yet, the road ahead isn't without its hurdles. The dominance of external suppliers remains a significant barrier, and breaking through this established system will require sustained efforts and strategic planning. For local farmers to truly benefit from these new initiatives, there needs to be a concerted effort to reduce these market limitations and create more opportunities for local produce to reach consumers.

The challenge is clear: while there's potential for growth in Arunachal Pradesh's agricultural sector, realising this potential will depend on overcoming the obstacles posed by external competition and limited local demand. Diversifying into cash crops such as large cardamom, palm oil and high value fruits such as kiwi, persimmon and avocado are being tried by many farmers. With the right support and continued improvements in infrastructure and market access, the state's farmers could play a much more significant role in its economic future. It's a challenge worth tackling, as the benefits could be substantial for the state's overall development.

5. Vicious Cycle of Cash for Votes

Sparse population of Arunachal Pradesh has a significant impact on its electoral politics, creating a unique and challenging dynamic. With only about 5,000 to 10,000 voters, on an average, per constituency, every single vote carries immense weight. This high-stakes environment often traps candidates in a cycle where they feel compelled to meet the immediate demands of voters, which frequently translates into spending large amounts of money on cash, contracts, and jobs only to secure electoral victory.

This cycle is more than just a challenge for candidates; it's a serious obstacle to the state's long-term development. When politicians are forced to prioritise short-term electoral gains over meaningful progress, governance suffers. Public resources, which should be directed toward sustainable development projects, are instead used to fulfil immediate promises made during campaigns. This not only stifles growth but also perpetuates a system where real, lasting improvements are continually pushed aside in favour of quick fixes.

Ajum, a prominent journalist mused, 'If the candidates have to spend so heavily to win an election, how can we expect them to carry out development work? His or her five-year tenure will be spent on recovering the money that they are spending now, and also, he or she has to get ready for the next election'[267].

The implications of this cycle are far-reaching. Over time, the focus on short-term electoral gains undermines the potential for long-term development, leaving the state stuck in a pattern of underachievement. This is an issue that cannot be ignored. Breaking this cycle is essential if Arunachal Pradesh is to move forward and realise its full potential.

Addressing this problem will require a concerted effort from all stakeholders, including politicians, voters, and civil society. It's about creating a political environment where long-term progress is valued over short-term gains, and where governance is focused on the betterment of the entire state rather than winning the next election. The stakes are high, but so are the potential rewards. Tackling this issue head-on is crucial for ensuring a brighter, more prosperous future for Arunachal Pradesh.

6. Demography and Development

Arunachal Pradesh is at a crossroads when it comes to demographic changes, driven largely by the demands of large-scale development projects like roads, power lines, and hydroelectric initiatives. These projects require a substantial labour force, but with the state's low population and limited pool of skilled workers, labour is often brought in from outside. This influx of external workers raises important concerns about the potential impacts on the local culture and social fabric.

Another area on which youth are getting restive is the possibility of intermarriage between these outsiders and tribal women. Such unions could lead to significant cultural shifts, potentially altering the traditional ways of life that have long defined the tribal communities of Arunachal Pradesh. The preservation of these cultural identities is crucial, and any changes to the demographic landscape need to be carefully considered in light of their long-term implications.

Addressing these issues head-on is essential. All of us must find ways to manage demographic changes in a way that respects and protects the traditions and rights of indigenous people while also accommodating the realities of development and migration.

7. Insurgency and Security

The ongoing insurgency in the Tirap, Changlang, and Longding (TCL) districts poses one of the most significant security challenges for Arunachal Pradesh. These areas have long been troubled by insurgent activities, which not only threaten the safety of the local population but also hinder the state's overall progress. Tackling this issue requires more than just a focus on security measures-it demands a deeper understanding of the underlying socio-economic factors that drive unrest in the region.

At the heart of the problem are long-standing socio-economic issues. These create an environment where such elements can gain influence. Addressing these root causes is essential for achieving lasting peace and stability in the region.

A holistic approach is needed-one that doesn't just rely on security forces to maintain order, but also prioritises development and social inclusion. This means investing in infrastructure, education, healthcare, and economic opportunities that can uplift these communities and provide alternatives to the entrenched narrative. By improving the quality of life and ensuring that the benefits of development reach everyone, such appeals can be diminished over time.

Security concerns in these districts are real and pressing, but the solution lies in a strategy that goes beyond force. By integrating security efforts with meaningful development initiatives, Arunachal Pradesh can work towards a more peaceful and stable future. It's a challenging path, but it's the only way to ensure that the peace achieved is not just temporary, but lasting and sustainable.

8. Conservation vs. Development

In Arunachal Pradesh, where ancient forests meet modern aspirations, the challenge isn't just about laying down roads or building bridges- it's about doing so without losing the soul of the land. This region's incredible biodiversity and deep-rooted cultural ties to nature make it unique, but they also create a complex dilemma: how to pursue development without unravelling the very fabric that holds the state together.

Balancing progress with preservation is no small feat. The push for infrastructure is real, and it promises to connect communities, boost the economy, and improve lives. Yet, if we charge ahead without considering the environmental costs, we risk damaging what makes Arunachal so special. The forests here aren't just a backdrop-they're a vital part of the state's identity and survival.

The solution lies in thoughtful planning that weighs economic gains against ecological impacts. This means sometimes choosing the slower, more expensive path because it ensures that the natural world remains vibrant and intact. Development projects must be designed with the environment in mind, even if that means rethinking how we measure economic costs. The real victory is in creating a future where Arunachal's landscapes remain as rich and diverse as its culture, allowing both to flourish side by side.

9. Harnessing power of the Water

As Arunachal Pradesh stands on the brink of a hydropower boom, the next decade could see the state generating around 13 GW of renewable energy. This surge in production could transform the region, potentially making it one of the wealthiest states in India, per capita. But with this immense opportunity comes a series of critical questions: How can we this new wealth be distributed fairly? And more importantly, how can we prepare ourselves to take benefits from such development?

The promise of economic growth through hydropower is undeniable, but it also brings its own set of challenges. Managing such a vast resource responsibly requires careful planning, not just in terms of infrastructure but also in ensuring that the benefits are shared equitably. There is a real risk that the wealth generated is likely to be fully spent within a small timeframe without careful financial planning. With a clear roadmap, this risk can be averted.

Moreover, preparing the next generation to handle these resources will be key. It's not just about teaching them to manage finances, but also instilling a sense of responsibility and caution. The future leaders of Arunachal will need to navigate a landscape where sustainable practices are not just a choice but a necessity.

10. Tourism: Balancing Development and Preservation

Tourism in Arunachal Pradesh is a double-edged sword-on one side, it offers a huge economic opportunity, and on the other, it raises concerns about preserving the state's delicate cultural and natural balance. The big question is: which path will the state choose? Will it follow the highly commercialised route of places like Manali, or take a more restrained and mindful approach, akin to Bhutan's model of sustainable tourism?

This decision is more than just a matter of economic growth. It's about defining the kind of tourism that aligns with Arunachal's identity. A rush toward unregulated development could bring in quick profits, but at the cost of eroding the very things that make this state special-its pristine landscapes, diverse wildlife, and rich cultural traditions. Contrarily, a more thoughtful approach to tourism could provide a long-term, sustainable boost to the economy while protecting these valuable assets-not an easy task though!

Sustainable tourism doesn't just happen; it requires deliberate planning and a clear vision. The focus needs to be on promoting experiences that respect local customs, protect the environment, and provide meaningful interactions between visitors and communities. This kind of tourism can bring in revenue while ensuring that the benefits reach everyone, from local artisans to small business owners. Rather such niche products command huge premium entailing higher profits with lesser carbon footprints.

The choice is urgent, and the time to act is now. Planning for a tourism industry that respects the essence of Arunachal Pradesh will require careful coordination, but it's a decision that will shape the state's future for generations. By choosing a path that balances development with preservation, Arunachal can unlock the full potential of its tourism sector without sacrificing what makes it truly unique.

11. Identity Assertion and Social Fabric

Arunachal Pradesh's diverse tribal communities represent both a deep-rooted heritage and a set of evolving challenges. As education and modernization spread, there's been a growing sense of individual tribal identity-a positive force in many ways, but one that also has the potential to create rifts. The stronger focus on distinct cultural identities can sometimes lead to tensions that unsettle the peace that has long been a hallmark of the state.

The challenge now is to find a way to preserve the rich variety of tribal identities without allowing divisions to take root. It's a delicate balance-one that requires finding common ground while respecting the uniqueness of each tribe. The future will depend on how well Arunachal Pradesh can maintain social cohesion while allowing space for its many cultures to thrive without conflict.

12. Degrees with No Skill

Youth of Arunachal Pradesh are faced with a unique dilemma. Firstly, the 'herculean task' to complete School and then College. Secondly, the degree earned after 15 years of education has very limited employability. The degree is without any skill! Further, dignity of labour is a concept alien to most parts of the State. *'Trained misfits' in their own society* is how Rustomji foresaw frontier youth acquiring education but losing their skill and *'nothing to contribute but idle discontent'*.

Arunachal Pradesh stands at this critical juncture. Unemployment pushes youth towards drugs, alcohol and even prostitution. Creating an ecosystem where youths have access to acquiring world class skill is urgent while our youths must inculcate the virtues of dignity of labour. In the same breath, we must also appreciate the fact that fewer youth prefer skills which require manual labour and therefore endeavour should be to tap their core competencies. To my mind, our girls and boys have inherently very high *Creative Quotient* (CQ)-art and music stands out. Further, the *'Political entrepreneurship'*- if there is such a phrase, is another strength of our youth- this is also a rare skill. How do we channelise these energies towards the benefit of the state?

13. Geopolitical Tensions and Opportunities

Arunachal Pradesh's borders present both challenges and opportunities. While growing tensions in the region cannot be ignored, there is also potential for fostering human interaction and trade, which could benefit the state's economy. Navigating these geopolitical dynamics will be crucial in determining the state's future role in regional stability and development. As Kiren Rijiju, the Union Minister who represents the State in the Lok Sabha has often observed, *"Arunachal Pradesh is a prisoner of both geography and geo-politics."* Yet, Arunachal Pradesh has immense potential to become the centre of international trade, commerce and tourism, especially with countries of South East Asia who share historical, religious and spiritual links with Arunachal. The Act East Policy demands the opening of land trade routes with neighbouring countries such as Bhutan. For instance, trading with Lhasa via Tsona, Nyingchi via Mechukha, Tuting, Taksing, Kibithoo, Bletting or Pangsau present viable economic and geo-political options, though constrained by international factors, often beyond the control of the State.

The decisions made today will shape the state's future, determining whether it can reconcile its rich cultural heritage with the demands of modernity and development. The path forward will require careful navigation, balancing tradition and progress, identity and unity, conservation and development. As the people of Arunachal Pradesh confront these challenges, their unmatched patriotism and fighting spirit will be their greatest assets in securing a prosperous and harmonious future.

In the National and Global Context

Both geographically and politically, Arunachal Pradesh occupies a unique and strategically significant position within India. With Bhutan, Tibet-China, and Myanmar as neighbours, the state serves as a critical frontier, especially in the context of recent geopolitical developments in the region, primarily arising out of the legacy we had detailed in this book. The Line of Actual Control (LAC) with China has made it a focal point in India's defence and foreign policy, with the Government ramping up infrastructure development and military presence to safeguard its borders. Arunachal Pradesh's rich cultural diversity and its location as a bridge between South and Southeast Asia offer immense potential for cross-border cultural exchanges and economic cooperation, though these opportunities are often weakened by the complexities of regional tensions and security concerns.

In the broader national context, Arunachal Pradesh is increasingly recognized for its contributions to India's strategic imperatives, including environmental conservation, hydroelectric power generation, and the preservation of indigenous cultures. As India seeks to strengthen its North-Eastern Frontier, Arunachal Pradesh's role has expanded beyond being a mere buffer state to becoming a crucial player in national security, ecological sustainability, and cultural diplomacy. The state's rich biodiversity and untapped natural resources also place it at the centre of national and global conversations on sustainable development and conservation, further elevating its significance on the global stage.

Some crystal gazing

As we look to the future of Arunachal Pradesh, the vision is clear: a state that grows and evolves without losing sight of its roots. The aspirations for this region go beyond building roads and boosting the economy. They include a deep respect for the rich cultural heritage that makes Arunachal unique. The challenge, and the opportunity, is to find a balance between progress and preservation.

Arunachal Pradesh has a lot to offer. Its strategic location makes it a gateway for trade and tourism, and there's untapped potential in its natural resources, especially in hydroelectric power. The focus on eco-friendly tourism is about more than attracting visitors-it's about doing so in a way that respects the environment and benefits local communities. Supporting local industries, like agriculture and handicrafts, is another key part of this vision, ensuring that the benefits of development are felt by everyone.

But as the state integrates more closely with the rest of India's growth story, there's a strong commitment to holding on to what makes Arunachal special. The languages, traditions, and indigenous cultures here are not relics of the past-they're living, breathing parts of the community. The future for

Arunachal is not about choosing between progress and tradition. Instead, it's about creating a path where both can thrive together, each enriching the other.

As we continue to move forward into the 21st century, the goal must be to build a resilient, self-reliant Arunachal Pradesh. A State that contributes to India's growth while staying true to its unique identity. Our future vision is one where development isn't a threat to culture, but rather, a way to celebrate and sustain it. This is the Arunachal Pradesh of tomorrow: a state where progress and tradition walk hand in hand, guiding each other forward.

For this, societies must be mindful of what they choose to honour, as, in the end, these values will shape what people aspire. As Plato wisely noted, the honours we bestow will ultimately be nurtured and replicated.

Final Thoughts

As we reach the end of our journey through some key moments of Arunachal Pradesh's history, it's clear that this state tells a remarkable story of endurance and growth. Nestled in the far northeast of India, surrounded by rugged mountains and remote valleys, Arunachal Pradesh has always faced unique challenges. Yet, through it all, we have shown an extraordinary ability to adapt and thrive, carving out a distinct place for ourselves within the Indian Union.

The road from its early days of NEFA to its current role as an essential part of India's narrative hasn't been easy. The challenges were many—geographical isolation, a sparse population, and the constant pressures of a complex geopolitical landscape. But the spirit of the people here is one of tenacity. We've preserved our rich heritage while also embracing the changes that come with modernity, proving that tradition and progress can coexist.

Looking ahead, there's much to be hopeful about. Arunachal Pradesh is a land of incredible cultural diversity and natural beauty, and its strategic importance continues to grow. With thoughtful planning and a clear vision, the state is set to be a model of sustainable development. The resilience that has carried the people of Arunachal through history will undoubtedly guide us into the future, one which is of absolute Happiness!

The future promises a vibrant Arunachal Pradesh-a place where the richness of tradition and the promise of progress come together-hand in hand. It's a future that not only holds prosperity for the state but also contributes significantly to India's broader journey toward progress and prosperity. Here, in this unique corner of India, we see the potential for a future where culture, nature, and development walk together in harmony.

But a word of caution is due here. There are stiff challenges staring at us today. We have discussed a few here. Only alert, aware and an informed citizenry led by a visionary leadership can equip us to overcome these inevitable obstacles. In the past, we could successfully overcome many formidable situations with grit and unity. This gives us optimism. However, how it unfolds is something we will all have to wait and watch.

'When the gem was mine
I cared not, and ignored its value
Now that the gem is lost to others,
Melancholy overwhelms me
As its pure worth dawns on me'.

– Sixth Dalai Lama

II. Arunachal Pradesh on the Rise

(Source: Department of IPR, Government of Arunachal Pradesh)

▲ **Figure 1:** Dr Manmohan Singh, Prime Minister at Itanagar, 2008

In Between The Blurry Lines

▲ **Figure 2:** Arunachal's first greenfield Donyi Polo Airport

▲ **Figure 3:** Shri Narendra Modi, Prime Minister of India in Arunachal Pradesh, 2019

▲ **Figure 4:** Shri Ram Nath Kovind, President of India presenting the Nari Shakti Puraskar to Smt. Tage Rita Takhe, founder of the Naara Aaba Winery

▲ **Figure 5:** Shri Narendra Modi, Prime Minister at Itanagar, 2022

▲ **Figure 6:** Smt. Draupadi Murmu, President of India at Statehood Day celebrations, 2023

▲ **Figure 7:** Interaction of Community Based Organizations (CBOs) with Shri Narendra Modi, Prime Minister in Delhi, 2023

▲ **Figure 8:** Arunachal Pradesh became the first State in the North East to achieve 100% saturation of Har Ghar Jal Programme.

▲ **Figure 9:** Shri Amit Shah, Union Home Minister at Kibithoo, India's first village during launch of the Vibrant Villages Programme

▲ **Figure 10:** Signing of MOU between Arunachal Pradesh and Assam to resolve the inter state border dispute

▲ **Figure 11:** Arunachal Pradesh hosts 77th Santosh Trophy Finals

▲ **Figure 12:** Arunachal Pradesh Legislative Assembly Building

▲ **Figure 13:** Bene Arch Bridge over Yomgo river, West Siang

▲ **Figure 14:** Taking governance to the people-Visit by Shri Pema Khandu, Chief Minister

▲ **Figure 15:** Shri Pema Khandu, Chief Minister addressing the G20 meet at Itanagar

▲ **Figure 16:** Inauguration of the Hump World War II Museum, Pasighat

▲ **Figure 17:** Celebration of International Year of Millets, 2023

▲ **Figure 18:** Kameng Hydroelectric Project

▲ **Figure 19:** Kiwi Plantation-Arunachal has the potential to become the fruit bowl of India

▲ **Figure 20:** Itanagar (Naharlagun) Railway Station

▲ **Figure 21:** New Age Learning Centre at Changlang

▲ **Figure 22:** Shri Jagdeep Dhankhar, Vice President of India at the Statehood Day Celebrations, 2024

▲ **Figure 23:** Shri Narendra Modi, Prime Minister at Itanagar, 2024

▲ **Figure 24:** RIWATCH, an institute dedicated to the empowerment of indigenous communities

▲ **Figure 25:** Women SHGs keeping alive indigenous traditions, handicrafts and cultures

▲ **Figure 26:** Rozgar Mela–handing over appointment letters to successful candidates appointed through APSSB

▲ **Figure 27:** Sela and Nechiphu Tunnels providing all weather connectivity to the strategic Tawang sector

▲ **Figure 28:** Super Car Rally on roads of Arunachal Pradesh

▲ **Figure 29:** The Vibrant Dambuk Orange Festival

▲ **Figure 30:** TRIHMS–first batch from the first MBBS college in the State passed out in 2023

▲ **Figure 31:** Empowering SHG women as Lakhpati Didis – Women Led Transformation

Additional Readings

Part I: Chapter 3[268]

Quest for the missing link of Tsangpo-Siang, Brahmaputra

"Eventually, all things merge into one, and a river runs through it"
– Norman Maclean.

"Most races have their promised land, and such legendary places must necessarily be somewhat inaccessible, hidden behind the misty barriers where ordinary men do not go…."
– Frank Kingdon Ward, The Riddle of the Tsangpo Gorges.

Sometimes it's the simplest questions that lead to the most profound discoveries. Consider this: where does the Tsangpo River, flowing through Tibet, eventually end up? This query, seemingly straightforward, sparked a series of daring explorations over many years, involving several determined souls-Kingdon Ward, Kinthup, Morshead, and Bailey. Each of them played a role in piecing together a puzzle that geography alone could not solve.

Our story begins with the intriguing geographical conundrum that the Tsangpo River, known for its rugged and elusive path through Tibet, posed to geographers and explorers alike. Was it connected to the Brahmaputra or did it flow into another river altogether? This wasn't just a question of mapping rivers-it was about venturing into uncharted lands, dealing with unpredictable elements, and encountering cultures vastly different from one's own.

The river begins its journey as *Tamchok Khambab*, aptly named for its mouth that resembles a horse's ear, emerging from the Angsi glacier on Mt. Kailash and flowing toward southern Lhasa. Here, it transforms into the mighty Yarlung Tsangpo, known as "the great river." As it meanders eastward from Lhasa for over 1,600 kilometers, it takes a dramatic turn, famously known as *"the great bend,"* plunging into a mysterious gorge that seems to vanish from sight, only to resurface magnificent and powerful as the Siang in Arunachal Pradesh, India.

The enigma surrounding this river has a long history, gaining new momentum thanks to Frank Kingdon Ward's search for the elusive "Rainbow Fall" near Pemako. His book, *The Riddle of the Tsangpo Gorge*, paints a vivid picture of a lush gorge overflowing with vibrant forests. This enchanting gorge stretches from Kongpo in Tibet to the Tuting-Gelling region in Arunachal Pradesh and is known as 'Pemakö'-an ancient Tibetan Buddhist realm of hidden treasures or *Beyul*. According to legend, Guru Padmasambhava concealed these mystical lands, proclaiming that only the chosen would be able to uncover them. This unfolding of secrets came to pass when Dudjom Drakgnak Lingpa, a tertön or 'revealer of treasures,' illuminated the area for the oppressed people of the Kham region.

This sacred landscape is said to embody *Vajravarahi*, or *Dorje Phagmo*, the Tibetan Goddess of Wisdom and Queen of the Dakinis. The river basin, where the Tsangpo meets the Siang, is believed to mirror her physical form. Her upper chakras are represented by the towering Kangri Karpo peak, symbolising her head, while the peaks of Namche Barwa and Gyala Pelri, on the Tibetan side, are likened to her breasts. On the Indian side, the holy mountain of Devakota is considered her sacred womb. The Yang Sang Chu, or "Secret River," a tributary of the Siang, winds alongside and is thought to carry the essence of the five wisdoms. The confluence of the Yang Sang Chu and the Siang is said to house her *secret* chakra.

This captivating mystique has drawn numerous explorers, who were also seekers on a pilgrimage, each yearning to experience the *Last Shangri-La*. Notable figures such as Ken Cox, Ian Baker and Ken Storme have been among those enchanted by this realm.

The name Siang itself is derived from two Adi words: "Asi," meaning "water," and "àpì-ang," meaning "heart." Thus, Siang translates to *the river that flows through our heart*, encapsulating its profound significance to the region and its people.

Frank Kingdon Ward, an explorer with a passion for botany, wasn't just drawn to the region for its flora. His expeditions across the harsh, mountainous landscapes were also driven by this geographical mystery. However, long before Ward made his mark, the groundwork was laid by earlier, equally brave explorers.

Perhaps the most compelling tale is that of Kinthup, a simple tailor who, against all odds, sought to prove the connection between the Tsangpo and the Brahmaputra. Sent by the British surveyors to track the river's course, Kinthup's journey was fraught with betrayal and hardship. He was sold into slavery, escaped, and still continued his mission. Imagine Kinthup, alone and unaided, tying notes to logs and releasing them into the river, hoping they would be found downstream to confirm his findings. It's the stuff of legend, yet it was all too real for him.

The Tsangpo was not just a river for Captain Morshead and F.M. Bailey. It represented a challenge of both intellect and endurance. Their expedition sought to answer questions left by previous explorers and to explore regions of Tibet cloaked in both physical and political mystery. Their journeys, fraught with danger from both nature and man, required a delicate balance of diplomatic savvy and raw determination.

Each of these explorers faced their own set of challenges. From political barriers set by wary local tribes and the Chinese government, to the physical hurdles posed by some of the world's most daunting terrains. The courage to push forward, often in the face of likely defeat, is a testament to their enduring spirit.

The outcome of these intrepid explorations was a triumph of perseverance and ingenuity. After enduring years of hardship and countless obstacles, the explorers finally confirmed that the Tsangpo River indeed flows into the Brahmaputra. This discovery was largely attributed to the combined efforts and data collected by these explorers over time. The conclusive piece of evidence came when logs released by Kinthup were found downstream in the Brahmaputra, matching the markers he had ingeniously placed. This pivotal moment not only solved the geographical mystery but also exemplified how collaboration, even across time and individual expeditions, can lead to monumental discoveries. The link between the Tsangpo and the Brahmaputra was no longer just a theory; it was a verified fact, charting new territories in the map of Asian rivers and enhancing our understanding of the region's intricate river systems.

What binds these stories is not just the quest to map a river, but a deeper, almost insatiable need to understand our world a little better. It's about how a simple question can lead to journeys across distant and dangerous lands, bringing together disparate threads of history, geography, and human endurance into a cohesive story that celebrates both human curiosity and resilience. The other outcome was that the explorers gained unparalleled deeper insights into the rich flora, fauna and the mysterious people living in these Terrains.

In retrospect, the journeys of these explorers were not just about discovering where a river ended, but also about the journeys we embark on to satisfy our curiosity. It's a powerful reminder that sometimes, to find our answers, we must be willing to travel into the unknown, armed with nothing but our questions, curiosity and the relentless human spirit.

Part I, Chapter 3[269]
The English Notes on the McMahon Line, March 1914

A. McMahon to the Lonchen Shatra, 24 March 1914

To

Lonchen Shatra

Tibetan Plenipotentiary

In February last you accepted the India-Tibet frontier from the Isu Razi Pass to the Bhutan frontier, as given in the map (two sheets), of which two copies are herewith attached, subject to the confirmation of your Government and the following conditions:

(a) The Tibetan ownership of private estates on the British side of the frontier will not be disturbed.

(b) If the sacred places of Tso Karpo and Tsari Sarpa fall within a day's march of the British side of the frontier, they will be included in Tibetan territory and the frontier modified accordingly.

I understand that your Government have now agreed to this frontier subject to the above two conditions.

You wished to know whether certain dues now collected by the Tibetan Government at Tsona Jong and in Kongbu and Kham from the Monpas and Lopas for articles sold may still be collected. Mr. Bell has informed you that such details will be settled in a friendly spirit, when you have furnished him with the further information, which you promised.

The final settlement of this India-Tibet frontier will help to prevent causes of future dispute and thus cannot fail to be of great advantage to both Governments.

Delhi   (Signed)

A. H. MCMAHON, British Plenipotentiary

B. The Lonchen Shatra to McMahon, 25 March 1914 (Translation)

To

Sir Henry McMahon,

British Plenipotentiary to the China-Tibet Conference

As it was feared that there might be friction in future unless the boundary between India and Tibet is clearly defined, I submitted the map, which you sent me in February last, to Lhasa for orders. I have now received orders from Lhasa, and I accordingly agree to the boundary as marked in red in the two copies of the maps signed by you subject to the conditions, mentioned in your letter, dated the 24th March, sent to me through Mr. Bell. I have signed and sealed the two copies of the maps. I have kept one copy here and return herewith the other.

Sent on the 29th day of the 1st Month of the Wood-Tiger year (25th March 1914) by Lonchen Shatra, the Tibetan Plenipotentiary.

Seal of the
Lonchen Shatra

Annotated translation on **"Tibetan Notes on the McMahon Line"**

This is in regards to how the British [Indo]-Tibetan boundary was demarcated. At first British India's Government through [Charles] Bell Sahib, give us a map showing from Dzayul to the lower part of Kongpo and then, another map from Dakpo-Kongpo to Tsona Dzong, saying that this map is the continuation of the previous map. [He] said that the ultimate aims is not to have any conflict over the border between British [India] and Tibet. Thus, the differences are to be decided now and also to be observed further whether it is possible or not. In the demarcated line, Tsari Sarpa, Tso Karpo, etc. and a vast region of Tawang, etc. from Tsona is also included. He points finger to the region and reasons how this Tibetan became part of British India, but it is not decided until the Government of Tibet did not order the demarcation of the British [Indo]-Tibetan border to be so. After having thorough discussion on the pros and cons on the dimension of the "three [borders] in actual, lost and visual," a border line was drawn. It was based upon after much area is drawn back [as claimed in the map]. The region, like Bathang, Lithang and Mili are not granted as per wishes of the British [India] Government, but nothing was left not to be considered heartily. Finally, it is said that British [India] Government will continue to support Tibetan, but still in whatever cases demarcation is necessary. Therefore, it is also said that Tibetan side also needed to consider deliberately, [because] British India continuously repeated the [importance of] demarcation.

Generally, Foreigner [British India] were currently powerful and systemic to their works, and opponents are losing to their steady development. Hence, it is needed to give [this region], because presently Tibet is in opposition to China; and we look for our temporary satisfaction to the British India's Government, as [given the example of] sometime the fatal poisonous turned into a medicine. Therefore, there aroused number of differences from every part to annex land and its subjects. At that time, a treaty was signed between Russia and Mongolia; I think it was mainly for the Russian greedy. Thus, this act leads upon one to compete against the second. Upon my reflection to those, I requested that [the Government of Tibet] should slightly consider on the border of Mon's side.

Therefore, in order to not to have further great tasks to be done by the Indian representative, Sne mgron mkhan chung was requested and dispatched to hold discussion and research in the country [Tibet]. Upon his successful returning, the line was prepared on the treaty's [map] of the three nations of China, Tibet and British [India]. Later on, the line was drawn red on the map as a boundary between British [India] and Tibet, and it was signed.

Thus, based upon letter given by the British [India]'s Foreign Minister, the followings are agreed: all the usual spiritual sources income will be remained intact to the private [estate], and of Mon [region, but] governmental taxation [from now on] will goes to British [India; if any Tibetan citizen, etc. falls into the British [India] side, one will not be accepted; and the sacred pilgrimage site as Tso Karpo and Tsari Sarpo will be reversed back to Tibet side, where if it falls within one day distances; and [finally], the routine collection of toll tax from the people of Mon and "Klo pa" can be settled at the mutual understanding.

Thus, the plenipotentiaries of British [India] and Tibet exchanged letters (= notes) on the Indo-Tibetan border. As you had stated that the Government of Tibet had confirmed the two maps given to them in recent month of February, which demarcated the Indo-Tibetan border from the Isu Razi Pass to the Bhutan frontier, it will be now based on the following notes:

a.   If any Tibetan citizen, etc. falls into the British [India] side, British India will not confiscate and impound his rights.
b.   The sacred pilgrimage site as Tso Karpo and Tsari Sarpa will be in Tibet side, where, if it falls within one day distances.

It is confirmed what you have heard that the Government of Tibet is happy with the above two conditions. Thus, I will be much delighted if you could kindly acknowledge yours confirmation.

A concern was raised by you, whether it is allowed to collect toll tax from Monpa and Klo pa who came to Tsona, Kongpo and Kham for trades. In that regards, as you had informed us that [Charles] Bell had been briefed details about the case. Thus, when he will talk those details to us, through mutual understanding, we can settle those [issues]. A great advantage will come to the nations of British [India] and Tibet after the clear demarcation of the Indo-Tibetan border. It is presented on 24th date of the 3rd month of the year 1914 by the British Plenipotentiary, A. H. McMahon.

Thus, accordingly the collection of the toll tax on goods from Mon should continue as per the principle statements of the agreement. [Besides that] after a final settlement on the Sino-Tibetan border, the talk on [the Indo-Tibetan border] must resume again.

Part II: Chapter 5

Amended Tibetan text with Annotated Translation of the 1952 document.[270]

An auspicious endorsement given by the Government of India to the three [traditional] domains of the Tawang monastery: the lands, the houses and the subjects.

Here is a concise [acceptance cum] requisition presented by us, the Tawang Monastery [officials] at the respected "great Indian Commissioner," whose method [of rule] is perfect, glorious and exalted.

This introduction to a letter from the Tawang Monastery to Major Bob reflecting acceptance and was followed by about 40 items of requisition.

Part II: Chapter 6

.....the broad framework of the following five fundamental principles:

1. People should develop along the lines of their own genius and we should avoid imposing anything on them. We should try to encourage in every way their own traditional arts and culture.
2. Tribal rights in land and forests should be respected.
3. We should try to train and build up a team of their own people to do work of administration and development. Some technical personnel from outside will, no doubt, be needed, especially in the beginning. But we should avoid introducing too many outsiders into tribal territory.
4. We should not over-administer these areas or over-whelm them with multiplicity of schemes. We should rather work through, and not in rivalry to, their own social and cultural institutions.
5. We should judge results, not by statistics or the amount of money spent, but by the quality of human character that is evolved.

Part II, Chapter 8

The Guilty Men: Reflections on 1962

D.R. Mankekar had, in his book-'The Guilty Men of 1962', made a bare it all analysis on the debacle of 1962. In this section I have tried to highlight some interesting extracts from the book.

As early as 1945-46, India's military leadership had begun to recognize the looming threat posed by a foreign power's control over Tibet. Lieutenant General Francis Tucker, then General Officer Commanding-in-Chief of the Eastern Command, sounded the alarm in a strategy paper. He wrote:

"From an enemy's perspective, the Tibetan plateau serves as the ideal launching pad for operations against eastern India. It offers airfields for bombardment campaigns and staging areas for future assaults on Uttar Pradesh, Bihar, and Bengal. For India, preventing China's military occupation of Tibet is not just strategic-it's imperative."

Despite such foresight, events unfolded in ways that India could not entirely anticipate. When the Dalai Lama fled to India in 1959, seeking refuge from Chinese persecution, he wasn't the only one to cross the border. Hidden among genuine Tibetan refugees were Chinese spies. Many infiltrated deep into Assam, establishing networks in places like Guwahati, Dibrugarh, and Silchar, often aided by pro-Chinese Indian communists.

In one instance, a Chinese spy ran a tea stall in a small hamlet north of Bomdila for two years before the invasion. Another operated a covert radio station in Chaku village for 18 months before being discovered. These were not isolated cases but part of a broader espionage operation, quietly laying the groundwork for the 1962 war.

When the Chinese attack finally came in 1962, it followed a route envisioned decades earlier by Chinese leader Dr. Sun Yat-sen. Back in 1921, he had proposed a railway line connecting Lhasa to Dirang Dzong and beyond via Tawang-strategic dreams that became handy for the PLA during their advance.

A question that has haunted many since is why India didn't use its air power to counter the Chinese invasion. The answer lies in an intelligence failure. Indian strategists grossly overestimated China's air strength, fearing massive retaliation. Ironically, we later learned that China's air force at the time was significantly weaker than assumed.

The Chinese, despite their initial military success, declared a unilateral ceasefire. Why? The harsh Himalayan winter and snow-blocked passes were cited, but deeper reasons emerged.

Miscalculating Tribal Loyalties

The Chinese had expected the local tribes to side with them. Instead, the tribes stood resolutely with India, rejecting Chinese overtures.

Underestimating Indian Resilience

Beijing assumed that a few military defeats would break India's spirit and force it to sue for peace. They anticipated a quick, decisive victory that would conclude before the world could react. But India didn't crumble.

Faulty Intelligence

Chinese diplomats and agents in Delhi, Kolkata, and other cities fed their military commanders wildly inaccurate predictions. They claimed that India was teetering on the brink of collapse, ripe for a communist revolution, and would fall apart with just a nudge. Instead, the invasion galvanized India. Political parties, including the Communist Party of India, set aside differences and rallied behind the government in a display of unprecedented unity.

The sight of a united India-resilient, patriotic, and resolute-was a rude awakening for Beijing. What they had hoped would be a swift conquest turned into a cautionary tale.

Part III: Chapter 10

Pioneers in the Frontiers-Early catalyst of State making

Vivekananda Kendra in Arunachal Pradesh Today

Today, the Vivekananda Kendra's impact in Arunachal Pradesh extends far beyond formal education. The Kendra operates through various wings, addressing multiple facets of community development:

- Vivekananda Kendra Vidyalayas (VKVs): Providing quality education to thousands of students across the state.
- Vivekananda College of Teacher Education (VKCTE): Training teachers to uphold high educational standards.
- Vivekananda Kendra Arun Jyoti (VKAJ): Engaging in non-formal education, health, hygiene, and skill training.
- Vivekananda Kendra Vidyalaya Alumni Association (VKVAA): Uniting alumni to contribute to societal development.
- Vivekananda Kendra Institute of Culture: – Arunachal Pradesh Chapter (VKIC-APC): Promoting cultural heritage and values.
- Vivekananda Kendra Centre for Human Excellence (VKCHE): Fostering leadership and personal development.

- Vivekananda Kendra Branch Centres: Operating in urban areas to extend their reach.

Through these initiatives, the Kendra involves 656 dedicated karyakartas, apart from regular staff, serving the society. This holistic approach ensures that the Vivekananda Kendra addresses both the educational and socio-cultural needs of the community, staying true to the vision of its founder, Mananeeya Shri Eknathji Ranade.

Impact of VKVs-Serving Society

The alumni of VKVs have made remarkable contributions across various fields. They serve as teachers, soldiers, doctors, engineers, entrepreneurs, agriculturists, financial consultants, and advocates. Their involvement in societal development has been significant, enhancing the human resource potential of Arunachal Pradesh.

- **Government Service:** 12 VKV alumni serve as IAS officers, and 70 have cleared the Arunachal Pradesh Civil Services (APCS) examination, with several holding key positions such as Superintendents and Deputy Superintendents of Police.
- **Education:** 18 alumni run 21 schools and three colleges, and 75 serve as faculty members in various colleges.
- **Cultural Contributions:** Many have initiated classical music and dance programs, while others have excelled in sports and established or actively participated in NGOs.

Indigenous/Traditional Faith and Education

Vivekananda Kendra, inspired by Swami Vivekananda and Mananeeya Eknathji, approaches the local communities, traditions, and faiths with respect and reverence. This manifests in three key ways:

- **Supporting Community Efforts:** Helping communities preserve their traditions in a rapidly changing world.
- **Inculcating Traditions in Schools:** Integrating local traditions into the Vidyalayas' curriculum.

- **Gurukul Initiative:** Deploying teachers to support the Donyi Polo Cultural and Charitable Trust's Gurukuls in Rang, Mwyw, Bam, and Pabo.

Conserving Human Resources – Challenges

One of the regular challenges faced by VKVAPT is the attrition of about 10% of its workforce. This is due to various factors such as personal aspirations, recruitment by state governments and Kendriya Vidyalaya Sangathan, direct postings as Senior Teachers/PGTs, and the multiple roles that teachers are required to play within VKVs and VKCTE. Despite these challenges, VKVAPT continues to scale up its operations gradually, based on experience and qualifications.

Gearing Up for Fifty Years

As VKVAPT prepares to celebrate 50 years of dedicated service, it is focused on several key areas:

Higher Education and Training: Enhancing opportunities for advanced learning.

Community Centers: Transforming every VKV into a hub for community activities. Teacher Training: Providing training for teachers from neighbouring schools and educational institutions.

Part IV: Chapter 12[271]

Share of states in central taxes

The share of states in the central taxes for the 2021-26 period is recommended to be 41%, same as that for 2020-21. This is less than the 42% share recommended by the 14th Finance Commission for 2015-20 period. The adjustment of 1% is to provide for the newly formed union territories of Jammu and Kashmir, and Ladakh from the resources of the centre.

Criteria for devolution

Table 1 below shows the criteria used by the Commission to determine each state's share in central taxes, and the weight assigned to each criterion. The criteria for distribution of central taxes among states for 2021-26 period is same as that for 2020-21. However, the reference period for computing income distance and tax efforts are different (2015-18 for 2020-21 and 2016-19 for 2021-26), hence, the individual share of states may still change. The individual share of states in the taxes devolved by the centre is provided in Table 2 in the annexure. We explain some indicators below.

▼ **Table 1:** Criteria for devolution

Criteria	14th FC 2015-20	15th FC 2020-21	15th FC 2021-26
Income Distance	50.0	45.0	45.0
Area	15.0	15.0	15.0
Population (1971)	17.5	-	-
Population (2011)#	10.0	15.0	15.0
Demographic Performance	-	12.5	12.5
Forest Cover	7.5	-	-
Forest and Ecology	-	10.0	10.0
Tax and fiscal efforts*	-	2.5	2.5
Total	**100**	**100**	**100**

*Note: #14th FC used the term "demographic change" which was defined as Population in 2011. *The report for 2020-21 used the term "tax effort", the definition of the criterion is same.*
Sources: Reports of the 14th and 15th Finance Commissions; PRS.

- **Income distance:** Income distance is the distance of a state's income from the state with the highest income. Income of a state has been computed as average per capita GSDP during the three-year period between 2016-17 and 2018-19. A state with lower per capita income will have a higher share to maintain equity among states.
- **Demographic performance:** The Terms of Reference of the Commission required it to use the population data of 2011 while making

recommendations. Accordingly, the Commission used 2011 population data for its recommendations. The demographic performance criterion has been used to reward efforts made by states in controlling their population. States with a lower fertility ratio will be scored higher on this criterion.

- **Forest and ecology:** This criterion has been arrived at by calculating the share of the dense forest of each state in the total dense forest of all the states.

- **Tax and fiscal efforts:** This criterion has been used to reward states with higher tax collection efficiency. It is measured as the ratio of the average per capita own tax revenue and the average per capita state GDP during the three years between 2016-17 and 2018-19.

▼ **Table 2: Individual share of states in the taxes devolved by the centre (out of 100)**

State	14th FC 2015-20	15th FC 2020-21	15th FC 2021-26
Andhra Pradesh	4.305	4.111	4.047
Arunachal Pradesh	**1.370**	**1.760**	**1.757**
Assam	3.311	3.131	3.128
Bihar	9.665	10.061	10.058
Chhattisgarh	3.080	3.418	3.407
Goa	0.378	0.386	0.386
Gujarat	3.084	3.398	3.478
Haryana	1.084	1.082	1.093
Himachal Pradesh	0.713	0.799	0.830
Jammu & Kashmir	1.854	-	-
Jharkhand	3.139	3.313	3.307
Karnataka	4.713	3.646	3.647
Kerala	2.500	1.943	1.925
Madhya Pradesh	7.548	7.886	7.850
Maharashtra	5.521	6.135	6.317
Manipur	0.617	0.718	0.716
Meghalaya	0.642	0.765	0.767
Mizoram	0.460	0.506	0.500
Nagaland	0.498	0.573	0.569

Odisha	4.642	4.629	4.528
Punjab	1.577	1.788	1.807
Rajasthan	5.495	5.979	6.026
Sikkim	0.367	0.388	0.388
Tamil Nadu	4.023	4.189	4.079
Telangana	2.437	2.133	2.102
Tripura	0.642	0.709	0.708
Uttar Pradesh	17.959	17.931	17.939
Uttarakhand	1.052	1.104	1.118
West Bengal	7.324	7.519	7.523
Total	**100**	**100**	**100**

Sources: Reports of 14th and 15th Finance Commission; PRS.

Part IV: Chapter 13

The Chinese Push and India's Response

The stretch of land where India meets China, known as the Line of Actual Control (LAC), has always been a place of strategic importance. But in recent years, it's become the stage for a silent, yet intense, contest. This chapter dives into the infrastructure race that's been unfolding along the LAC-a race that's not just about roads and tunnels, but about power, control, and the future of this high-stakes region.

China's Infrastructure Drive: Building for Dominance

Imagine this: towering mountains, treacherous passes, and an environment that challenges even the toughest soldiers. This is where China has been building, not just to survive, but to dominate. Over the past few years, China has ramped up its infrastructure efforts along the LAC with a clear objective in mind-to make sure its military can move swiftly and efficiently, no matter the terrain.

Despite the CCP's dominance over Tibet dating back to the early 1950s, it wasn't until China's launch of the 'Go West Campaign' in 1999 as part of its 'West Development Strategy' that the scale of regional development intensified… "The total road network in Tibet in 1959 was only 7,300 km which amplified to 1,20,000 km by early 2022 expanding at approximately *5 km per day* since 1959". "Under its 10th and 11th Five Year Plans, China invested $ 4.2 billion and $ 21 billion to undertake 117 and 188 key infrastructure and development projects in Tibet".

The roads China has built, like NH G-318 is the longest China NH (5,476 km). The 14th Five Year Plan plans extension of G 318 which connects Shanghai to Tibet through Chengdu in Sichuan. It then enters Nepal near Zhangmu near the China-Tibet border. The road passes through Nyingchi close to the China-India border near Arunachal Pradesh and a feeder road originating from G 318 also reaches opposite Tawang, are more than just paths through the mountains. They're lifelines for the People's Liberation Army (PLA), allowing troops to be mobilised at a moment's notice. These routes cut down travel time, giving China the ability to position itself quickly in key areas, which could be crucial in any potential conflict.

But roads are just the beginning. China's been busy constructing bunkers, camps, and underground shelters-all designed to withstand harsh weather and potential attacks. Artillery positions and radar sites have sprung up, turning the region into a fortified zone. On top of that, there's been a noticeable increase in the number of rail networks, fighters, drones, and air defense systems stationed along the LAC. It's clear that China isn't just preparing for today-it's gearing up for any future challenges as well.

One of the more subtle yet significant moves by China has been the construction of dual-use "Xiaokang"-628 villages (427 first line and 201 second line villages) border villages. These aren't just settlements; they're strategic outposts that double as civilian and military facilities. By planting these villages near the border, China is reinforcing its territorial claims and creating a network that can support military operations if needed.

India's Strategic Counter: Building to Defend and Deter

India has watched these developments closely, and it's not been idle. While China has been building, so has India-each road, each tunnel, a step in fortifying its own defenses along the LAC. The Indian government has made it clear that it's not just going to sit back and let China have the upper hand.

Take the Sela Tunnel Road, for example. Recently completed and inaugurated by the Prime Minister, it is the world's longest bi-lane tunnel above 13,000 feet ASL, cutting through the rugged terrain to provide a faster, safer route to the border. This isn't just about convenience; it's about ensuring that Indian troops can move quickly and reliably, even in the harshest conditions.

The Border Roads Organisation (BRO) has been at the forefront of these efforts, with its budget seeing a significant boost in recent years. In the 2023-24 fiscal year alone, the BRO's budget was substantially increased, a clear indication of how serious India is about closing the infrastructure gap with China. The BRO has completed numerous projects across the border states, ensuring that India's troops have the roads, tunnels, and other infrastructure they need to operate effectively.

But it's not just about roads and tunnels. India has also focused on improving the living conditions and logistical support for its troops stationed along the LAC. New solar-heated shelters and insulated bunkers have been established to help soldiers endure the freezing winters, ensuring that they remain ready for any situation. The upgrades in living facilities are about more than comfort-they're about keeping the troops at peak readiness, no matter what the weather throws at them.

The Vibrant Village Program is a befitting counter to the 'Xiaokang' project. By far, our biggest advantage remains the residents of these border villages, fiercely patriotic, while living under the harshest of conditions. Best of defence infrastructures cannot beat the high spirits of our Border Villagers.

The Infrastructure Race: A Game of Strategy

When you compare the infrastructure developments of India and China along the LAC, it's like watching a high-stakes chess match. China, with its extensive road networks and rapid construction of dual-use villages, seems to be playing a game of speed and scale. It's about being able to mobilise quickly and assert control over strategic areas.

India, on the other hand, is focusing on strategic positioning. While it might not match China in sheer numbers, India is investing in quality-like the strategically placed tunnels and upgraded airfields that provide crucial advantages in the difficult terrain. India's approach is less about matching China move for move and more about creating a defense that's both resilient and responsive.

This infrastructure race isn't just about who can build more, faster. It's about creating a balance of power along the LAC, where both sides know that the other is prepared and capable. This balance is what keeps tensions from boiling over into conflict-it's a delicate dance, where each side builds and fortifies, always with an eye on what the other is doing.

As we look at the developments along the LAC, it's clear that this is more than just an infrastructure race. It's a contest for influence, control, and security in one of the most strategically important regions in the world. China's aggressive push to build and fortify has certainly raised the stakes, but India's strategic and thoughtful response has ensured that it's not left behind.

The LAC will continue to be a focal point of geopolitical tensions between these two powerful neighbours. The infrastructure being built today isn't just for show-it's a critical component of the ongoing struggle for dominance and security in the region. As both nations continue to fortify their positions, the challenge will be to maintain this delicate balance, ensuring that these developments lead to stability rather than conflict.

In this high-altitude chess game, every road, every tunnel, every bunker is a move that could shape the future of the region. And for India, the goal is clear: to defend, to deter, and to ensure that its borders remain secure in the face of any adversity. Doklam in Sikkim, Galwan Valley in Ladakh and Yangtze In Arunachal Pradesh were clear examples of how far India can go to protect every inch of her land. With the local residents in the borders fiercely guarding the territory, the other side will not err to meet-a totally Indian Arunachal Pradesh, yet again.

List of Figures

I. Select Photographs from NEFA Period

Figure 1:   Verrier Elwin and Nari K Rustomji with Mishmis of Arunachal Pradesh, 1954 148

Figure 2:   Contingent from NEFT participating in the Republic Day Parade in Delhi, 1956 149

Figure 3:   Farewell of Shri Jairamdas Daulatram, Governor of Assam at Shillong, 1956 150

Figure 4:   His Holiness the Dalai Lama disguised as a layman during his escape from Tibet, 1959 151

Figure 5:   Shri P.N. Luthra, IFAS, Adviser to Governor & Brig. Mami, 1962 . 152

Figure 6:   Mr. Luthra and Mrs. Luthra with Rinchin Dondup, Political Interpreter (PI) of Tawang at Shillong, 1962 153

Figure 7:   Rinchin Dondup, Political Interpreter (popularly known as Nyerpa Khau) of Tawang praying to Lord Buddha in Shri Luthra's residence in Shillong, 1962 154

Figure 8:   Indian Army in the Frontiers during the 1962 War 155

Figure 9:   Anini, Headquarter of Dibang Valley, 4 December 1965 155

Figure 10:   Smt. Indira Gandhi, Prime Minister at Naharlagun 156

Figure 11:   Giani Zail Singh, Union Home Minister at Raj Niwas 157

Figure 12:   Mask dance by the Memba Lama at Tuting 158

Figure 13:   Shri Yashwantrao Chavan, Union Home Minister at Along (Aalo), 1969 159

Figure 14:   Tawang Monastery, 1969 160

Figure 15:   Bhalukpong Petrol Pump 161

Figure 16:   Governor Shri BK Nehru at Deomali Plywood Factory 162

Figure 17:   Governor Shri BK Nehru at Tawang Monastery, 1 May 1969 163

Figure 18:   Handmade Paper (Mon-Shug) making in Mukto village, 1969 164

Figure 19:   Shri Vidya Charan Shukla, Minister of Information and Broadcasting interacting with locals at Ziro, 11 February 1970 165

Figure 20:   Union Territory Announcement by Smt. Indira Gandhi, Prime Minister, 1972 166

Figure 21:   Opening of Pahung Hydel Project by Shri KAA Raja, Chief Commissioner on 28 August 1972 167

Figure 22:   Shri R N Mirdha, Union Home Minister at Deomali, 24 March 1974 168

Figure 23:   Assembly House at Itanagar, 19 August 1975 169

Figure 24:   Itanagar Bazar in 1976 - 1st Mall of Itanagar 170

Figure 25:   Along (Aalo) Hydel Project, 1976 171

Figure 26:   New Hayuliang Cooperative Bus, 14 January 1977 172

Figure 27:   Silver Jubilee Seminar at Shillong, 7 September 1977 173

Figure 28:   Shri Morarji Desai, Prime Minister at Arunachal Pradesh, 3
              November 1978 174

Figure 29:   Shri Neelam Sanjiva Reddy, President of India at Along (Aalo),
              1979 175

Figure 30:   Shri KAA Raja demits charge and leaves Arunachal Pradesh, 16
              January 1979 176

Figure 31:   VV Giri, President of India at Sarada Mission School. 177

Figure 32:   Visit of His Holiness the 14th Dalai Lama to Itanagar, 1983 178

Figure 33:   Laying foundation stone of Centre for Buddhist Studies by His
              Holiness the 14th Dalai Lama, 5 May 1983 at Itanagar 179

II. Arunachal Pradesh on the Rise

Figure 1:   Dr Manmohan Singh, Prime Minister at Itanagar, 2008 303

Figure 2:   Arunachal's first greenfield Donyi Polo Airport. 304

Figure 3:   Shri Narendra Modi, Prime Minister of India in Arunachal
              Pradesh, 2019 304

Figure 4:   Shri Ram Nath Kovind, President of India presenting the Nari
              Shakti Puraskar to Smt. Tage Rita Takhe, founder of the Naara
              Aaba Winery 305

Figure 5:   Shri Narendra Modi, Prime Minister at Itanagar, 2022 306

Figure 6:   Smt. Draupadi Murmu, President of India at Statehood Day
              celebrations, 2023 306

Figure 7:   Interaction of Community Based Organizations (CBOs) with
              Shri Narendra Modi, Prime Minister in Delhi, 2023 307

Figure 8:   Arunachal Pradesh became the first State in the North East to
              achieve 100% saturation of Har Ghar Jal Programme. 307

Figure 9:   Shri Amit Shah, Union Home Minister at Kibithoo, India's first
              village during launch of the Vibrant Villages Programme 308

Figure 10:   Signing of MOU between Arunachal Pradesh and Assam to
              resolve the inter state border dispute 308

Figure 11:   Arunachal Pradesh hosts 77th Santosh Trophy Finals 309

Figure 12:   Arunachal Pradesh Legislative Assembly Building 309

Figure 13:   Bene Arch Bridge over Yomgo river, West Siang 310

Figure 14:   Taking governance to the people-Visit by Shri Pema Khandu,
             Chief Minister 310

Figure 15:   Shri Pema Khandu, Chief Minister addressing the G20 meet at
             Itanagar 311

Figure 16:   Inauguration of the Hump World War II Museum, Pasighat 311

Figure 17:   Celebration of International Year of Millets, 2023 312

Figure 18:   Kameng Hydroelectric Project 312

Figure 19:   Kiwi Plantation-Arunachal has the potential to become the
             fruit bowl of India 313

Figure 20:   Itanagar (Naharlagun) Railway Station 313

Figure 21:   New Age Learning Centre at Changlang 314

Figure 22:   Shri Jagdeep Dhankhar, Vice President of India at the
             Statehood Day Celebrations, 2024 314

Figure 23:   Shri Narendra Modi, Prime Minister at Itanagar, 2024 315

Figure 24:   RIWATCH, an institute dedicated to the empowerment of
             indigenous communities 315

Figure 25:   Women SHGs keeping alive indigenous traditions, handicrafts
             and cultures 316

Figure 26:   Rozgar Mela–handing over appointment letters to successful
             candidates appointed through APSSB 316

Figure 27:   Sela and Nechiphu Tunnels providing all weather connectivity
             to the strategic Tawang sector 317

Figure 28:   Super Car Rally on roads of Arunachal Pradesh 318

Figure 29:   The Vibrant Dambuk Orange Festival 318

Figure 30:   TRIHMS–first batch from the first MBBS college in the State
             passed out in 2023 319

Figure 31:   Empowering SHG women as Lakhpati Didis – Women Led
             Transformation 319

List of Maps

Map 1:   The Course of Tsangpo (1886-87) to illustrate Colonel Tanner's ... 40

Map 2:   Railway Map of China showing proposed Line from Lhasa to
            Tezpur via Tawang and Dirang, 1921. ... 41

Map 3:   Route Map from Assam to Sichuan Province, China prepared
            by Noel Williamson ... 68

Map 4:   Sheet I of Map of the Northern Frontier of India as settled at the
            Simla Conference, March 1914 (the McMahon Line) ... 69

Map 5:   Sheet II of Map of the Northern Frontier of India as settled at
            the Simla Conference, March 1914 (the McMahon Line) ... 70

Map 6:   Map to illustrate Article 9 of the Simla Convention, 1914,
            initialled by the British Representative and signed by the
            Chinese and Tibetan Representatives. The two latter did not
            merely initial the Convention but also signed ... 71

Map 7:   Map I attached to Simla Convention signed by Representatives
            of Great Britain and Tibet, 1914 ... 72

Map 8:   Map II attached to Simla Convention signed by Representatives
            of Great Britain and Tibet, 1914 ... 73

Map 9:   Sketch Map of some parts of Southern and Eastern Tibet as
            prepared by Christian Missionaries in 1871. The boundary
            shown in the map approximates to what later became known as
            the McMohan Line ... 74

Map 10:   Map of Sadiya Frontier Tract– 1933 ... 75

Map 11:   Political Map of India, 1959 ... 120

Map 12:   Tribal Boundaries Map of Assam, including present day
            Arunachal Pradesh, 1946 ... 121

Map 13:   Map showing NEFA Administrative Divisions, 1971 ... 216

Map 14:   Map showing Schools in NEFA, 1971 ... 217

Map 15:   Map showing Social Welfare Centres in NEFA, 1971 ... 218

Map 16:   Map showing Post Offices, Telegraph Offices, Telephone and
            Electricity Lines in NEFA, 1971 ... 219

Map 17:   Map showing Craft Centres and Cooperative Societies in
            NEFA, 1971 ... 220

Map 18:   Map of Airports, Advanced Landing Grounds and Helipads in
            Arunachal Pradesh, 2024 ... 267

Select Bibliography

1. Hamilton, In Abor Jungles of North-East India
2. D.P. Choudhury, The North-East Frontier of India 1865-1914
3. Manilal Bose, British Policy in the North-East Frontier Agency
4. H.K Barpujari, Problem of the Hill Tribes: North-East Frontier 1822-42
5. H.K Barpujari, Problem of the Hill Tribes: North-East Frontier 1843-72
6. F. Kingdon Ward, Assam Adventure
7. L.W. Shakespear, History of Upper Assam, Upper Burmah and North-Eastern Frontier
8. M. L. Bose, History of Arunachal Pradesh
9. Verrier Elwin, A Philosophy for NEFA
10. Berenice Guyot Rechard, Shadow States- India, China and the Himalayas, 1910-1962
11. INNER LINE REGULATION AND MIZORAM. Zahluna, J. "INNER LINE REGULATION AND MIZORAM." *The Indian Journal of Political Science* 72, no. 1 (2011): 221–25. http://www.jstor.org/stable/42761822.
12. P N Luthra, Constitutional & Administrative growth of Arunachal Pradesh
13. *YouTube*, 17 April 2020, https://dspace.gipe.ac.in/xmlui/bitstream/handle/10973/49675/GIPE-031640.pdf?sequence=3&isAllowed=y. Accessed 13 July 2022.
14. Kundra, Ashish. "Understanding the history of the Inner Line Permit in the Northeast." *Hindustan Times*, 22 December 2019, https://www.hindustantimes.com/analysis/understanding-the-history-of-the-inner-line-permit-in-the-north
15. *YouTube*, https://archive.org/details/dli.pahar.3101/page/9/mode/1up. Accessed 28 July 2022.
16. Bailey, F. M. "No Passport to Tibet."
17. https://en.wikipedia.org/wiki/McMahon_Line
18. *YouTube*, https://archive.org/details/dli.pahar.3101/mode/1up. Accessed 27 July 2022.
19. Bailey, Frederick Marshman. "Frederick Marshman Bailey." *Wikipedia*, https://en.wikipedia.org/wiki/Frederick_Marshman_Bailey. Accessed 27 July 2022.
20. "File:1913 North-Eastern Frontier and Tibet by Morshead and Bailey from RE Journal 1921.jpg." *Wikimedia Commons*, https://commons.wikimedia.

org/wiki/File:1913_North-Eastern_Frontier_and_Tibet_by_Morshead_ and_Bailey_from_RE_Journal_1921.jpg#filehistory. Accessed 27 July 2022. (MAP OF THE TRAIL)

21. Gould, Basil. "The Tibet Journal." *THE NORTHERN FRONTIERS OF INDIA,*

22. LW Shakespear, History of Upper Assam, Upper Burmah and North Eastern Frontier

23. Adventures of Jean- Baptiste Chevalier in Eastern India (1752-1765) - Historical Memoir and Journal of Travels in Assam, Bengal and Tibet, Translated by Caroline Dutta- Baruah and Jean Deloche.

24. https://www.claudearpi.in/wp-content/uploads/2021/02/2014-Lobsang-Tenpa-The__Centenary_of_the_McM_Line_and_the_Status_of_ Monyul_1951-2-libre.pdf. Accessed 27 July 2022.

25. "Henry Morshead." *Wikipedia,* https://en.wikipedia.org/wiki/Henry_ Morshead. Accessed 27 July 2022.

26. Lt. Gen Baljit Singh, AVSM, VSM TIBET AND TRAIL BLAZING THE MCMAHON LINE IN 1913 | Salute

27. Oshong Ering, The Lingering Memories

28. Kalha, RS. "The McMahon Line: A hundred years on | Manohar Parrikar Institute for Defence Studies and Analyses." *IDSA,* 3 July 2014, https://idsa. in/idsacomments/TheMcMahonLine_rskalha_030714. Accessed 27 July 2022.

29. "Simla Convention." *Wikipedia,* https://en.wikipedia.org/wiki/Simla_ Convention. Accessed 27 July 2022.

30. Singh, Baljit. *TIBET AND TRAIL BLAZING THE MCMAHON LINE IN 1913 | Salute,* 16 January 2020, https://salute.co.in/tibet-and-trail-blazing-the-mcmahon-line-in-1913/. Accessed 28 July 2022.

31. "Wikipedia." *Wikipedia,* https://en.wikipedia.org/wiki/McMahon_Line. Accessed 27 July 2022.

32. Parshotam Mehra, The McMahon Line and After

33. J.P Dalvi, Himalayan Blunder

34. PARLIAMENT AND INDIA'S FOREIGN POLICY WITH PARTICULAR REFERENCE TO SINO- INDIA BORDER DISPUTE, 1962

35. Gen JJ Singh, The McMahon Line, A Century of Discord

36. Shurmo Ngawang Choidraks & Shurmo Lobsang Phuntsok, 1962, When The Mountains Cried

37. http://www.archieve.claudearpi.net/maintenance/uploaded_pics/Tibet_ India_1947_1950.pdf

38. D R Mankekar, Guilty Men of 1962

39. Claude Arpi, 1962 and the McMahon Saga

40. Vijay Gokhale, The Long Game

41. John W Garver, China's Decision for war with India in 1962

42. BB Pandey, Arunachal Pradesh; Village State to Statehood

43. Ram Chandra Guha, Savaging the Civilised, Verrier Elwin, His Tribals and India

44. https://www.indiatoday.in/magazine/cover-story/story/19980518-line-of-actual-control-remains-sore-point-between-india-and-china-826413-1998-05-18

45. Lintner, China's India War (2018) PP 210-211

46. https://www.orfonline.org/research/operation-falcon-when-general-sundarji-took-the-chinese-by-surprise/

47. https://www.firstpost.com/world/sikkim-standoff-india-should-be-ready-for-long-haul-as-impasse-may-go-beyond-wangdung-incident-3775047.html

48. https://web.archive.org/web/20060524151804/http://www.indiatodaygroup.com/itoday/22021999/obit.html

49. Managing the 1986-87 Sino-Indian Sumdorong Chu Crisis- Manjeet S Pardesi -(pages 534-551)

50. https://economictimes.indiatimes.com/news/defence/dhola-sadiya-bridge-not-enough-china-still-miles-ahead-of-india-in-infrastructure-along-lac/articleshow/58879677.cms

51. https://theprint.in/opinion/for-operation-falcon-maj-gen-jimmy-asked-for-mules-but-army-chief-sundarji-gave-helicopters/421730/

52. https://caravanmagazine.in/interview/general-v-n-sharma-indian-china-conflict-wangdung-tawang-1987-mcmahon-line

53. https://theprint.in/past-forward/sumdorong-chu-ladakh-like-india-china-face-off-which-took-9-yrs-to-end-but-without-violence/451517/

54. https://idsa.in/idsacomments/CurrentChineseincursionLessonsfromSomdurongChuIncident_msingh_260413

55. https://opentopomap.org/#map=14/27.78704/91.78047

56. https://idsa.in/idsacomments/CurrentChineseincursionLessonsfromSomdurongChuIncident_msingh_260413

57. https://indianexpress.com/article/india/latest-news/no-compromise-on-arunachal-territory-issue-advani/

58. https://eparlib.nic.in/bitstream/123456789/676905/1/3009.pdf

59. Claude Arpi, 'Dharamshala and Beijing: The Negotiations that never were', Lancer Publishers and Distributors, 2009, pp 138-139.

60. Rajiv Gandhi's 1988 visit broke ice between India and China: Chinese diplomat

61. https://www.thebetterindia.com/163207/arunachal-pradesh-hindi-news/amp/

62. Nefamese - Wikipedia

63. Impact of Multilingualism and Multiculturalism on English Language Education: The Case of Arunachal Pradesh, India

64. Yankee Modi, The complexity and emergence of Hindi as lingua franca in Arunachal Pradesh

65. Losel Nyinje Charitable Society & Monyul Social Welfare Association, Crossing of the Frontier, The exile route of His Holiness the 14th Dalai Lama-1959

66. Denma Gyalsey Tulku, The Clear Mirror, Reflection of Monyul in the history of Tawang Monastery, Translated by Yeshi Dhondup

67. North & Northeastern Frontier Tribes of India, Compiled- Intelligence Branch Division of the Chief of the Staff Army Headquarters India.

68. Takhe Kani, Compiled and edited, Tour Diary of Imdad Ali, Political Officer, Balipara Frontier Tract

69. Neville Maxwell, India's China War

70. Yvonne Wagstaff & Shiela Shaw, Letters from the Empire, A Soldier's account of the Boer war and the Abor Campaign in India

71. Ian Baker, The Heart of the World, A Journey to the Last Secret Place

72. George Dubnar, Frontiers

73. Jamyang Norbu, Echoes from Forgotten Mountains

74. https://www.lookandlearn.com/blog/25415/in-1959-the-dalai-lama-became-the-centre-of-world-media-attention/

75. https://kclpure.kcl.ac.uk/ws/portalfiles/portal/57863066/MAS_Article_Accepted.pdf

76. Tenpa, Lobsang. "The Centenary of the McMahon Line (1914-2014) and the Status of Monyul until 1951-2." *The Tibet Journal*, vol. 39, no. 2, 2014, pp. 57–102. *JSTOR*, http://www.jstor.org/stable/tibetjournal.39.2.57. Accessed 8 June 2024.

77. John S.R. Khathing, 'The Life of the Unsung Hero Maj Ralengnao 'Bob' Khathing.

78. Nari Rustomji, Imperilled Frontiers, India's North eastern Borderlands

79. Nari Rustomji, Enchanted Frontiers, Sikkim, Bhutan and India's North-Eastern Borderlands.

80. Nirupama Rao, The Fractured Himalaya, India Tibet China 1949-1962

81. Shiv Kunal Verma, 1962 The War that Wasn't

82. Kanti Bajpai, India versus China, Why They are not friends.

83. https://lawschoolpolicyreview.com/2020/06/22/sardars-patels-tibet-letter-was-short-on-facts/

84. https://www.usiofindia.org/publication-journal/1962-war-the-unknown-battles-operations-in-subansiri-and-siang-frontier-divisions.html

85. Bertil Lintner, China's India War, Collision Course on the Roof of the World

86. Christopher Lee, Viceroys, The Creation of the British

87. Prof. Sachidananda Mohanty, Betrayal, Early Warnings Unheeded, Lessons from Sardar Patel and Sri Aurobindo.

88. Dr. Tandon, Study of the Great Assam Earthquake of August 1950 and its aftershocks | MAUSAM

89. Brenece Guyot Rechard Relief, Rehabilitation, and Nation-Building in North- Eastern India after the 1950 Assam Earthquake

90. https://www.indiabudget.gov.in/budget2015-2016/es2014-15/echapvol1-10.pdf

91. https://fincomindia.nic.in/asset/doc/commission-reports/14th-FC/14thFCReport.pdf

92. https://arunachalobserver.org/2020/02/09/31335/

93. https://www.baaa-acro.com/operator/kalinga-airlines

94. http://magazines.odisha.gov.in/Orissareview/2017/May/engpdf/41-43.pdf

95. https://vishwabhaarat.com/webpage/detailnews/3/16

96. https://rsdebate.nic.in/bitstream/123456789/545217/2/IQ_43_30041963_U190_p1377_p1378.pdf

97. https://newsable.asianetnews.com/india-defence/from-the-iaf-vault-the-colourful-history-of-lilabari-airfield-ru6so3

98. https://books.google.co.in/books?id=YmOKEAAAQBAJ&pg=PT123&lpg=PT123&dq=kalinga+airlines+in+nefa&source=bl&ots=I4iDh_RWIz&sig=ACfU3U0zNaQs_ywdTk7qEuCah-PXhz6eaAQ&hl=en&sa=X&ved=2ahUKEwi0nsrc5JGHAxVU2jgGHZZpALE4HhDoAXoECCYQAw#v=onepage&q=kalinga%20airlines%20in%20nefa&f=false

99. Lowangcha Wanglet, Headhunting Nagas of Arunachal Pradesh

100. Tade Sangdo, POSA SYSTEM: A CASE STUDY OF THE BRITISH-NYISHI RELATIONS

101. *The East India Company: The World's Most Powerful Corporation* by Tirthankar Roy

102. The Making of a Frontier: Five Years' Experiences and Adventures in Gilgit, Hunza, Nagar, Chitral, and the Eastern Hindu-Kush by Algernon Durand

103. The Himalayan Frontier: India, China, and Bhutan by Dorothy Woodman

104. North East strife… rooted in history by W Chandrakanth
105. https://in.boell.org/en/2019/12/20/we-will-give-blood-not-our-land-citizenship-amendment-act-protests-context-northeast?amp
106. https://indiancitizenshiponline.nic.in/Documents/UserGuide/E-gazette_2019_20122019.pdf
107. Reid, History of the Frontier areas
108. George Dunbar, Frontiers
109. The Frontier Policy of the Government of India by Sir Olaf Caroe
110. https://www.tibetrightscollective.in/op-eds-commentaries/110th-anniversary-of-the-13th-dalai-lamas-tibetan-declaration-of independence#:~:text=The%20Declaration%20of%20Independence,Tibet%2C%20outside%20of%20China's%20auspices.
111. Captain H.T. Morshead, R.E, Report on an Exploration on the North East Frontier 1913
112. https://idsa.in/idsacomments/TheMcMahonLine_rskalha_030714
113. https://core.ac.uk/download/pdf/144519401.pdf
114. Arunachal Pradesh State Archives, Appreciation of services rendered and grant of rewards for relief work-earthquake 1950
115. 'Assam tea gardens face ruin', Times of India (24 August 1950)
116. https://www.claudearpi.net/wp-content/uploads/2020/08/The-Balipara-Frontier-Tract-towards-Tawang.pdf
117. https://www.friendsoftibet.org/sardarpatel.html
118. Vijay Gokhale, The Long Game
119. https://www.dalailama.com/messages/transcripts-and-interviews/india-should-share-its-ancient-knowledge-with-the-world-the-dalai-lama
120. McMahon, "International Boundaries", Journal of the Royal Society of Arts.
121. IP Gupta, Journey of a Bureaucrat, From the Hills to the Beaches, a Memoir
122. Diigok Rolii (The Call of the Dawn), Souvenir of Itanagar Solung Festival Celebration-2006
123. https://arunachaltimes.in/index.php/2022/01/03/the-founding-fathers-of-arunachal-pradesh/#google_vignette
124. https://www.india.gov.in/my-government/constitution-india/amendments/constitution-india-thirty-seventh-act-1975
125. https://cenjows.in/chinas-infrastructure-development-along-the-line-of-actual-control-lac-and-implications-for-india/
126. https://www.indiabudget.gov.in/budget2015-2016/es2014-15/echapvol1-10.pdf
127. https://fincomindia.nic.in/asset/doc/commission-reports/14th-FC/14thFCReport.pdf

128. https://www.indiabudget.gov.in/budget2015-2016/es2014-15/echapvol1-10.pdf
129. https://fincomindia.nic.in/asset/doc/commission-reports/XVFC%20VOL%20I%20Main%20Report.pdf
130. https://en.wikipedia.org/wiki/India%E2%80%93China_Border_Roads#Border_airport_and_ALG_projects
131. https://rsdebate.nic.in/bitstream/123456789/545217/2/IQ_43_30041963_U190_p1377_p1378.pdf
132. https://arunachaltimes.in/index.php/2022/11/20/pm-inaugurates-donyi-polo-airport/
133. https://en.wikipedia.org/wiki/First_Indira_Gandhi_ministry
134. https://x.com/PemaKhanduBJP/status/1559490391338098689
135. https://arunachaltimes.in/index.php/2024/03/25/perils-of-festival-of-elections/#google_vignette
136. https://arunachaltimes.in/index.php/2020/11/05/chow-khamoon-gohain-namshum-arunachals-first-mp-and-a-pioneer/

Endnotes

1   Dr. D Pandey, History of Arunachal Pradesh, page 330

2   https://in.boell.org/en/2019/12/20/we-will-give-blood-not-our-land-citizenship-amendment-act-protests-context-northeast?amp

3   Berenice Guyot Rechard, *Shadow States-India, China and the Himalayas, 1910-1962*, page-20

4   Dr. D Pandey, History of Arunachal Pradesh, page 331

5   Tade Sangdo, POSA SYSTEM: A CASE STUDY OF THE BRITISH-NYISHI RELATIONS, page 1054

6   Dr. D Pandey, History of Arunachal Pradesh, page 330

7   M. L. Bose, History of Arunachal Pradesh, page 194

8   Dr. D Pandey, History of Arunachal Pradesh, page 331

9   Arunachal Pradesh State Archives

10   Dr. D Pandey, History of Arunachal Pradesh, page 334

11   Arunachal Pradesh State Archives

12   *The East India Company: The World's Most Powerful Corporation* by Tirthankar Roy

13   The Making of a Frontier: Five Years' Experiences and Adventures in Gilgit, Hunza, Nagar, Chitral, and the Eastern Hindu-Kush by Algernon Durand

14   M. L. Bose, History of Arunachal Pradesh, page 195

15   Kundra, Ashish. "Understanding the history of the Inner Line Permit in the Northeast." *Hindustan Times*, 22 December 2019

16   M. L. Bose, History of Arunachal Pradesh, page 200

17   *Ibid*, page 206

18   *Ibid*, page 207

19   The Himalayan Frontier: India, China, and Bhutan by Dorothy Woodman

20   Dr. D Pandey, History of Arunachal Pradesh, page 338

21   W Chandrakanth, North East strife… rooted in history,

22   Dr. D Pandey, History of Arunachal Pradesh, page 340

23   Kundra, Ashish. "Understanding the history of the Inner Line Permit in the Northeast." *Hindustan Times*, 22 December 2019,

24   https://in.boell.org/en/2019/12/20/we-will-give-blood-not-our-land-citizenship-amendment-act-protests-context-northeast?amp

25   https://indiancitizenshiponline.nic.in/Documents/UserGuide/E-gazette_2019_20122019.pdf

26   Berenice Guyot Rechard, *Shadow States-India, China and the Himalayas, 1910-1962*, page 37

27   M L Bose History of Arunachal Pradesh, page 74

28   *Ibid*, page 81

29   Berenice Guyot Rechard, *Shadow States-India, China and the Himalayas, 1910-1962*, page 35

30   *Ibid*, page 36

31   D Pandey, History of Arunachal Pradesh, page 308

32   Prayas, APLS Magazine, poem by Kennong Darang, Abors: The Unsung Freedom Heroes

33   D Pandey, History of Arunachal Pradesh, page 307-8

34   Berenice Guyot Rechard, *Shadow States-India, China and the Himalayas, 1910-1962*, page 39

35   M L Bose History of Arunachal Pradesh, page 81

36   D Pandey, History of Arunachal Pradesh, page 314

37   Berenice Guyot Rechard, *Shadow States-India, China and the Himalayas, 1910-1962*, page 39

38   George Dunbar, Frontiers, page 144-170

39   Reid, History of the Frontier areas, page 229-321

40   George Dunbar, Frontiers, page 144-170

41   D Pandey, History of Arunachal Pradesh, page 316

42   *Ibid*, page 315

43   The Frontier Policy of the Government of India by Sir Olaf Caroe

44   Dr. D Pandey, History of Arunachal Pradesh (Earliest times to 1972 AD), page 324

45   https://en.wikipedia.org/wiki/McMahon_Line

46   *Ibid*

47   *Ibid*

48   https://claudearpi.blogspot.com/2017/06/when-china-did-not-claim-what-is-todays.html

49   Berenice Guyot Rechard, Shadow States-India, China and the Himalayas, 1910-1962

50   *Ibid*

51   Tibet Rights Collective-110th Anniversary of the 13th Dalai Lamaâ€™s Tibetan Declaration of Independence

52   Berenice Guyot Rechard, Shadow States-India, China and the Himalayas, 1910-1962, page 50

53   Notes-Additional Readings

54   Henry Morshead." *Wikipedia*, https://en.wikipedia.org/wiki/Henry_Morshead. Accessed 27 July 2022.

55   Bailey, F. M. "No Passport to Tibet".

56   Captain H.T. Morshead, R.E, Report on an Exploration on the North East Frontier 1913, page 83

57   Parshotam Mehra, The McMahon Line and After, page 175

58   Bailey, F. M. "No Passport to Tibet.

59   Simla Convention." *Wikipedia*, https://en.wikipedia.org/wiki/Simla_Convention. Accessed 27 July 2022.

60   Parshotam Mehra, The McMahon Line and after, page 283

61   Bailey, No Passport to Tibet

62   Simla Convention." *Wikipedia*, https://en.wikipedia.org/wiki/Simla_Convention. Accessed 27 July 2022.

63   *Ibid*

64   Brenece Guyot Rechard, Shadow States-India, China and the Himalayas, 1910-1962, page 51

65   Claude Arpi,1962 and the McMahon Saga, page 168

66   DP Choudhury, BRITISH POLICY ON THE NORTH-EAST FRONTIER page 243

67   Lt. Gen Baljit Singh, AVSM, VSM TIBET AND TRAIL BLAZING THE MCMAHON LINE IN 1913 | Salute

68   Brenece Guyot Rechard, Shadow States-India, China and the Himalayas, 1910-1962, page 52

69   https://en.wikipedia.org/wiki/Rongbatsa_Agreement#:~:text=Facing%20military%20defeat%2C%20China%20requested,Tibet%2C%20and%20was%20supplemented%20by

70   Brenece Guyot Rechard, Shadow States-India, China and the Himalayas, 1910-1962, page 55

71   Dr. D Pandey, History of Arunachal Pradesh (Earliest times to 1972 AD), page 326

72   Brenece Guyot Rechard, Shadow States-India, China and the Himalayas, 1910-1962, page 56

73   Bailey, No Passport to Tibet

74   Parshotam Mehra, The McMahon Line and After, page 418

75   *Ibid*, page 420

76   Brenece Guyot Rechard, Shadow States-India, China and the Himalayas, 1910-1962, page 56

77   Parshotam Mehra, The McMahon Line and After, page 428

78   PARLIAMENT AND INDIA'S FOREIGN POLICY WITH PARTICULAR REFERENCE TO SINO-INDIA BORDER DISPUTE, 1962 page 161-162

79   The McMahon Line: A hundred years on | Manohar Parrikar Institute for Defence Studies and Analyses

80   *Ibid*

81   PARLIAMENT AND INDIA'S FOREIGN POLICY WITH PARTICULAR REFERENCE TO SINO-INDIA BORDER DISPUTE, 1962, page 166

82   The McMahon Line: A hundred years on | Manohar Parrikar Institute for Defence Studies and Analyses

83   *Ibid*

84   *Ibid*

85   PARLIAMENT AND INDIA'S FOREIGN POLICY WITH PARTICULAR REFERENCE TO SINO-INDIA BORDER DISPUTE, 1962, page 169

86   *Ibid*, page 170

87   The McMahon Line: A hundred years on | Manohar Parrikar Institute for Defence Studies and Analyses

88   Arunachal Pradesh State Archives

89   Brenece Guyot Rechard Relief, Rehabilitation, and Nation-Building in North-Eastern India after the 1950 Assam Earthquake

90   Dr. Tandon, Study of the Great Assam Earthquake of August 1950 and its aftershocks | MAUSAM

91   https://www.jstor.org/stable/44003801?seq=4

92   Brenece Guyot Rechard Relief, Rehabilitation, and Nation-Building in North-Eastern India after the 1950 Assam Earthquake

93   https://arunachaltimes.in/index.php/2020/11/05/chow-khamoon-gohain-namshum-arunachals-first-mp-and-a-pioneer/

94   Brenece Guyot Rechard Relief, Rehabilitation, and Nation-Building in North-Eastern India after the 1950 Assam Earthquake, page 8

95   *Ibid*, page 8

96   Arunachal Pradesh State Archives, Appreciation of services rendered and grant of rewards for relief work-earthquake 1950

97   *Ibid*

98   *Ibid*

99   *Ibid*

100   Arunachal Pradesh State Archives

101   Brenece Guyot Rechard, Shadow States-India, China and the Himalayas, 1910-1962, page 99

102   'Assam tea gardens face ruin', Times of India (24 August 1950)

103   Brenece Guyot Rechard Relief, Rehabilitation, and Nation-Building in North-Eastern India after the 1950 Assam Earthquake

104   *Ibid*

105   *Ibid*

106   *Ibid*

107   *Ibid*

108   *Ibid*

109   *The Clear Mirror'* penned by Denma Gyalsey Trulku and translated by Yeshi Dhondup

110   *Ibid*

111   *Ibid*

112   Purshotam Mehra, McMahon Line and After, page 420

113   Berenice Guyot Rechard, Shadow States-India, China and the Himalayas, 1910-1962

114   *Ibid*

115   Claude Arpi The Balipara Frontier Tract Towards Tawang

116   *Ibid*

117   Berenice Guyot-Rechard, Shadow States India, China and the Himalayas, 1910-1962, page 65

118   *Ibid*

119   *Ibid*, page 67

120 *Ibid*, page 68

121 Vijay Gokhale, The Long Game

122 Sardar Patel's Letter to Nehru (Nov 7, 1950) | Friends of Tibet

123 Nirupama Rao, The Fractured Himalaya, page 87

124 John S.R. Khathing, 'The Life of the Unsung Hero Maj Ralengnao 'Bob' Khathing

125 *Ibid*

126 *Ibid*

127 *Ibid*

128 Nari Rustomji, Enchanted Frontier, page 126

129 John S.R. Khathing, 'The Life of the Unsung Hero Maj Ralengnao 'Bob' Khathing.

130 Tenpa, Lobsang. "The Centenary of the McMahon Line (1914-2014) and the Status of Monyul until 1951-2." *The Tibet Journal*, vol. 39, no. 2, 2014, pp. 57–102. *JSTOR*, http://www.jstor.org/stable/tibetjournal.39.2.57. Accessed 8 June 2024.

131 John S.R. Khathing, 'The Life of the Unsung Hero Maj Ralengnao 'Bob' Khathing.

132 *Ibid*

133 *Ibid*

134 Nari Rustomji, Enchanted Frontiers, Sikkim, Bhutan and India's North-Eastern Borderlands.

135 John S.R. Khathing, 'The Life of the Unsung Hero Maj Ralengnao 'Bob' Khathing.

136 Reid, R.,' Assam', Journal of the Royal Society of Arts, vol. XCII (April, 1944), page 27

137 Nari Rustomji, Imperilled Frontiers, India's North eastern Borderlands

138 *Ibid*

139 List of Padma Bhushan award recipients (1960–1969)-Wikipedia

140 Ram Chandra Guha, Savaging the Civilised, Verrier Elwin, His Tribals and India

141 Verrier Elwin, A Philosophy for NEFA (1959)

142 *Ibid*

143 Nari Rustomji, Enchanted Frontiers

144 *Ibid*

145 The Tribal World of Verrier Elwin: An Autobiography

146   Nari Rustomji, Imperilled Frontiers

147   Ram Chandra Guha, Savaging the Civilised, Verrier Elwin, His Tribals and India

148   Oshong Ering, The Lingering Memories

149   Authors conversation with Anupam Tangu, son of JM Tangu

150   *Ibid*

151   Excerpt from the Press Release of The Dalai Lama issued from Tezpur, 18th April 1959

152   Ramachandra Guha, India After Gandhi

153   Kanti Bajpayee, India versus China, Why they are not friends, page 4

154   Claude Arpi India Tibet relations 1947-1949 India begins to vacillate Paper presented on the occasion of the International Conference on Exp

155   Vijay Gokhale, The Long Game

156   Shiv Kunal Verma, 1962 The War that Wasn't, page 4

157   Vijay Gokhale, The Long Game, page 49

158   Shiv Kunal Verma, 1962 The War that Wasn't, page 14

159   *Ibid*, page 17

160   Losel Nyinje Charitable Society & Monyul Social Welfare Association, Crossing of the Frontier, The exile route of His Holiness the 14th Dalai Lama-1959

161   *Ibid*

162   Rene Cutforth, a BBC correspondent

163   *Ibid*

164   https://www.dalailama.com/messages/transcripts-and-interviews/india-should-share-its-ancient-knowledge-with-the-world-the-dalai-lama

165   McMahon, "International Boundaries", Journal of the Royal Society of Arts.

166   George Dunbar, Frontiers (Introduction)

167   Claude Arpi, 1962 and the McMahon Line Saga, page 228

168   Shiv Kunal Verma, 1962, The War that Was'nt, page 17

169   John Graver, page 92-93

170   Berenice Guyot-Rechard, Shadow States, page 187

171   Kanti Bajpai, India versus China, page 98

172   Berenice Guyot-Rechard, Shadow States India, China and the Himalayas, 1910-1962, page 189

173   *Ibid*, page 185

174   *Ibid*, page 208

175	Kanti Bajpai, India versus China, page 102

176	John W Garver, China's Decision for War with India in 1962

177	Claude Arpi, 1962 and the McMahon Line Saga, page 486

178	Some lessons of the 1963 NEFA Debacle, Lt. Gen A. M. Vohra Pg 1400

179	Stories of Heroism: PVC & MVC Winners, B. Chakravorty, page 11

180	*Ibid*, page 11

181	*Ibid*, page 11

182	Defenders of the Dawn

183	1962 War – The Unknown Battles: Operations in Subansiri and Siang Frontier Divisions, Major General GG Dwivedi, SM, VSM and Bar (Retd), Major General PJS Sandhu, (Retd) 1962 War - The Unknown Battles: Operations in Subansiri and Siang Frontier Divisions

184	*Ibid*

185	https://www.usiofindia.org/publication-journal/the-red-cross-and-the-1962-sino-indian-conflict.html#:~:text=For%20the%20Indian%20nation%2C%20the,the%20experience%20was%20particularly%20harrowing.

186	John W Garver, China's Decision for War with India in 1962

187	*1962, When the Mountains Cried"* by Shurmo Ngawang Choidraks and Shurmo Lobsang Phuntsok

188	*Ibid*

189	*Ibid*

190	Arunachal Pradesh State Archives, Stories of Human Interest-Behaviour of local tribals during the last Chinese invasion

191	*Ibid*

192	*Ibid*

193	*Ibid*

194	John S.R. Khathing, 'The Life of the Unsung Hero Maj Ralengnao 'Bob' Khathing.

195	Nari Rustomji, Imperilled Frontiers, India's North eastern Borderlands

196	*Ibid*

197	*Ibid*

198	Nari Rustomji, Enchanted Frontiers

199	*Ibid*

200 Nari Rustomji, Enchanted Frontiers, Sikkim, Bhutan and India's North-Eastern Borderlands.

201 Brenice Guyot-Rechard, Shadow States, page 26

202 M. L. Bose, History of Arunachal Pradesh, page 235

203 P N Luthra, Constitutional & Administrative growth of Arunachal Pradesh

204 M. L. Bose, History of Arunachal Pradesh, page 236

205 *Ibid*, page 238

206 *Ibid*, page 239-40

207 *Ibid* page 238

208 https://www.claudearpi.net/wp-content/uploads/2016/12/IFAS.pdf

209 *Ibid*

210 *Ibid*

211 *Ibid*

212 I.P Gupta, Journey of a Bureaucrat, From the Hills to the Beaches, a Memoir, page 5

213 *Ibid*, page 11

214 *Ibid*, page 74

215 *Ibid*, page 246

216 Arunachal Pradesh-Wikipedia

217 Diigok Rolii (The Call of the Dawn), Souvenir of Itanagar Solung Festival Celebration-2006, page 42-45

218 M. L. Bose, History of Arunachal Pradesh page 241-42

219 https://arunachaltimes.in/index.php/2020/11/05/chow-khamoon-gohain-namshum-arunachals-first-mp-and-a-pioneer/

220 M. L. Bose, History of Arunachal Pradesh, page 247

221 Dani Sulu, https://arunachaltimes.in/index.php/2022/01/03/the-founding-fathers-of-arunachal-pradesh/#google_vignette

222 Shiva Swaroop-Wikipedia

223 Interview of retired official

224 BB Pandey, Arunachal Pradesh, Village State to Statehood. page 200

225 *Ibid*, page 194

226 https://www.india.gov.in/my-government/constitution-india/amendments/constitution-india-thirty-seventh-act-1975

227 BB Pandey, Arunachal Pradesh, Village State to Statehood, page 194

228 *Ibid*, page 195

229 Interview with Pradip Behera, a senior journalist of Arunachal Pradesh

230 https://www.researchgate.net/publication/291568148_Impact_of_Multilingualism_and_Multiculturalism_on_English_Language_Education_The_Case_of_Arunachal_Pradesh_India, page 667

231 *Ibid*, page 665

232 *Ibid*, page 666

233 https://en.wikipedia.org/wiki/Indira_Miri

234 Yankee Modi, The complexity and emergence of Hindi as lingua franca in Arunachal Pradesh, page 162

235 https://en.m.wikipedia.org/wiki/Nefamese

236 Census of India

237 https://www.researchgate.net/publication/291568148_Impact_of_Multilingualism_and_Multiculturalism_on_English_Language_Education_The_Case_of_Arunachal_Pradesh_India, page 668

238 *Ibid*, page 668

239 *Ibid*, page 669

240 https://cenjows.in/chinas-infrastructure-development-along-the-line-of-actual-control-lac-and-implications-for-india/

241 Lessons from Somdurong Chu Incident | Manohar Parrikar Institute for Defence Studies and Analyses

242 No compromise on Arunachal territory issue: Advani | India News-The Indian Express

243 https://eparlib.nic.in/bitstream/123456789/676905/1/3009.pdf

244 https://main.sci.gov.in/jonew/judis/14617.pdf

245 Finance Commission-Wikipedia

246 Thirteenth Finance Commission-Wikipedia

247 Ways and means advances-Wikipedia

248 The Fourteenth Finance Commission (FFC) – Implications for Fiscal Federalism in India?

249 https://fincomindia.nic.in/asset/doc/commission-reports/14th-FC/14thFCReport.pdf page 152

250 *Ibid*, page 97

251 *Ibid*, page 95

252 https://www.indiabudget.gov.in/budget2015-2016/es2014-15/echapvol1-10.pdf, page 129

253   *Ibid*, page 132

254   https://fincomindia.nic.in/asset/doc/commission-reports/XVFC%20 VOL%20I%20Main%20Report.pdf, page 155

255   *Ibid*, page 160

256   https://fincomindia.nic.in/asset/doc/commission-reports/XV-FC%20 -VOL%20II%20Annexes.pdf, page 272

257   Lowangcha Wanglet, Headhunting Nagas of Arunachal Pradesh

258   https://en.wikipedia.org/wiki/Kalinga_Airlines

259   http://magazines.odisha.gov.in/Orissareview/2017/May/engpdf/41-43.pdf, page 40

260   https://rsdebate.nic.in/bitstream/123456789/545217/2/IQ_43_ 30041963_U190_p1377_p1378.pdf, page 1377

261   https://en.wikipedia.org/wiki/India%E2%80%93China_Border_ Roads#Border_airport_and_ALG_projects

262   https://arunachaltimes.in/index.php/2022/11/20/pm-inaugurates-donyi-polo-airport/

263   https://arunachalobserver.org/2022/08/17/is-advani-right-arunachal-delhi-se-door-hey-par-dil-se-nahin/

264   https://en.wikipedia.org/wiki/First_Indira_Gandhi_ministry

265   Source: Planning Department, Govt of Arunachal Pradesh

266   https://x.com/PemaKhanduBJP/status/1559490391338098689

267   https://arunachaltimes.in/index.php/2024/03/25/perils-of-festival-of-elections/#google_vignette

268   https://www.globalonenessproject.org/library/photo-essays/river-heart-world

269   Tenpa, Lobsang. "The Centenary of the McMahon Line (1914-2014) and the Status of Monyul until 1951-2." *The Tibet Journal*, vol. 39, no. 2, 2014, pp. 57–102. *JSTOR*, http://www.jstor.org/stable/tibetjournal.39.2.57. Accessed 8 June 2024.

270   *Ibid*

271   https://prsindia.org/policy/report-summaries/report-15th-finance-commission-2021-26

About the Author

Sonam Chombay, a dedicated civil servant for over 21 years, has expertise in Revenue, Finance, Tourism, IT, Hydropower, and Aviation. Hailing from the picturesque Tawang district of Arunachal Pradesh, he is Monpa by birth and proudly identifies as an Arunachalee. His career spans multiple sectors and reflects a strong commitment to public service.

Sonam has an equally eclectic academic background. After leaving dentistry, he studied literature at Hindu College, Delhi University, and earned a Master's in Regional Development from JNU. He has also attended programs at the Indian School of Business, Duke University, and other prestigious institutions. Outside of work, Sonam enjoys reading non-fiction and is a passionate musician with a love for the blues. This debut book offers a fresh perspective shaped by his unique and wide-ranging interests and experiences.

9 798896 327189